Nuffield Co-ordina

47

BIOLOGY

HERSCHEL GRAMMAR SCHOOL
NORTHAMPTON AVE.
SLOUGH SL1 3BW

BoC— 674199.

Published for the Nuffield–Chelsea Curriculum Trust by
Longman Group UK Limited

General Editors,
Nuffield Co-ordinated Sciences
Geoffrey Dorling
Andrew Hunt
Grace Monger

Author and General Editor, Biology
Grace Monger

Co-ordinating Editor, Biology
Tim Turvey

Contributors
D. R. B. Barrett
Barbara Case
Elizabeth Fenwick
Neil R. Ingram
Peter Openshaw
John Peters
Dr Graham Walters

Consultants
The General Editors acknowledge with thanks the advice of Pamela Rivaz on language and
the General Editor, Biology, is grateful to J. Parkyn for his help on medical matters.

Longman Group UK Limited
Longman House, Burnt Mill, Harlow, Essex CM20 2JE, England and
Associated Companies throughout the World.

First published 1988
Fifth impression 1990
Copyright © The Nuffield-Chelsea Curriculum Trust

Illustrations by
Peter Edwards, Hardlines, Oxford Illustrators Ltd., and Chris Ryley
Cover illustration by Plus 2 Design

Filmset in Times Roman
Produced by Longman Group (FE) Ltd
Printed in Hong Kong

ISBN 0 582 04257 7

All rights reserved; no part of this publication may be reproduced, stored in a retrieval system,
or transmitted in any form or by any means, electronic, mechanical, photocopying, recording,
or otherwise, without either the prior written permission of the Publishers or a
licence permitting restricted copying in the United Kingdom issued by the Copyright
Licensing Agency Ltd, 33–34 Alfred Place, London WC1E 7DP

Contents

Acknowledgements

Photographs

Allinson: 6.13c

Heather Angel: 1.7e, f and h, 1.12, 2.1e and k, 2.2, 2.6a and b, 2.7a and b, 2.8, 2.11, 2.12a, b and c, 2.14, 2.20, 2.21, 2.22a, b and c, 2.25, 3.3b and d, 3.8, 3.15, 4.2b, d and g, 8.4, 10.5, 10.9e, 11.4, 13.2, 13.5b, c and d, 13.6d, 13.13a, b, c and d, 14.3c, 14.6a, 15.10a, 15.19, 16.5b, 16.10a and b, 16.12, 16.15, 16.23, 16.25, 16.27, 17.3, 17.7, 17.18, 17.20, 17.25, 18.14, 18.25a, b and c, 18.27, 18.33, 19.2, 19.5b, 19.8d and f, 19.12b and f, 19.15; G. Kinns 19.24b; B. M. Rogers 15.23

Ardea London: I. Beames 21.1; Y. Arthus-Bertrand 4.1 (left); J. P. Ferrero 2.18, 4.3; B. Gibbons 19.3a; J. M. Labat 19.10; A. Lindau 17.17; J. L. Mason 15.15; P. Morris 23.25a; W. Weisser 1.10; J. Whiteman 4.1 (right)

Associated Sports Photographers: 9.10

Professor D. Baker, Department of Biological Sciences, Wye College, University of London: 8.3

Barnaby's Picture Library: 6.1, 10.1, 22.27a

A. C. Barrington-Brown, from Watson, J. D. The double helix Weidenfeld & Nicolson, 1968: 7

Biophoto Associates: 1.11j, 2.1d, f, g and h, 2.5, 2.13a, 2.15, 2.23, 2.24c, 5.3c, 7.9, 7.12, 8.5a, 8.8, 8.13, 8.19 (right), 9.6, 10.3, 10.6, 10.8a and b, 11.12, 11.20, 11.21, 12.9, 13.4c, 14.7a, d, g and h, 15.2, 15.7i, 16.5a 16.7, 16.8a, 19.1a and b, 19.3b, 19.4, 20.13, 21.14, 22.7, 22.8, 22.13, 22.22, 22.23b, 23.20, 23.26a and b

Anthony Blake Photo Library: 6.2a, 6.2b, 6.6a, b, c, e, f, h, k and l, 6.13a and b; G. Buntrock, 6.2e

Professor C. C. Booth: 5.8

Bob Bray: 22.2a

Bridgeman Art Library: 20.12 (by courtesy of Christies, London), 23.4, 23.27b

X-rays, Department of Radiodiagnosis, Bristol Royal Infirmary: 5.11

British Coal: 23.24

By courtesy of the Trustees of the British Museum (Natural History): 18.26, 23.1, 23.23b

Cadbury Ltd: 6.6j

J. Allan Cash Ltd: 1.2, 1.11p and q, page 31, 4.2f, 6.6i, 6.13d, 7.2a, page 155, 13.1a, 13.4d, 14.3b, 14.12a, 15.1, 15.6, 15.7a, 15.7iv, 16.2, 16.8b, 16.18a, 16.20, 17.1, 17.29, 18.12, 18.13, 18.18b, 20.18a and c, 23.8, 23.14

Philip Chapman: 15.11

Bruce Coleman Ltd: B. and C. Alexander 13.1b; J. Burton 14.6b, 23.15, 23.16, 23.23a; E. Creighton 3.4; G. Cubitt 13.4e, 22.24; M. P. L. Fogden 1.7g, 16.1a; M. Freeman 23.13; D. Green 19.5a; P. A. Hinchliffe 15.9; Rogers and Sullivan 16.31a; F. Sauer 3.1, 10.4, 16.1c; K. Taylor 15.7ii; J. Van Wormer 17.26

The Contract Journal: 9.1

D. A. Cox Ltd: 10.18

Gene Cox: 8.9, 8.18

Daily Telegraph Colour Library: R. Hallman 18.15; Space Frontiers 23.27a

Roy DeCarava: 22.10b

Dollond & Aitchison Group Ltd: 22.5

The Electricity Council: 6.6h

Electron Microscopy Group, Clinical Research Centre, Northwick Park Hospital, Harrow: 14.7b

An Esso photograph: 17.27

Barbara Flanagan: 22.2b

The Alan Fletcher Research Station, Land Administration Commission, Queensland, Australia: 17.10, 17.11, 17.12

Dr R. Franklin and Professor R. Gosling, Department of Biophysics, King's College, London: 8

Malcolm Fraser: 7.8, 8.6, 11.1

The Fresh Fruit and Vegetable Information Bureau: 6.13e

Elizabeth Gent: 5.7

From Glowacinski, Z. and Jarvinen, O. Ornis. Scand 6 33. 1975: 13.12a, b, c, d, e and f

Sally and Richard Greenhill: page 7, 7.15

Taken from the film "The first days of life" by Guigoz. Distributed by Boulton-Hawker Films Ltd, Guigoz-Claude-Edelmann-Baufle: 20.6

Guinness Superlatives Ltd: 6.3

Philip Harris Biological Ltd: B. J. F. Haller, 9.3

Health Education Authority: 7.17

Department of Haematology, St Helier Hospital, Carshalton, Surrey: 8.10

Marc Henrie: 1.4, 1.5, 2.17, 11.3

Eric and David Hosking: 1.7d, 1.11l and w, 2.1a, 3.3c, 9.13, 10.9a, b and c, 13.4b, 15.7iii and v, 15.21, 16.11, 16.29, 17.14, 17.24, 18.1, 18.20, 19.8b, 19.12a and d; John Hawkins 18.32; D. P. Wilson 1.7b, 2.1i, 2.9, 2.10b, 2.13b and c, 16.14a and b

Imperial Chemical Industries plc: Fertilizers Division 15.5; Plant Protection Division 17.6

Institute of Horticultural Research: 3.11, 3.13a and b

Professor M. R. B. Keighley: 5.2

Frank Lane Picture Agency Ltd: R. Austing 4.2c, 9.15; C. Carvalho 1.7a; A. Christiansen 13.11; G. Dodd 3.3a; W. Eisenbeiss 13.4a; A. R. Hamelin 1.11e; F. Hartman 2.16, 12.4c; P. Heard 1.11f and k, 15.7e, 16.9; J. Hutchings 17.2; A. Johnson 1.7c; D. Jones 15.10b, 18.8; F. W. Lane 4.4; S. McCutcheon 18.5; M. Newman 18.29; M. Nimmo 2.24b; R. Van Nostrand 1.13, 18.28; F. Polking 18.30; A. J. Roberts 4.2e, 17.19; W. W. Roberts 12.4b; D. A. Robinson 1.11r; L. Robinson 19.11; L. Lee Rue 4.2a, 16.31b, c and d, 16.33b; Silvestris 10.9d, 18.3; J. Swale 15.7c; R. Tidman 1.11x, 18.18a, 18.31; J. Watkins 1.11m; L. West 2.4; A. Wharton 16.16; R. Wilmshurst 1.11s, u and v, 13.5a, page 235; W. Wisniewski 2.10a, 13.6c; M. B. Withers 1.11b

Dr R. E. Lawrence: 7.5

Professor R. M. Leech, University of York: 3.6

Mansell Collection Ltd: 22.16, 23.5

John May: 22.23a

Tony Morrison: 17.21, 18.6

The National Blood Transfusion Service: 8.14

National Dairy Council: 6.2c

Natural History Photographic Agency Ltd: A. Bannister 1.7i; S. Dalton 10.20

Andrew Neal: 1.8

Network Photographers: M. Abrahams 22.27b; M. Goldwater 20.18b

R. H. Noailles: 19.9 (left)

Dr R. Owen, Department of Surgery, University of Liverpool: 2.7c

Oxfam: 6.7; J. Hartley 17.5

Oxford Scientific Films Ltd: G. I. Bernard 1.6b, 8.7, 15.20, 16.22, 19.12c, 19.19a, b and c, 19.20a, b and c, 19.24a, 23.11a and b; D. Cayless 15.7b; J. A. L. Cooke 11.11, 19.3di and dii, 23.9, 23.25b; S. Dalton 19.8a; C. G. Gardener 8.19 (left); M. P. L. Fogden 10.2; Z. Leszczynski 19.22; Mantis Wildlife Films 19.17; M. B. Milne 16.33a; P. Parks 13.3, 19.21a , b, c and d; D. Renn 9.8; A. Shay 19.12e; D. Thompson 19.13; G. J. Wren 22.1

The Photo Source Ltd: 8.1, 21.16

Dr A. W. Pike, Department of Zoology, University of Aberdeen: 14.7c and f, 14.9

Promotion Australia: G. Robertson 2.19

R. H. S. Wisley: W. Halliday, F.R.P.S. 3.7

Reproduced by Gracious Permission of Her Majesty the Queen: 2.3 (right)

Rentokil Ltd: 2.24a

M. B. V. Roberts: 4.7a

Reproduced by permission of Her Majesty's Royal Armouries: 2.3 (left)

Reproduced by kind permission of the President and Council of the Royal College of Surgeons of England: 7.6

Royal Society for the Protection of Birds: S. and B. A. Craig 1.11i; S. C. Porter 1.11h, n and o; M. W. Richards 1.11a, c and t; D. Sewell 1.11g

St Bartholomew's Hospital, London, Department of Medical Illustration: 6.9

Eugen Schuhmacher: 12.4a

Science Photo Library Ltd: 8.15; M. Dohrn 1.6a, 12.3; Lepus 14.12b; H. Morgan 2, 12.12; L. Mulvehill 1; C. Nuridsamy and M. Perennou 11.2a and b; D. Parker 3; S. Patel 7.2b; D. J. Patterson 2.1c, 14.3a; D. Schaf 4.10; S. Stammers 14.7e; J. Stevenson 7.14a and b

Seaphot Ltd: 13.6a and b, 16.1b

Shell Photograph: 4, 17.4, 22.4

Harry Smith Horticultural Photographic Collection: 19.8e, 21.8, 21.9

Sport and General Press Agency: 9.9

Painting by Margaret Stones, reproduced by courtesy of the Royal Botanic Gardens Kew: 22.17

Swedish Institute: 5

Dr Nick Taylor-Delahoy: 19.8c, 23.11c

The Times: 6

Courtesy of the Tropical Development and Research Institute, Crown Copyright: 15.7d

Unilever Research: 22.11a and b

Van den Berghs & Jurgens Ltd: 6.2d, 6.6d

G. Villermet, Institute of Ophthalmology: 22.20

Dr Graham Walters: 13.10a, b, c(i) and (ii), 16.3, 16.4, 16.6, 16.17, 16.19, 16.21, 18.17, 18.18c, 18.19, 18.21, 18.22, 18.23, 18.24

By courtesy of the Wellcome Museum of Medical Science: 4.6

Dr C. W. Wells, Electronmicroscopy Unit, Department of Pathology, St Bartholomew's Hospital, London: 2.1j, 2.11

Susan M. Wells: 17.13, 17.15

From Wheater, P. R., Burkitt, H. G., Daniels, V. G. Functional histology Churchill Livingstone, 1979: 5.10, 9.2

Diagrams and tables

Data from Adlard, P., Department of Growth and Development, Institute of Child Health,

University of London: 21.11

From Arnold, G. *Aid and the Third World* Robert Royce, 1985: 14.8b

Data from ASH Factsheets: 7.16, 7.18

Based on *Atlas of body and mind* Mitchell Beazley, 1976: 11.16, 20.1, 20.5, 20.7a and b, 20.8a and b, 21.12

Based on Austin, C. R. and Short, R. V. *Reproduction in mammals* Book 2, 2nd edition, Cambridge University Press, 1982: 19.23

From Barker, J., "Guts" *Journal of Biological Education* 16 No. 1, Spring 1982: 5.1

Based on Beckett, B. S. *Biology, a modern introduction* 2nd edition, Oxford University Press, 1976: 11.17, 11.18

From Bell, G. H., Emslie-Smith, D. and Patterson, C. R. *Textbook of physiology and biochemistry*, Churchill Livingstone, 1978: 12.6, 12.7

From Bloom, A. L. *The surface of the Earth* Prentice-Hall Inc., 1973: 15.17

Based on Bolin, B. "The carbon cycle", © 1970 by *Scientific American* Inc., 223, 124–132, all rights reserved: 15.14

From Boorer, M., Hamlyn All-Colour Paperbacks *Mammals of the world* 1970, illustration by John Beswick: 10.19

Brown, A. W. A., ed. White Stevens, R. H. *Pesticides* Vol. 2, Ch. 12, Marcel Dekker, New York, 1968: 17.9

Based on graph from Cain, A. J. and Shepard, P. M., "Natural selection in *Cepaea nemoralis*", *Genetics* 39 89–116, 1954: 23.18

Based on Cairncross, S. and Feachem, R. G. *Environmental health engineering in the tropics, an introductory text* John Wiley & Sons, 1983: 14.8c

Based on data from *Climates of the States* G. Res. Co. Detroit, 1978: 1.9b

Based on data from "Climatology of the United States", *Decennial census of the US climate* 81–4 The National Oceanic and Atmospheric Administration, 1981: 1.9c

Map based on the data from *Christian Aid/Oxfam* Educational Productions Ltd: 14.8a

Adapted from Cloudsley-Thompson, J., "Water relations and diurnal rhythm of the activity in the young Nile monitor" *British Journal of Herpetology* 3 296–300, 1967: 13.8, 13.9

Based on Dale, A. *An introduction to social biology* Heinemann, 1953: 20.11

From map by David & Charles (Publishers) Ltd, 1980: 18.11

Based on Delwiche, C. C. "The nitrogen cycle" © 1970 by *Scientific American* Inc., 223, 136–46, all rights reserved: 15.18

Adapted from Demarest, R. J. and Sciarra, J. J. *Conception, birth and contraception* Hodder & Stoughton/McGraw–Hill Book Company, 1969: 20.10, 20.14a, b, c and d; 20.16b

Based on Emerson, E. B. *Alcohol and Man* by permission of the Macmillan Company of New York, 1967: 11.24

Based on Family Planning Information Service: 20.16a, 20.17a and b

Data from *Finding out about medicines and drugs* Find Out the Facts series, CRAC Publications, Hobsons, 1985: 11.22

Data from *Finding out what happens when I drink* Find Out the Facts series, CRAC Publications, Hobsons, 1983: 11.25

Map from The Forestry Commission *Bulletin No. 63* HMSO, © Crown copyright 1987: 18.4

Based on maps from Frazer, D. *Reptiles and amphibians in Britain* Collins, 1983: 18.9

From the Geological Museum *The story of the Earth* 3rd impression, Crown copyright, HMSO, 1977: 23.3

Based on Gregory, R. L. *The eye and brain* George Weidenfeld & Nicolson, 1985: 11.10

Adapted from Hardy, A. C. *The open sea, its natural history: Part 2, Fish and fisheries* Collins, 1959: 14.2

From Hardy, R. N. *Temperature and animal life.* Studies in Biology No. 35. Edward Arnold, 1979: 12.5

Alan Harris: 1.11d

From Hawkey, R. *Sport science* Hodder & Stoughton, 1984: 11.13

By courtesy of The Health Education Authority: 6.5, 6.8

From Huxley, A., Gaia Books *Green inheritance* Collins, 1984: 17.22

Based on maps from Kerney, M. P. and Cameron, R. A. D. *A field guide to land snails of Great Britain and North-West Europe* Collins, 1979: 16.18b and c, 16.26

Based on King, T. J. *Ecology* Selected Topics in Biology, Nelson, 1980: 17.23

Based on Mackean, D. G. *Introduction to biology* colour edition, John Murray 1978: 5.9, 7.7, 10.7

Data from MacLulich, D. A., "Fluctuations in the numbers of the varying hare (*Lepus americanus*)" University of Toronto Studies in Biology series, No. 43, 1937: 16.34

Map from Mallinson, J. *The shadow of extinction* Macmillan, 1978: 18.2

Based on Marshall, W. A. and Tanner, J. M., "Variations in the pattern of pubertal changes in girls" *Archives of Disease in Childhood* 44 291–303, 1969: 20.2

Based on Marshall, W. A. and Tanner, J. M.

"Variations in the pattern of pubertal changes in boys" *Archives of Disease in Childhood* 45 13–23, 1970: 20.3

Based on data from McCance, R. A. and Widdowson, E. M. *The composition of foods* 4th revised edition by Southgate, D. A. T. and Paul, A. A., HMSO, 1978: 6.10

After Mourant, A. E. *Blood groups and the study of mankind* Ministry of Health, 1962: 23.12

From the Nature Conservancy Council *Wildlife, the law and you* HMSO, 1982: 18.34

Based on Odum, H. T., "Trophic structure and productivity of Silver Springs, Florida" *Ecological Monographs* 27 55–112, 1957: 14.11, 14.15

From map made and published by the Director General of the Ordnance Survey, Crown copyright, 1961: 18.10

Maps based on *Philip's modern school atlas* George Philip & Son Ltd, 74th edition, 1976: 16.13, 16.26

Based on Quiring, D. P. *Functional anatomy of vertebrates* McGraw-Hill Book Company, 1950: 4.16

From Rasmussen, D. L. "Biotic communities of Kaibab Plateau, Arizona", *Ecological Monographs*, 11 229–275, 1941: 16.30 and 16.32

From *Road Atlas of Great Britain* published by W. and A. K. Johnston and G. W. Bacon, 1968: 18.16

From Roberts, M. B. V. *Biology for life* Nelson, 1986: 9, 1.7, 11.14, 23.21

From Simpkins, J. and Williams, J. I. *Advanced biology*. Bell and Hyman, 1984: 9.14

From Stafford–Miller Ltd: 4.12

After Strachal, G. and Ganning, B. *Boken om Lavet* Forskning och. Framsteg, Stockholm, 1977: 15.4

Adapted from Tinbergen, N. *The study of instinct* Clarendon Press, 1951: 19.14

Based on Varley, G. C., "The concept of energy flow applied to a woodland community, quality and quantity of food" *Symposium of British Ecological Society* Blackwell, 1970: 14.13, 14.14

Based on Vines, A. E. and Rees, N. *Plant and animal biology* Volume 1, 4th edition, Pitman, 1972: 4.15

Data from Whitaker, J., *An almanack*, J. Whitaker & Sons Ltd, 1987: 21.19

From Wolcott, G. M. "An animal census of two pastures and a meadow in Northern New York" *Ecological Monographs* 7 1–90, 1937: p. 176, table in **Q20**

Data from *World reference encyclopaedia* Octopus, 1979: 21.18

Introduction

What is science?

Before you can join in and be a scientist you need to know something of what scientists have already discovered and how they do their work. All the people pictured in figures 1 to 4 are scientists. What is special about being a scientist? What do scientists do and how do they do it?

Figure 1

Figure 2

Figure 3

Figure 4

Some people compare being a scientist with playing a game. It can be great fun but it is also very competitive. Scientists like to be first to publish new results and theories and they may win awards and be remembered for their work. Scientists, like sports professionals, need plenty of training and have to work hard for success.

Often scientists work in teams and enjoy the excitement of working out ideas and making discoveries as a group. Members of a team play the game according to agreed rules. One of the rules in the game of science is that the results of experiments are not accepted until they have been published and checked by other scientists. The editors of science journals send new articles to "referees" to make sure that they are written according to the rules and are fit to print.

Figure 5
The Nobel medal which is given to the winners of the annual prizes for physics, chemistry, medicine, literature, and the promotion of peace. The awards are made from the bequest of Alfred Nobel, the Swedish inventor of dynamite, who died in 1896.

Science helps us to make sense of the world we live in. Every day we experience regular patterns: the Sun rises each morning, sugar always dissolves in water, plants wilt without water. This gives us a sense of order which lets us make predictions: the Sun will rise tomorrow morning, the next spoonful of sugar will dissolve in a cup of tea, the rubber plant will die if we forget to water it.

So scientists look for order in what they observe. To see order, they must first make observations and take measurements. In this way they collect much information about the world we live in. They look for patterns in their knowledge.

For example, meteorologists are scientists who study the weather. They record huge numbers of measurements of air pressure, rainfall, temperature and windspeed. The measurements are not taken at random. Meteorologists have theories about which are the important readings to take. Computers are programmed according to these theories to process the mass of data.

We see one way of making a pattern out of all the facts about the climate every time we watch a weather forecast on television. The lines on the weather map have been worked out from all the measurements and satellite observations.

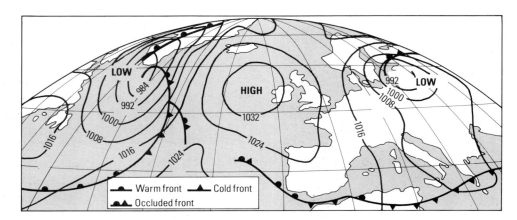

Figure 6
Weather maps like these are published in newspapers.

Once scientists have found patterns it becomes possible to make predictions. Some predictions are very reliable. Astronomers can predict the movement of the planets and comets very accurately. Sometimes the predictions are less certain, as you will know if you have ever been misled by a weather forecast.

As they are collecting facts and looking for patterns scientists also seek explanations. Why is the world as it is? Why do things behave in the way that they do? Inventing theories to explain what we know is an important part of science.

One of the things that you will be doing as you study this science course is seeing for yourself some of the things which scientists have already found. We will be taking you on a "conducted tour" to give you firsthand experience of what scientists have discovered.

While on this tour you will be taught some of the practical skills needed to use scientific equipment and methods. Learning skills needs practice, as you will know if you play a musical instrument or are learning to type. The practice may not always be enjoyable but it is necessary.

If you have ever been a tourist on holiday you will know that it can be interesting – at least for a time. However in the end being a tourist is not as interesting as living your own life where you belong. So it is with science.

To understand science you need to have experience of asking questions and planning investigations. You have to be involved in experiments where the answer is not known in advance. We hope that by the end of this course you will have had several opportunities to join in and be a scientist, using your knowledge and skills to carry out investigations.

Biology is the life science. As members of the living world human beings have always been interested in studying living organisms. At the beginning of the twentieth century biologists spent a great deal of time collecting and recording information about all forms of life. Observation played a very important part in their work and it led to an awareness of the enormous variety that exists among organisms. You can begin to look at this *diversity* in the first two chapters of this book and also to see, in Chapter **B**23, how it led Darwin and Wallace to put forward their theory of evolution.

It is obvious that no one person could ever be expected to know about all the different forms of life. Fortunately, biology is not just a collection of facts. Today biologists are concerned with acquiring an understanding of life and using it to solve problems which affect humans. As in all science, *observation* has an important role in biology. Having made the observations, the next stage is to look for *patterns* or generalizations. A pattern must be *tested* and when it is established that a pattern exists it can be used to make *predictions* about other organisms. In this way the task of a biologist is simplified because it becomes possible to have an understanding of organisms which have never been studied at first hand. The diversity of organisms may be impressive but it is equally remarkable to find that there are patterns which establish that there is also an underlying *unity* among organisms. The key to understanding both the diversity and unity of life was provided by a very exciting discovery which was announced in May 1953. This was a discovery in which knowledge and expertise from biology, chemistry and physics merged to solve the structure of a molecule called DNA.

DNA stands for deoxyribonucleic acid and it is the chemical substance of which genes are made and is therefore found in chromosomes. It is the hereditary material of all cells. The way in which the atoms are arranged to form a molecule of DNA was one of the most exciting discoveries of the twentieth century.

James Watson and Francis Crick (figure 7), two scientists who were working at the Cavendish Laboratory in Cambridge, suggested that the structure of the molecule is like a twisted ladder, an arrangement which has become known as a *double helix*.

Two other scientists, Rosalind Franklin and Maurice Wilkins, who were experts in a technique called X-ray crystallography, took photographs which supported the idea that the molecule was a double helix. (See figure 8.)

The "rungs" of the ladder are formed from pairs of *bases*. There are only four different bases and they are known by their initial letters A, C, T and G. A always pairs with T and C with G. (See figure 9.)

In 1962 the Nobel Prize for Medicine and Physiology was awarded to Francis Crick, James Watson and Maurice Wilkins for the part they played in establishing the structure of DNA. Sadly, Rosalind Franklin had died in 1958 at the age of thirty-seven but she also should be remembered for the outstanding part she played in the discovery of the structure of this remarkable molecule as a double helix.

Figure 7
James Watson and Francis Crick standing in front of the double helix model.

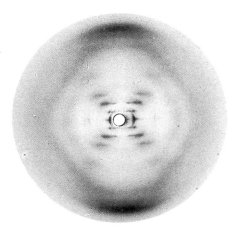

Figure 8
Rosalind Franklin's X-ray photograph of DNA. It was taken in 1952.

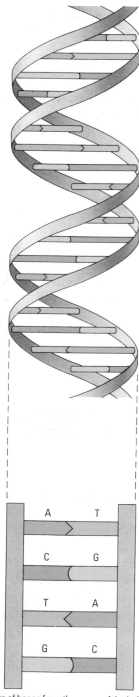

pairs of bases form the rungs of the ladder
Figure 9
A diagram showing the structure of DNA.

You can find out about chromosomes and genes in Chapter **B**22. Because we now know the structure of DNA we know that what living organisms inherit is a chemically coded message: a message which lies in the order of the four bases. There are almost endless possible arrangements for the order of these four bases. This is what gives DNA the unique property of being able to carry all the information which is passed from one generation to the next.

DNA is the hereditary material of all living organisms but different species have different amounts of it. It distinguishes a bacterium from a horse and a mushroom from an oak tree and so it accounts for both the unity and the diversity of life.

A knowledge of the structure of DNA has led to enormous advances in many areas of science, from getting nearer to understanding what causes cancer to helping to solve the world food problem.

One of the aims of studying biology is to help us to understand how living organisms *function* and much of this book is about that. In addition we need to understand that all organisms interact with each other and with the environment in which they live. This important aspect of biology – called *ecology* – is the subject of Chapters **B**13 to **B**18. We have already cut down a large part of the rain forests and have hunted some animals so much that they are in danger of disappearing. These things were done without people realizing the results they would have. If we can think "biologically" about such matters we can avoid making similar mistakes and may even be able to put right some of the damage already done. We need a supply of food and it has to come from other living organisms but we must have a balanced approach to how we use other organisms for our own purposes. If we are aware of the consequences then we can conserve our resources for the future.

Co-ordinated Sciences

This is a Co-ordinated Science course. You may have seen the word *co-ordinated* used elsewhere. What do you think the following newspaper story means?

"Police carried out a *co-ordinated* raid on ten warehouses in the London area last night. As a result fifteen people were arrested and are being held for questioning."

To be *co-ordinated* the raid must have been carefully organized. Each person in the police team knew exactly what was happening elsewhere and when it was happening. That is what we and your teachers have tried to do with this science course.

You have different books for Biology, Chemistry and Physics, but the separate parts of the course have been carefully co-ordinated so that ideas you meet in one subject can be used in another. For example you will need to use ideas about energy in all your sciences. You will learn about energy first in Physics. When you come to use energy ideas in Physics and Chemistry, your teachers will know and expect to use what you have learned in Biology.

To help you to make the most of this co-ordination we have included a large number of cross references in each of the books. For example when you first come to the subject of photosynthesis in Biology you will be reminded that you can find out more about colour in your Physics book and about the making of starch and sugar in Chemistry.

Sciences are only a part of your school timetable. Your work in this course will also have links with other subjects such as Mathematics, CDT,

Geography and Home Economics. You should be on the look out for opportunities to take advantage of these links.

How to use this book

This book is divided into four topics. It is possible that you will study them in the order in which they are printed. But your teacher may decide on another order. You will have to make use of the knowledge and understanding you have gained in Chemistry and Physics to make sense of all the chapters.

The commentary text advises you on how to go about different parts of your work. Commentary text is printed in type like this.

You do not have to know everything in this book. The book contains more than you have to study so that you and your teacher have some choice about the way you will learn.

Your teacher will guide you. The commentary text will also help you to decide which bits to study in detail, which parts to read for interest and which sections to leave out all together.

Throughout this book, there are symbols to help you to recognize the skills and processes which you need to apply. When one of these is used in the work of this book you will often see the appropriate word in the margin. However, you will find there are often opportunities which are not marked in this way. Here are the skills and processes we shall emphasize.

Observation

This is the skill we use when we look carefully at organisms and how they work. We also use it when we watch what is happening in an experiment.

Measurement

This is an important skill that we use when we are obtaining and recording results.

Interpretation

We shall use this word to mean any activity that involves trying to find new things from observations or measurements. "Interpretation" may mean "making a deduction", or "making a prediction", or "relating observations and measurements to some other ideas in science".

Application

Applying what you have learned and understood is an important skill.

Planning

Planning is a very important part of any scientific investigation. Before making measurements, and often before making detailed observations, you must decide what it is you want to do and what you hope to gain from the investigation.

You will also be able to plan your own experiments. You will find some suggested problems to investigate in this book. You may have better ideas of your own. Successful investigations require careful planning and your teacher will give you guidance about how to set up a scientific inquiry.

Reading a textbook is not the same as reading a story. You have been familiar with stories ever since you started to read. You know the ways in which story books are organized. Textbooks are different. You will have to learn how to make sense of technical writing. You may be given worksheets by your teacher which will help you to make sense of some of the types of text in this book.

Topic B1   The variety of organisms

You recognize people by their characteristics.

Chapter B1

What's what?

B1.1   Sorting things out

Would you make a good witness of an accident? Most people think that they would, but the police are continually amazed at how many eye-witnesses give different, even conflicting accounts of an event. Unfortunately, not many of us are budding Sherlock Holmeses. As the great detective once complained, "You see, but you do not observe".

Figure 1.1
"You see, but you do not observe."

The problem is that although we notice many different things, we are not always able to work out and remember which are the most important and, as a result, we forget nearly everything that we see.

There are hundreds of thousands of types of organism, each with a different name. In Chapters **B**1 and **B**2 you can see something of the diversity of organisms in the world, and the reasons for their complex names.

Organisms have bodies that are built of many different parts and it is possible to describe the many features, or *characteristics*, that they may have. The colour of your eyes or hair and your height are all characteristics that you and your friends have in common. That is not to say that you all have blue eyes or that you are all the same height. In fact you recognize your friends by the combination of characteristics they have.

---

1 What characteristics do you use to recognize your friends?

How do biologists recognize different organisms? They start by looking very carefully for the similarities and differences between organisms. Worksheet **B**1A will help you to do this.

Figure 1.2
Not all of these woodlice are the same.

Figure 1.2 shows a number of animals called woodlice. They are found in damp, dark places, particularly under stones and rotting vegetation. At first sight they all look the same, but if you look carefully you will see that there are differences between them.

---

2 How many different sorts of woodlice are there in figure 1.2?

If you study woodlice carefully, you will find that they are not always found in the same places. Some types of woodlice are found in drier conditions than others. Also, they do not all behave in the same way when handled – some are capable of rolling themselves into a small ball, while others are not.

Studying woodlice under natural conditions is difficult, because they live in dark places. If you keep them in the laboratory, however, you will find that a woodlouse of one type will only breed successfully with another of the same type. The same is true for all the other kinds of woodlice.

This suggests that there are natural groups of organisms, which the organisms themselves seem to recognize. Biologists call these groups *species*.

But what exactly is a species? How similar do organisms of the same species have to be? Unfortunately there is no simple answer to this question, and some biologists have argued for years about whether certain organisms belong to the same or different species. One thing that is always true is that members of the same species must be able to breed successfully to produce offspring which can themselves reproduce.

For example, a horse and a donkey are different species, even though they can breed together to produce a mule (figure 1.3). We know they are different species because the mule is sterile, and normally cannot breed.

Bulldogs and basset hounds look very different from each other but they are the same species and can breed together successfully.

There are some species of mosquito which are so similar that biologists cannot tell them apart. However they belong to separate species because they cannot interbreed with each other.

Figure 1.3
A donkey, a horse and a mule.

Figures 1.4 and **1.5**
A bulldog and a basset hound can breed together successfully. Can you imagine what their puppies would look like?

a　　　　　　　　　　　　　　　　　　b

Figure 1.6
These mosquitoes belong to different species. You cannot easily see any difference between them.

B1.2　Countless different types

How many different species are there in the world? No one really knows, and no one ever will. It is a sad fact that there are many species in the tropical rain forests that are being destroyed before they have been properly described.

e

f

g

h

i

j

k

l

m

n

o

p

q

r

s

t

u

v

w

x

possible to see unusual birds even in the middle of cities. This is particularly true in winter, when many birds move into towns, searching for food. It is worth finding out what is the best food to put into your garden or even on the windowsill in order to attract birds.

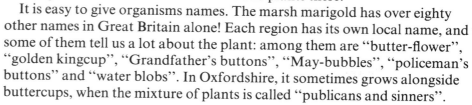

12 Males and females of some bird species look different. Which birds are they? How would you distinguish the sexes?

Keys are concerned with the **differences** between organisms and are useful for identification. However, they don't tell us much about the **similarities** between the organisms that we are studying. For example, a key would help us to identify blackbirds, starlings and song thrushes, but would not tell us that blackbirds have more in common with song thrushes than with starlings.

B1.5 What's in a name?

Figure 1.12
The marsh marigold – its scientific name is *Caltha palustris*.

Suppose a friend has just told you that a ginger-coloured animal has dug a hole by some white flowers in the garden. You may suspect that the ginger tom cat from next door has been trying to manure the roses, but there is just a chance that a lion has escaped from the zoo and is hiding in the camellias. You can see that unless you use names it is impossible to give any accurate information. It is little wonder that Adam's first job in the Garden of Eden was to give names to all of the animals and plants there!

It is easy to give organisms names. The marsh marigold has over eighty other names in Great Britain alone! Each region has its own local name, and some of them tell us a lot about the plant: among them are "butter-flower", "golden kingcup", "Grandfather's buttons", "May-bubbles", "policeman's buttons" and "water blobs". In Oxfordshire, it sometimes grows alongside buttercups, when the mixture of plants is called "publicans and sinners".

INTERPRET

13 From this list of names what do you imagine this plant to be like? Look at figure 1.12 to see if you are correct.

Figure 1.13
This is the American robin. Compare it with the British robin in figure 1.11.

Attractive as local names are, unless everyone is familiar with them all there is a great risk of confusion.

Sometimes the same name is used for two different organisms. Americans, for example, use the name "robin" to mean a different bird from the British one. This is not satisfactory, and you need to say "American robin" or "British robin" to be sure that everyone understands exactly which organism you are talking about. (See figures 1.13 and 1.11.)

To avoid this sort of confusion, biologists use a single system of naming organisms that is recognized throughout the world. This method was devised by Carl von Linné (or Linnaeus as he is often called), and he wrote about it in a book called *Systema naturae* which was published in 1735. The principles of his method (and indeed many of his original names) are still in use today.

Each organism has a unique name that consists of two parts. This system of naming organisms is called the *binomial system*. Each part of the name is usually of Latin or Greek origin, which is why scientific names look strange to people who have not learned those languages. Worksheet **B**1D will help you to practise using this system of naming organisms.

Review

In this chapter we have seen that there is a great variety of different organisms living on the Earth. It is necessary to have a method of naming them so that everyone knows exactly which organism you are referring to. Biologists also find it convenient to put organisms into groups – a different activity called classification, which we shall look at in the next chapter.

Many forms of life

Figure 2.1
a Carp – *Carassius* sp.
b Field mushroom – *Agaricus campestris*.
c *Peranema* sp. (× 250)
d This causes influenza. (× 59 000)
e *Mucor hiemalis* on tomato.
f *Amoeba*. (× 84)
g An orchid – *Cephalanthera damasonium*.
h *Herpes* – this causes cold sores on your mouth. (× 98 000)
i Sea anemone, *Actinia equina* – this organism catches small aquatic organisms in its sticky tentacles.
j The thin wavy lines are *Treponema* – this organism causes syphilis. (× 790)
k Coconut palm tree.
l *Streptococcus* – this causes a sore throat. (× 1370)

B2.1   The kingdoms of the Earth

You may think that all the organisms in the world are either animals or plants. Unfortunately it is not as simple as that! There are a number of organisms that do not fit into either the animal or the plant kingdoms.

One quite clear difference between organisms is that they either consist of a single cell (are *unicellular*), or many cells (*multicellular*). In unicellular organisms, the single cell has to perform all of the functions necessary for life. In multicellular organisms some cells are specialized and carry out certain functions. We call organisms that are too small to be seen with the naked eye *microscopic*, whilst those that are visible are called *macroscopic*.

Figure 2.1 shows photographs of twelve organisms. Some are animals, some are plants and some are definitely neither! You may use Worksheet **B2B** to find out to which kingdoms these twelve organisms belong.

a

b

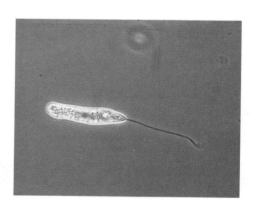

c

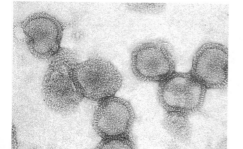

d

e

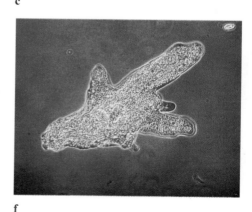

f

B2.2 Inside the animal kingdom

Read carefully the descriptions of the various animal groups that follow. You should have examples of various organisms displayed in the laboratory.

Invertebrates

This group contains all the animals that do not have a backbone. A backbone is part of an internal skeleton made out of bone or cartilage. Invertebrates do not have this bony internal skeleton, and must have some other way of supporting their bodies.

One of the largest phyla (groups) of invertebrates is the arthropods.

Arthropods

All these animals have a body divided into distinct parts (called *segments*). Their bodies are supported by a hard external skeleton called an *exoskeleton*. All have limbs that are jointed.

There are four classes of arthropod.

Crustaceans

These are usually aquatic animals which breathe oxygen dissolved in water through their gills. They always have two pairs of antennae and more than four but fewer than twenty pairs of legs.

Living in a suit of armour. The exoskeleton of a crab may be useful because it protects the delicate parts of the animal, but it does cause problems when

g

h

i

j

k

l

Figure 2.2
A crab, *Carcinus maenas*. Note the exoskeleton, jointed limbs and antennae.

the animal grows. We can imagine what it is like by comparing the exoskeleton to a suit of armour.

A warrior in the sixteenth century had to have a made-to-measure suit of armour. As King Henry VIII grew larger so his armour had to increase in size. Henry was fortunate because he did not need to wear his armour all of the time. For an arthropod, an exoskeleton is like a suit of armour that it does have to wear all of the time.

Figure 2.3
These are just two of the suits of armour that were made for King Henry VIII. As he grew older his armour had to be made taller and broader.

1 How do you think that crabs manage to grow if they live inside a rigid exoskeleton?

On the beach you may have found parts of crab skeletons. This gives you a clue to what happens when an arthropod grows in size.

2 Biologists call the shedding of the exoskeleton *ecdysis*. What is the more common name for it?

3 What dangers would you foresee for a crab when it is undergoing this change?

Insects

These are the largest class of arthropods, and are also the most widespread, living in all parts of the world. They usually live on land and many are capable of flying, sometimes for considerable distances. Their bodies are divided into three parts, called the head, the thorax and the abdomen. On the thorax there are three pairs of legs and usually one or two pairs of wings (figure 2.4). During their lives insects often pass through several stages, some of which may be aquatic.

Figure 2.4
A housefly. You can see the head, the thorax to which the wings are attached and the abdomen.

Figure 2.5
Close up, a spider can look quite
frightening. This is the garden cross
spider, *Aranea diadema*.

Arachnids

Now is the time for a number of you to start wishing that you had stayed in
bed this morning! Arachnids rarely feature in pet shop windows, because they
include the spiders, the scorpions, the mites and the ticks.

Spiders are useful to have in the house because they eat insect pests, and are
a natural form of fly-killer! There are many different forms of spider in
Britain (at least 584 different species), and they are all predatory (figure 2.5).
They look ferocious , and all produce webs made of silken threads in which to
trap and store their food. On a late summer's morning you can often see webs
covered in dew, and the beautiful geometrical shapes become visible. If you
ever see a spider spinning a web then stay and watch how it does it, because it
is a very impressive piece of engineering. Spiders are unusual amongst the
arachnids because their bodies are divided into only two parts. All
arachnids have four pairs of legs.

Myriapods

Question: What goes "ninety-nine bonk, ninety-nine bonk"?
Answer: A centipede with a wooden leg.

An awful joke, which is not even accurate! A centipede does not have 100
legs and a millipede does not have a thousand (or even a million). So how
many do they have?

---

4 Figure 2.6 shows close-up photographs of a millipede and a centipede. Notice that
their bodies are divided into a large number of segments. Count the number of legs on
each segment.

Figure 2.6
A centipede and a millipede. Which is which?

Centipedes and millipedes form a class called myriapods. They are land-
dwelling animals and their heads have jaws. The total number of legs they
have depends upon the number of segments in their bodies.

---

5 Now try to place any arthropod specimens you have in the laboratory in their
appropriate classes.

"Worms"

What is a worm? That is not an easy question to answer, because so many different sorts of animals are called worms. You will probably recognize the one in figure 2.7a. It is an *earthworm*, which is segmented and is a member of the annelid phylum. Figure 2.7b shows a *roundworm*, which belongs to the nematode phylum. The third worm, in figure 2.7c, is a *flatworm* which belongs to the phylum called platyhelminthes.

Figure 2.7
a A segmented worm, the earthworm – *Lumbricus terrestris*.
b A roundworm – *Ascaris* sp.
c A flatworm, the tapeworm – *Taenia* sp.

a

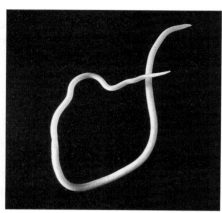
b

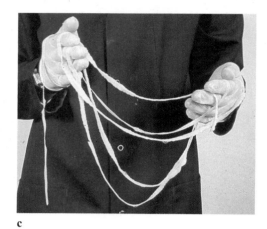
c

6 What features do you see in all the animals shown in figure 2.7 that could be described as "worm-like"?

Flatworms (platyhelminthes)

Some worms from this phylum, such as tapeworms (figure 2.7c) and liver flukes, are common parasites found in many parts of the world. All members of this phylum have flattened bodies which may be divided into sections.

Roundworms (nematodes)

If you looked at freshly dug soil under a microscope, you might be able to see fine white worms that look like pieces of cotton. They may be uninteresting to look at but roundworms can have a remarkable effect upon other organisms. When a dog has worms it is usually infected with parasitic roundworms (although it could have a tapeworm!). Many are parasites in the roots of crop plants. The threadworms (also called pinworms) that are very common parasites of young children are members of this group.

Segmented worms (annelids)

Earthworms have probably done more than any other invertebrate to help farmers in Britain. They improve the texture of the soil by dragging leaves from the surface into their underground burrows. The burrows themselves create valuable air spaces and improve drainage. Fertile soil contains large numbers of earthworms. There are many other species in the annelid phylum, including marine worms and the leeches.

7 Try to place any "worm" specimens you may have in the laboratory into their appropriate groups.

Here are some other examples of invertebrate phyla.

Sponges

These are aquatic animals, with holes through which water circulates. Bath sponges are usually made of plastic nowadays, but a real bath sponge once lived in a tropical sea.

Jellyfish group

These are mostly marine animals, and the group includes sea anemones (see figure 2.1i, page 19). Inside them is a simple cavity with just one opening where they digest their food. The mouth is surrounded by tentacles which may possess stinging cells. The notorious Portuguese man of war has trailing tentacles that contain a poison powerful enough to paralyse a human.

a

b

Figure 2.10
Two molluscs: (**a**) a snail and (**b**) an octopus.

Molluscs

These have an unsegmented soft body, often with a shell, and a large single muscular "foot". The group includes snails, slugs and squids.

This is the only other invertebrate group, apart from crustaceans, that is commonly eaten by humans. Snails of many sorts are often eaten and some people think that squid is a great delicacy.

Echinoderms

This phylum includes sea urchins and starfish. They have a spiny skin with hard plates. Starfish have five arms, which radiate outwards like the spokes of a wheel.

8 Examine some of the specimens of these groups as carefully as you can. Try to see the features mentioned above.

Figure 2.8
A living sponge in its natural habitat.

Figure 2.9
A Portuguese man of war.

Figure 2.11
An echinoderm, the sea urchin – *Echinus esculentus*.

Seafood platter. Worksheet **B2C** contains questions on crabs, lobsters, prawns, shrimps, cockles, mussels and whelks. Use the photographs in figures 2.12 and 2.13 and, if possible, actual specimens to help you answer the questions on the worksheet. You should also look at the live lobster in figure 1.7 (page 11). The hard exoskeleton is a bluish colour and you can see the hard antennae and walking legs.

a   b   c

Figure 2.12
a A live prawn, *Leander* sp. **b** Cooked prawns. *c* A cooked lobster. These crustaceans are very tasty.

a   b   c

Figure 2.13
Delicacies among the molluscs.
a A cockle, *Cardium edule*. **b** A mussel, *Mytilus* sp. **c** A whelk, *Nucella lapillus*.

Vertebrates

These are animals with an internal skeleton which is usually made of bone. They have a backbone surrounding a hollow nerve tube running down the whole of the back of the animal.

The following groups are included among the vertebrates.

Figure 2.14
The common goldfish. Notice the scal and the fins.

Fishes
Fishes are animals that live exclusively in water and breathe through gills. They have a number of fins which enable them to swim upright. Their skin is covered with scales.

Amphibia
These animals can live on land, but they mostly return to water in order to breed. Their sperms and eggs are shed into the water and fertilization is external.

Figure 2.15
One of the British amphibians, the frog –
Rana temporaria. Notice its limbs and its
soft skin.

Figure 2.16
A crocodile, which has a number of ways of avoiding the loss of much water.

Reptiles

Unlike amphibians, reptiles are able to live in dry regions, away from water. They have a dry scaly skin, which is waterproof. Fertilization of the eggs takes place inside the female's body. The eggs have a leathery shell. Reptiles have lungs for breathing air.

One feature of the two remaining vertebrate classes is remarkable. Unlike any other animals, all birds and mammals have the ability to regulate their body temperature. It will not normally fluctuate even though the temperature of the environment may vary. So, for example, a penguin (figure 12.4, page 147) can live and breed in the Antarctic, where the temperature is seldom above 0 °C; its body temperature remains around 39 °C.

We say that birds and mammals are *homoiothermic*; all other animals are *poikilothermic* – the body temperature fluctuates with the environment.

Figure 2.17
All mammals can suckle their young.

Birds

Birds are covered in feathers and have wings for flight (see figure 1.11w, page 15, in which the primary wing feathers show clearly). They breathe air with lungs. Fertilization in birds is internal and the eggs are covered with a hard shell.

Mammals

Their skin has hair and sweat glands. All mammals, even the aquatic ones, such as whales, use lungs for breathing. There is a diaphragm which divides the body cavity into two parts: the *thorax* and the *abdomen*. Fertilization of the eggs is internal. Female mammals produce milk from special glands (called *mammary glands*) to feed the young (figure 2.17).

9 Try to place the vertebrate specimens you may have in the laboratory into their appropriate classes.

Figure 2.18
A duck-billed platypus.

An astonishing animal – what is it? In Australia there lives a rare example of an animal that seems not to fit comfortably into any of the classes of the vertebrates (figure 2.18). It is about the size of a rabbit. It is homoiothermic and is covered in fur. It has webbed feet with claws on the end of its toes. Its reproductive organs are like those of a reptile, and it has a large flat beak like a duck. It lays eggs, which have soft shells. It is a diving animal, and can close the entrance to its ears with a muscular flap of skin when it dives. It produces milk from glands underneath its body. It looks a bit like a collection of spare parts joined together!

10 **Which of these characteristics of this animal are normally associated with**
a **reptiles**
b **birds**
c **mammals?**

The bill of this animal is not made of the same hard material as that of a bird. Also, the animal lacks feathers and the eggs lack a hard shell. It is unlikely to be a bird.

The majority of its characteristics are those of mammals, and so it is grouped with the mammals.

Marsupials. These are a group of mammals which include the kangaroos and wallabies (figure 2.19), whose young are born at a very early stage in their development.

The offspring of a kangaroo are about 2 cm long when they are born, and they have to crawl up the fur on the abdomen of the mother to reach a pouch. The journey takes about three minutes and, once established inside the pouch, they begin to feed on milk produced from nipples that line the pouch.

Figure 2.19
The young of the kangaroo are born very early in their development and spend a long time being suckled inside the mother's pouch.

11 **What are the advantages to the kangaroo of being able to suckle its offspring inside a pouch?**

The majority of mammals, including humans, develop to quite an advanced stage inside the uterus of the mother, nourished directly by her. (See figures 20.11, page 258, and 19.23, page 248.)

12 **The placenta is a structure that enables the mother's blood supply to flow near that of the developing offspring (called a *foetus*). What substances pass from the mother to the foetus? Which pass from the foetus to the mother? (See figure 20.11, page 258.)**

Many baby mammals are born in quite an advanced state, and are usually capable of movement within a few hours after they are born, although they may need a considerable amount of care by the parent for the first weeks (years in the case of humans) of life. One exceptional group of mammals is the ungulates (including horses, zebras and antelopes) which are able to run quickly almost as soon as they are born, although they tend to remain near to their mothers.

13 **Bearing in mind the lifestyle of the ungulates, why is it a considerable advantage to the newly born animals to be able to run?**

OBSERVE

B2.3   The silent producers

In this section we are going to look at some of the major plant groups in order to discover what their main characteristics are.

What is a plant? If you have done Worksheet **B2B** you may have some idea. One thing that is quite clear is that most plants are certainly different from most animals. This is because they get their food in a completely different way from animals which **eat** their food. Their green colour enables them to make their own food by a process called *photosynthesis* which is discussed in Chapter **B**3. Because they **make** their own food they are often called *producers*, in contrast to animals which are known as *consumers*.

Bryophytes

This is a distinctive group of land plants. Bryophyte is the Greek word for "moss-like plant", and this group contains the *mosses*, as well as plants called liverworts.

You will have an opportunity to find out more about mosses if you do Worksheet **B2D**.

Pteridophytes

These plants are the *ferns*. They have xylem in their stems (see page 89). They were much more numerous in the past than they are now. In the Carboniferous age (three hundred million years ago), the Earth was covered with forests of tree ferns. The tree ferns that survive today give us a clue about what those old forests were like (see figure 2.20).

Figure 2.20
A modern tree fern. The carboniferous forests, from which our coal deposits were formed, contained many huge ferns rather like this one.

Worksheet **B2D** helps you to examine the life history of ferns.

Figure 2.21
A pine tree – *Pinus sylvestris*. This tree sheds its leaves slowly throughout the year.

Some plants have a more successful way of reproducing that does not involve spores. These are the *seed-producing plants*. Their seeds contain an embryo and a food supply. They are surrounded by a tough protective coat and are more robust than spores. Seeds are more likely to germinate successfully than spores. Plants that produce seeds are now the most common types of plant on this planet. They belong to two major groups, represented by the *conifers* and the *flowering plants*.

Conifers

These are trees or shrubs that have roots and stems which contain xylem. They have leaves which are often like *needles*. Many of them are evergreen (figure 2.21), because they shed their leaves steadily throughout the year, and do not lose all of them during the autumn. The European larch is a deciduous conifer tree, and does lose its leaves during the autumn.

All conifers produce *cones* which bear the seeds.

The Scots pine produces two types of cone. Pollen is produced inside the male cone. The seed develops inside the female cone (figure 2.22).

a

b

c

Figure 2.22
These cones are where pollen and seeds are made in the pine. The male cone (**a**) produces clouds of pollen, and the seed develops inside the female cone (**b**). The seeds lie between the woody scales of the large ripe cone (**c**).

Figure 2.23
You can see the parallel veins in the leaf of this monocotyledon, maize (*Zea mays*).

Angiosperms

These are plants that produce flowers. Flowering plants have roots, stems and leaves all of which contain xylem. They produce seeds, which are contained inside fruits. They are divided into two groups, the *monocotyledons* and the *dicotyledons*.

Monocotyledons include the grasses, cereals and sugar cane. Oil palms are unusual monocotyledons because they are trees. Monocotyledons usually have long thin leaves with veins that run parallel to the edges of the leaf (see figure 2.23).

The shapes of leaves of the dicotyledons are much more variable and they have different patterns of veins. Differences in the structure of the seeds are investigated in Worksheet **B**2D. Dicotyledons include almost all of the flowering trees (oak, ash, chestnut etc.) as well as plants which lack wood, such as broad bean, pea, daisy, dandelion and buttercup.

B2.4   The other three kingdoms

We are not going to spend so much time thinking about the organisms in the remaining kingdoms. Worksheet **B2B** gives you some details about each of them and the photographs that follow, together with their captions, will give you a chance to think more about them.

Bacteria

These are among the oldest forms of living organisms, as well as being the simplest. They belong to the kingdom called **Monera**. They are of great significance to humans because many of them cause disease. Others are decomposers and in the chapters that deal with ecology you will be told how important they are. Bacteria are almost everywhere and there are times when we are aware of their presence. However, individual species are hard to identify and only experts can do that! (See the photograph of *Streptococcus* in figure 2.1, page 19.)

14 Give two examples of times when you have been aware of the presence of bacteria.

Fungi

Most people have heard of fungi and you have almost certainly eaten some. The edible mushrooms are all members of this kingdom. (See figure 2.1b, page 18.)

Like all the other kingdoms, the fungi are of importance to humans in all kinds of ways. Not only do we eat them, but some species attack and destroy our food crops (see figures 2.1e and 2.24c); others damage the woodwork in our buildings (figure 2.24a).

a

b

c

Figure 2.24
Many fungi are not welcomed by humans.
a House beams can be rotted away by the dry rot fungus;
b Elm trees are killed by a fungus that causes Dutch elm disease;
c Potato crops can be infected with a destructive fungus, potato blight.

Not all fungi are a nuisance to humans, however.

---

15 In what ways do we all benefit from the widespread ability of fungi to digest the various chemicals that have been made by plants?

You may have personal experience of fungi. If you have ever had athlete's foot you have been infected by a species of fungus that causes disease. On the other hand, there are certain foods that would not exist were it not for the work that fungi do in preparing them for you.

---

16 Apart from mushroom soup, what foods do you eat that need fungi to make them?

17 Before going any further, can you think of any organism that does not fit into one of the four kingdoms that you have learned about so far?

Figure 2.25
Some of the biggest protists are the brown seaweeds, like the oarweeds and thongweed.

There are quite a lot of organisms that do not fit into any one of the four kingdoms mentioned so far. They are all grouped into the kingdom **Protista**. Some of them are unicellular. Others are multicellular, like the brown seaweeds that are found around much of the British coastline at the low tide mark (figure 2.25). These protists may reach a length of 3 metres or more.

If you examine a drop of pond water under a microscope you are likely to see a number of unicellular protists such as *Peranema* (see figure 2.1c, page 18).

Many of the protists are photosynthetic, like plants. But others feed in a similar way to animals. *Amoeba* (see figure 2.1f) is a unicellular protist that may be found in ponds and puddles, or living in the soil. One or two species are even parasites of humans and can be very dangerous. *Amoeba* feeds on tiny organisms such as bacteria.

Topic **B**2   The processes of life

Sunlight streaming through leaves.

Chapter B3   Light means life

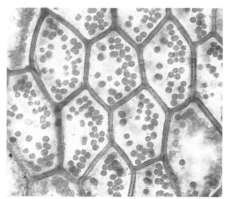

Figure 3.1
The cells in a leaf of the moss *Mnium* seen under a microscope.

B3.1   A leafy world

By far the most common colour in the natural world is green and this natural greenness is provided mainly by the leaves of plants.

Why do leaves look green? To find the answer to this question we can begin by looking inside a leaf. A good leaf to choose is that of a moss, because it consists of just a single layer of cells which we can see easily by using a microscope (figure 3.1).

Where do we find the "greenness"? You can see that it is not everywhere in the cells of the leaf but only in the rounded structures which are called *chloroplasts*. If a leaf is ground up in a liquid such as propanone (water won't do – why not?) a solution of the green colour is formed. The green substance is called *chlorophyll*.

The colours of the spectrum and chlorophyll

The spectrum is obtained by passing white light through a prism (figure 3.2).

1 Which colours can you see in the spectrum of white light?

2 How is the spectrum changed when the light is passed through a chlorophyll solution?

3 What must have happened to the colours which are missing from the spectrum when white light is passed through a chlorophyll solution?

4 After studying figure 3.2 explain why, when you look upwards towards the sky through the leaves of a tree, the leaves look green.

Figure 3.2
a The spectrum (rainbow colours) obtained from white light. The spectrum is obtained by passing white light through a prism, for instance, so that the light is split up into its different colours.
b The spectrum obtained by passing white light through a chlorophyll solution.

a

b

P
PLAN

5 How would you use a projector and a screen, a prism and a chorophyll solution to find out for yourself the effect of passing light through chlorophyll?

A spectrum such as the one produced by light which has passed through a chlorophyll solution is called an absorption spectrum (figure 3.2b).

There is more about colour in the Physics book, Chapter P15.

Coloured substances like chlorophyll are called pigments. If you wanted to, you could find out more about the pigments in a solution of chlorophyll by using the technique called chromatography as in Worksheet **B**3A. At the moment you should realize that chlorophyll is a remarkable molecule because it "harvests" the energy of sunlight and uses it in the process of making food molecules (*photosynthesis*). This, however, is only the beginning of the story of why light means life.

One way of finding out more about leaves and light is to do some experiments yourself (see Worksheet **B**3B). Another is to look at other people's results.

Worksheet **B**3C gives some results and some information about three investigations into leaves and light.

a

B3.2   Why is photosynthesis important?

Animals eat food because it is a source of energy. All living things need a constant supply of energy if they are to grow, reproduce or move, among other things, or indeed, just stay alive. Plants don't eat food but, as we have seen, they do have some in the form of starch in their leaves.

When we eat food we are giving our bodies a source of energy. All the plants and animals shown in figure 3.3 have a link with the food people eat.

b

c

d

Figure 3.3
Some plants and animals which provide our food.

6 No matter what food you eat, its energy has always come from one source in the first place. What is that source?

So one of the reasons why photosynthesis is important is that all animals, including humans, depend on it for a supply of food.

Plants and food

Such an important process needs to be looked at more closely. First of all, not all plants make starch. All plants make the sugar called glucose. Some change it into another sugar, called sucrose, and others change it into starch. The presence of starch in leaves is therefore often taken as a sign that photosynthesis has taken place.

7 Of the plants shown in figure 3.3 choose one which you think makes only sugar and one which makes starch as well. (See Chapter **C3** in the Chemistry book for information on the chemical nature of glucose, sucrose and other sugars.)

What do plants need in order to make glucose (or starch)?

You may perhaps have seen that light, chlorophyll and carbon dioxide are needed for starch to be made in a leaf. However, carbon dioxide contains only atoms of carbon and oxygen – as its name suggests. Sugars and starch on the other hand, both contain atoms of hydrogen as well. The substance most likely to supply the hydrogen atoms is water as it contains hydrogen and oxygen atoms and is readily available in the surroundings of most plants.

We can therefore write a word equation for the process of photosynthesis like this:

$$\text{carbon dioxide} + \text{water} \xrightarrow{\text{light and chlorophyll}} \text{glucose} + \text{oxygen}$$

(Remember that the glucose is changed to starch in many plants.)

The chemical equation for this reaction is written like this:

$$6CO_2 + 6H_2O \xrightarrow{\text{light and chlorophyll}} C_6H_{12}O_6 + 6O_2$$

(See Chapter **C3** in your Chemistry book.)

You can carry out experiments yourself to find out if the four factors, carbon dioxide, water, light and chlorophyll, as suggested in the equation, are all needed for starch to be made in a leaf. See Worksheet **B3B**.

Controlled experiments

As in other biological investigations you must include a *control*. In this case it is also important to make sure that the leaves of the plant you are going to use do not contain starch already. You should therefore use a plant which has been in the dark for a few days. Also, you should then test one of its leaves to check that there is no starch there. If there is none, we say that the plant is *de-starched*. It can then be used in the investigation. In this experiment, the control with which you will compare the other results is a plant which you will give *everything* you think is needed for it to make starch. You then take another de-starched plant and give it everything you think it needs except the one factor you want to investigate. Then after a suitable length of time you test for starch. In this way you can investigate each factor in turn.

Figure 3.4
Variegated leaves of a silver queen plant,
Euonymous fortunei.

You can easily obtain plants which have been without light by putting them in the dark for a time. You will need to obtain leaves without chlorophyll from plants like the one shown in figure 3.4, in which part of the leaf is cream or white because it has no chlorophyll in it.

To get plants which have no carbon dioxide in their surroundings you have to put an alkaline substance, such as soda lime, near the leaves in a closed container and to grow them in these conditions for a day or two. It is not so simple to show that water is needed because it is obvious that if you removed all the water from a plant you would certainly kill it.

An experiment for you to design

8 Design an experiment in which you could grow plants:
a in the dark and with carbon dioxide in their surroundings
b in the light but without carbon dioxide
c in darkness but with no carbon dioxide.
Describe your apparatus and explain how you would use it to find out if plants really do need light and carbon dioxide in order to make starch. (See Worksheets **B3B** and **B3D**.)

Green plants, then, are unique because they can "harvest" energy from the sun and use it to make food. The raw materials used are carbon dioxide and water and the products are glucose and oxygen. The amount of glucose that is made by different plants varies quite a lot. Sugar cane growing on 1 square metre of land can produce up to 7 kilograms of glucose in a year. (To give you an idea how much this is, remember that sugar is usually sold in 1-kilogram bags.) In Britain the agricultural crops produce between 0.15 and 0.8 kilogram of glucose per square metre each year. Animals cannot make food in this way – they have to eat plants or other animals which have eaten plants. They may even eat animals which have eaten animals which have eaten plants! It is therefore true to say that all animals depend on plants for their food (see Chapter **B4** and Chapter **B14** in this book and Chapter **P12** in your Physics book).

B3.3 Leaves and gases

Carbon dioxide

You probably know that human beings and other animals give out carbon dioxide to the atmosphere around them. This is the result of *respiration*, which is a process carried out by all living organisms, including green plants (see Chapter **B9**). Vast quantities of carbon dioxide are being added to the Earth's atmosphere all the time. Industrial processes, as well as respiration, produce carbon dioxide which is released into the atmosphere; one estimate is that 500 000 000 000 tonnes of this gas are added each year. In spite of this, the amount of carbon dioxide in the atmosphere has remained remarkably constant over the years although it is increasing at the present time. The reason it has remained so constant until recently is mainly that it is removed by photosynthesis, although vast amounts are also absorbed by the waters of the oceans.

Oxygen

The numbers that follow are only to give you an idea of the huge amounts of oxygen involved. You are not expected to remember them.

The oxygen produced by photosynthesis on the land and in the sea amounts to 368 000 000 000 tonnes in a year. The four thousand million or so people living on the Earth (without counting all the other organisms) need about 1 000 000 000 tonnes of oxygen a year for respiration. Add to this the oxygen used by other organisms and by industry and we find that about 500 tonnes of oxygen are disappearing every second. The oxygen produced by photosynthesis plays an important part in restoring the balance although there is an enormous reservoir of oxygen in the atmosphere, which amounts to 1 200 000 000 000 000 tonnes; we also rely on this.

So photosynthesis is also important because it helps to keep the balance between carbon dioxide and oxygen in the atmosphere.

B3.4   Made for the job

You know that food is made in the leaves of plants and you know what is needed for photosynthesis to take place. Keeping these facts in mind you should be able to design an "ideal" leaf. See also Worksheets **B3E**, **B3F** and **B3G**.

You are now in a position to consider the close relationship between the structure of a leaf and the important process which it carries out. You already know that photosynthesis takes place in the chloroplasts because that is where the chlorophyll, which "harvests" the light, is found. So first of all, notice how the thinness of the leaf means that vast numbers of chloroplasts are very close to the upper surface. Note too, that the upper epidermis itself has no chloroplasts in it. This means the light can pass through it to the cells underneath. The air spaces allow gases to circulate inside the leaf and the stomata in the lower epidermis allow gases to pass in and out of the leaf. The sugars made in the cells are carried away in the veins of the leaf, which form the transport system. (See figure 3.6.)

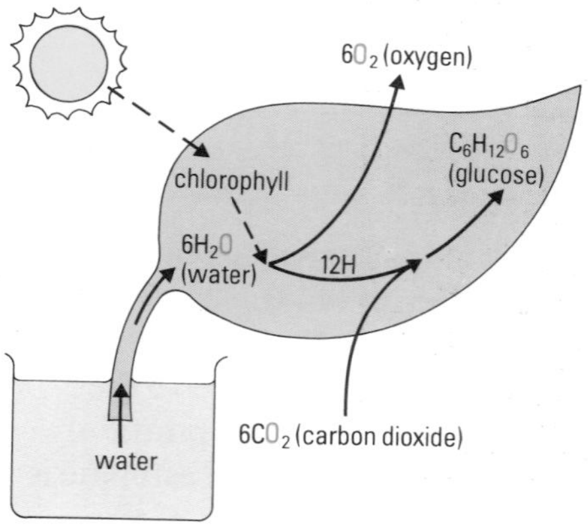

B3.5   More about photosynthesis

It would be a good idea to consult your teacher before starting this section.

9 Work out the path which is taken by a carbon atom from the time it enters a leaf in a molecule of carbon dioxide until it becomes part of a glucose molecule.

Figure 3.5
The changes taking place during photosynthesis.

We can follow the path the carbon atom takes in photosynthesis but another question we might ask is, "Where does the oxygen which is given off from the leaf come from?". It could come from the carbon dioxide or it could come from the water taken in by the plant, as both of these molecules contain oxygen atoms. From the results of experiments carried out by other people, we know that the water molecules are split into oxygen and hydrogen and it is this oxygen which is given off from the leaves. The hydrogen combines with the carbon dioxide to form glucose. An outline of all the changes taking place in photosynthesis is shown in figure 3.5.

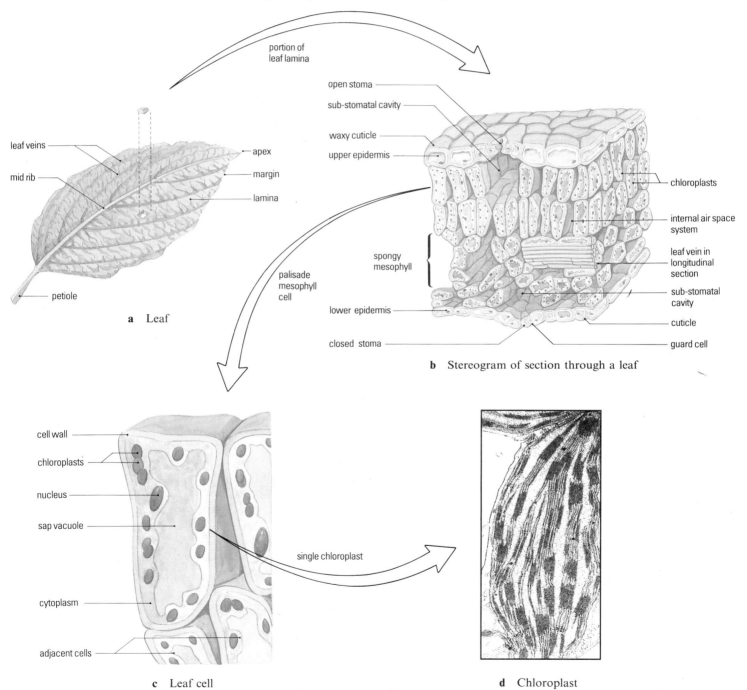

Figure 3.6
Where in a leaf does photosynthesis take place?
Note: Chloroplasts are extremely small but under an electron microscope (**d**) they are magnified many thousands of times.

B3.6   **What are the best conditions for photosynthesis?**

Earlier in this chapter we saw that sugar cane makes more sugar than crops grown in Britain. One of the reasons for this may be that the climate in the countries where sugar cane grows is better for photosynthesis than the British climate.

10 What conditions do you think may affect photosynthesis?

Let us look at each of the conditions you may have suggested in answer to question **10**.

Temperature

Sugar cane grows well in a hot climate. This is because the higher the temperature, the greater the **rate** of photosynthesis. (*Rate* always involves time, so that the rate at which photosynthesis takes place could be measured by the amount of glucose made in a given time.) However, above temperatures of about 40 °C photosynthesis begins to slow down and if the temperature continues to rise it stops altogether. This is because the enzymes which take part in the chemical reactions of photosynthesis are destroyed at the higher temperatures (there is more about enzymes in Chapter **B**5.) One of the reasons why some plants produce such a good crop in a glasshouse is the higher temperature (but the temperature should not be too high).

Figure 3.7
Grapes growing in a glasshouse.

Light

The light is also very bright in countries where sugar cane grows and this will certainly make photosynthesis take place more quickly. Plants do not grow in dark caves.

It is also true to say that the brighter the light, the greater the rate of photosynthesis. Many plants have their leaves spread out in such a way that each leaf gets as much light as possible and the lower leaves are not shaded by the ones above. This arrangement is called a *leaf mosaic* (see the photograph facing page 30).

However, there are exceptions to this because some woodland plants photosynthesize more efficiently in dim light than in bright light. Because of this they are called *shade plants* (figure 3.8).

An investigation into the effects of light on the rate of photosynthesis

It is possible to investigate the effect of light on the rate of photosynthesis by modifying the apparatus often used to collect the gases given off by a water plant. This time the bubbles given off in a specific time are counted by using the arrangement of apparatus shown in figure 3.9.

Figure 3.10 shows some typical results from such an experiment.

Figure 3.8
Wood sorrel growing in bright light. This plant has a feature which reduces the amount of light falling on the leaves. Can you see what it is?

Figure 3.9
Counting the number of bubbles of gas given off by a water plant under different light intensities.

Distance between plant and light source in m	Number of bubbles given off in 1 minute
1.0	7
0.5	26
0.25	110

Figure 3.10

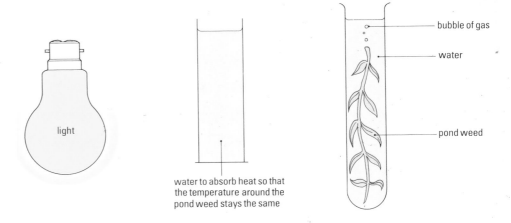

bubble of gas
water
pond weed

water to absorb heat so that the temperature around the pond weed stays the same

INTERPRET

11 From these results suggest what the relationship may be between the rate of photosynthesis and the amount of light received by a plant. (See Worksheet **B3H**.)

Getting the ''right'' light

Many plant growers use artificial light in their glasshouses because they find the plants grow faster and larger than when they are grown in natural light.

We saw earlier that chlorophyll does not absorb all the colours in white light.

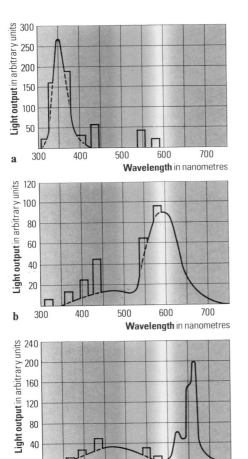

Figure 3.12
Graphs which show the colours given by three different types of light bulb.

Figure 3.11
Plants growing in a glasshouse under artificial lighting.

12 Which light bulb would you advise a plant grower to use?

13 What would you say about the light from the bulb and about plants that might convince the grower that the right type of light should be used? (See Worksheet **B3H**.)

Concentration of carbon dioxide in the air

It is not surprising that scientists had the idea of adding carbon dioxide to the air around plants in order to increase the amount of sugar made in photosynthesis. This would improve the growth of the plants and that would mean better crops. It is difficult to do this out in a field but it is possible in a glasshouse. It is very common for growers to pump carbon dioxide into glasshouses and, as you can see from figure 3.13, this makes a considerable difference to the growth of lettuces. The concentration of carbon dioxide in the air is normally 0.03 per cent. Increasing the level to 0.1 per cent gives a much higher yield of crop. Doing this costs the grower money but is worth

Graph A

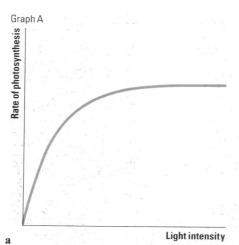

a

a

b

Figure 3.13
Lettuces growing in greenhouses. Those in **a** were grown in air containing more carbon dioxide than those in **b**.

Graph B

b   Carbon dioxide concentration

Figure 3.14
Graphs showing
a light and
b carbon dioxide,
acting as limiting factors.

while because of the increased crop yield. Above the level of 0.1 per cent there is often not enough light for the plants to be able to use any extra carbon dioxide and we say that light is *limiting* the rate of photosynthesis. At much higher levels of carbon dioxide photosynthesis stops altogether. This is partly because the stomata in the epidermis close and the gases cannot pass in and out of the leaf.

Water

A wilting plant will not make much sugar but the lack of water will affect other processes besides photosynthesis, so it is difficult to investigate the effect of water alone on the rate of photosynthesis.

imiting factor.

These four factors, temperature, light, carbon dioxide and water do not, however, act separately in the effect they have on the rate at which plants make food by photosynthesis. We have already seen that light may limit the rate when there is plenty of carbon dioxide present. They interact with each other and so each one can be a *limiting factor*, depending on the conditions.

INTERPRET

14 Study figure 3.14. Suggest why the rate of photosynthesis shown in graph A does not continue to increase although light intensity does.

15 Suggest why the rate of photosynthesis shown in graph B slows down, although the concentration of carbon dioxide continues to increase.

16 Which factors do you think limit the rate of photosynthesis in the following cases?
a In a field of wheat early on a summer morning (the carbon dioxide concentration is high as a result of respiration which the plants carried out during the night). (See figure 3.3.)
b In the same field of wheat in the middle of the day.
c Among the plants growing under the trees in a forest in the summer (figure 3.15).

Figure 3.15
Plants growing in a forest in summer.

Review

So long as light is available from the sun, photosynthesis is the process which supports all the living organisms on this planet. There are two very important features of it which must be mentioned here but which are dealt with in more detail elsewhere (see Chapters **B**14 and **B**15). Firstly, photosynthesis takes part in the mechanism whereby carbon atoms move in a cycle from one organism to another. Carbon dioxide, produced during respiration (see Chapter **B**9), is one of the raw materials used to produce glucose during photosynthesis. Some of the glucose is used as the building blocks for the bodies of plants and animals, but most of it becomes a source of energy in the process of respiration and carbon dioxide is again released. This pattern is called the *carbon cycle* (see Chapter **B**15). Whenever humans cut down forests or pollute oceans they are gambling with the carbon cycle.

Secondly, while the carbon atoms are recycled, **energy flows** continuously in one direction. Energy from the sun is transferred to leaves where it is used to make carbohydrate molecules during photosynthesis. Animals and plants get energy from these molecules during respiration. Finally, most of the energy is transferred to the surroundings and eventually back out to space and cannot be useful to living organisms again. (See Chapter **B**14.)

So we, like every other living organism on this Earth, depend on photosynthesis for every activity of our lives.

Chapter B4   How do animals feed?

B4.1   Lazers or grazers?

Animals depend on food as a source of energy but unlike green plants they cannot make it for themselves.

1 How do animals get their food?

Enormous herds of animals such as wildebeestes, zebras and gazelles live in grassland areas such as the famous Serengeti Plain in East Africa. They make up some of the largest herds of animals to be found anywhere in the world and they spend most of their time feeding. Lions live in much smaller groups in the same grassland areas but they spend most of their time resting.

Figure 4.1
Lions laze while zebras graze.

2 What explanation can you give for lions lazing while the zebras graze?

B4.2   Different ways of feeding

3 Sort out the animals shown in figure 4.2 into two groups — those which are plant eaters and those which eat animals.

Figure 4.2
Some animals eat plants, some eat other animals and some eat both.
Can you tell what eats what?

Animals which eat plants are called *herbivores* and those which eat other animals are called *carnivores*. Worksheet **B4A** looks at the quantity of food eaten by different animals.

B4.3   Different teeth for different food

OBSERVE   INTERPRET

4 What differences can you see between the horse's teeth and those of the tiger (see figures 4.3 and 4.4)?

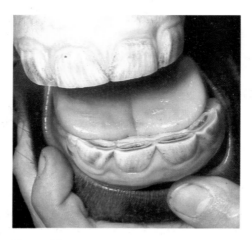

Figure 4.3
The teeth of a horse. What do you think it eats?

Figure 4.4
The teeth of a tiger. Notice the differences from the horse's teeth.

It is easier to see differences in mammals' teeth if you look at skulls which have the teeth still in place in the jaws. It is quite obvious that not all mammals have the same numbers of the different kinds of teeth. The way that the different numbers and kinds of teeth are arranged in mammals' jaws is called their *dentition*. It is interesting to see the way in which the dentition of mammals varies and how it is related to the food a mammal eats. (See Worksheet **B4B**.)

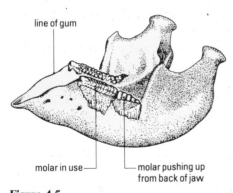

line of gum

molar in use — — molar pushing up from back of jaw

Figure 4.5
The large molars in the lower jaw of an elephant.

Eating plants is not easy

Over its lifetime an African elephant wears down a total of 24 molar teeth, although usually only two in each jaw are in use at any one time. An elephant's molar tooth is about the size of a housebrick and it is made up of layers. As the tooth wears, it moves forward in the jaw and the layers drop off until none of the tooth is left. Another tooth grows forward from the back of the jaw to replace it. When the sixth molar in each side of the jaw has worn out there are no more to replace them. The elephant then has difficulty in eating – this happens when it is about 66 years old.

Figure 4.6
The cheek teeth of sheep.

5 Name some other mammals you would expect to have teeth like those of a sheep and explain why.

6 Which type of teeth do sheep lack?

The meat eaters

a

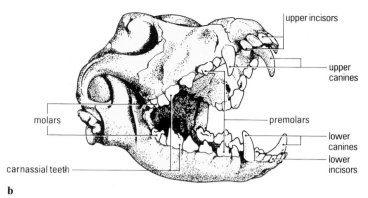

b

Figure 4.7
a Give a dog a bone.... Which teeth is it using?
b You can see the different kinds of teeth clearly in the skull of a dog.

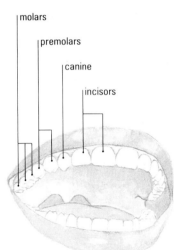

Figure 4.8
Human adult teeth.

7 Which of the dog's teeth seem particularly well developed? Why do you think this is (see figure 4.7)?

8 In what ways do the cheek teeth of a plant-eater and a meat-eater differ? Explain the way this affects the state of the food when it is swallowed.

The easiest set of teeth for you to examine is your own – Worksheet **B4B** will help you. You already know that not all your teeth are the same and you can see the different kinds of teeth named in figure 4.8.

Because humans usually eat both plants and animals as food we are called *omnivores*.

9 Of the animals shown in figure 4.2, which ones have teeth that are something like ours?

Your own teeth are very important and it will help you to look after them properly if you know about their structure.

B4.4 Teeth should last a lifetime

Acrobats can hang by their teeth. Some people crack nuts with their teeth and even use them to wrench the tops off bottles. No one can recommend this if you want your teeth to last a lifetime. But it gives you some idea of just how strong they are. The *enamel* that covers your teeth is the hardest substance in the body.

Smile at yourself in a mirror. Your gums should be pale pink and firm and should not bleed when you brush your teeth. Don't worry if your teeth look more ivory than sparkling white. However, there should be no discoloration of the gums around the margins or between the teeth.

Why do teeth decay?

If teeth are so strong, how is it that dentists manage to stay in business?

One reason is that although tooth enamel is very hard, it can be "eaten away" by acid. If you feel your teeth with the tip of your tongue just before brushing them, they may seem slightly rough and sticky in places. What you feel is a substance called *plaque* which collects, especially between the teeth and around the edges of the gums (figure 4.10).

Figure 4.9
A section cut through a tooth to show its structure.

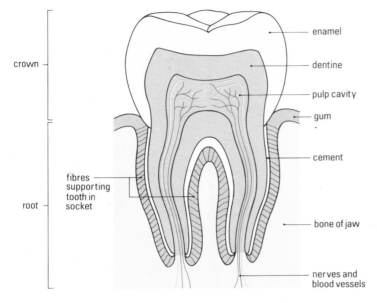

crown

root

enamel

dentine

pulp cavity

gum

cement

fibres supporting tooth in socket

bone of jaw

nerves and blood vessels

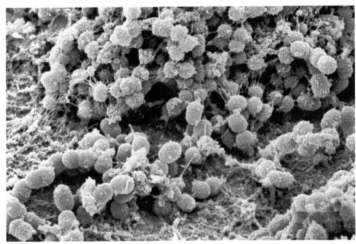

Figure 4.10
An electronmicrograph of plaque on teeth.

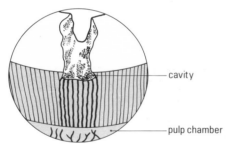

cavity

pulp chamber

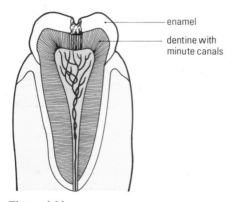

enamel

dentine with minute canals

Figure 4.11
How a cavity forms in a tooth. Once the hard enamel has been eroded, bacteria enter the tiny canals in the dentine. If not treated they eventually reach the pulp cavity.

Plaque consists of saliva, food particles and bacteria. If any sugar is present, the bacteria will react with it and produce acid. Acid which is allowed to stay in contact with the teeth will "eat" through the enamel into the *dentine*. Worksheet **B**4C tells you how to show up any plaque there may be on your teeth.

Running through the dentine are tiny canals that lead to the "live" part of the tooth – the *pulp cavity* – that contains its nerve and its blood supply. Once the dentine is exposed, the bacteria will be able to enter these canals and reach the centre of the tooth, inflaming the pulp and causing toothache. This process of tooth decay is called *caries* (figure 4.11).

B4.5   Prevention is better than cure

Another reason for the fact that dentists are seldom out of work is that, although we know what causes caries, we don't always take steps to prevent it. Where your teeth are concerned, prevention is always better than cure. Decayed teeth have to be filled – and every filling will weaken the tooth a little. A tooth which has become badly decayed may even have to be pulled out. Dentists nowadays do all they can to save a tooth rather than pull it out, but about 25 % of British adults have a complete set of false teeth and have none at all of their own.

It is impossible to keep the mouth sterile (bacteria-free). But there are other ways of reducing the chances of caries developing.

A
APPLY

10 Can you think of two such ways, and suggest how they might work?

Keeping your teeth clean

The first and most effective step is to brush your teeth regularly, last thing at night and after every meal. This removes the plaque and so prevents the formation of the acids which make teeth decay.

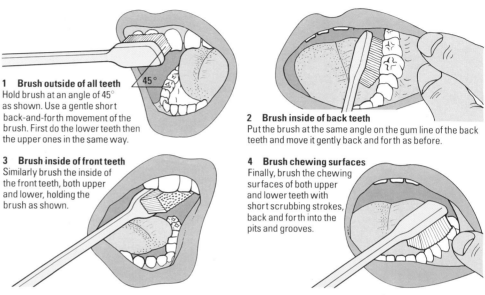

1   Brush outside of all teeth
Hold brush at an angle of 45°
as shown. Use a gentle short
back-and-forth movement of the
brush. First do the lower teeth then
the upper ones in the same way.

2   Brush inside of back teeth
Put the brush at the same angle on the gum line of the back
teeth and move it gently back and forth as before.

3   Brush inside of front teeth
Similarly brush the inside of
the front teeth, both upper
and lower, holding the
brush as shown.

4   Brush chewing surfaces
Finally, brush the chewing
surfaces of both upper
and lower teeth with
short scrubbing strokes,
back and forth into the
pits and grooves.

Figure 4.12
The way to brush your teeth.

Figure 4.12 shows how you should brush your teeth from side to side, up and down and at the back of the teeth as well. Dental floss, drawn to and fro between the teeth so that the side of each tooth is rubbed, will remove traces of plaque in the gaps. Most dentists recommend using a small toothbrush, which will clean the crevices between the teeth better. Brushing your teeth properly will help to prevent gum disease (gingivitis) too. If plaque is allowed to build up, it will irritate the edges of the gums. These become sore and inflamed. They may swell, so that between the tooth and the gum a "pocket" forms in which more plaque can accumulate. Eventually the plaque hardens, and cannot be removed simply by brushing – the dentist will need to "de-scale" the teeth, using a special instrument. Then the dentist will polish the teeth because plaque is less likely to form on a smooth surface. Worksheet **B**4C will help you to find out more about how well you clean your own teeth.

The dangers of a sweet tooth

The more sugar and sugary foods your diet contains, the more chance there is that acid will be produced by the bacteria in your mouth, and the greater the risk of tooth decay. Cutting down the amount of sugar you eat will help to limit tooth decay. Even if you can't resist sugary foods, try to cut down the amount of time your teeth are exposed to them. A 50 g bar of chocolate eaten all at once, for example, will be less harmful than 50 g of toffees sucked throughout a whole afternoon.

If you cannot brush your teeth easily after a meal, eat a piece of cheese instead. Cheese neutralizes the acid formed, and is a better way to end a meal than the traditional apple (which contains sugar).

Worksheets **B**4C, **B**4D and **B**4E help you to find out about some of the things which may be responsible for patterns of tooth decay.

Worksheet **B**4F helps you to compare different toothpastes.

B4.6   Different guts for different diets

It is not only the teeth that differ between one animal and another. Different diets require different guts. The gut of an animal is almost always a tube which begins at the mouth and ends at the anus. An earthworm is an example of an animal with a gut which is a straight tube.

The structure of guts varies a lot and depends on the amount and kind of food that is eaten.

The human gut is an example of one that belongs to an omnivore (figure 4.13).

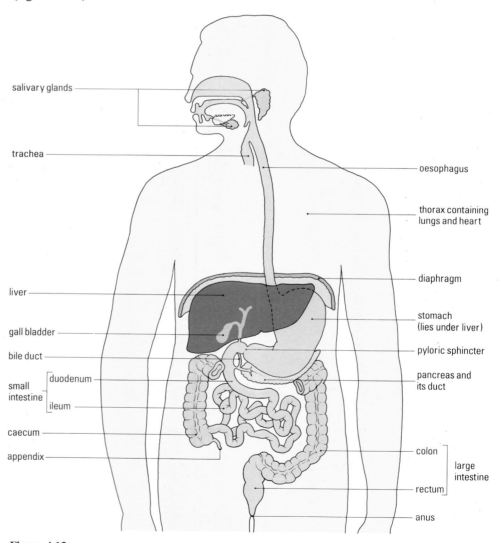

Figure 4.13
The parts of the human gut.

We have already seen that herbivores eat a lot. Also plant food is not easy to digest. It takes about two and a half days for food to pass through an elephant's gut. Even so, elephant dung contains a great deal of undigested plant material. This is because the walls of plant cells are made of cellulose which most animals cannot digest. There are, however, some bacteria that do digest cellulose. The plant eaters, therefore, often have these bacteria in a part of their gut and they digest the cellulose.

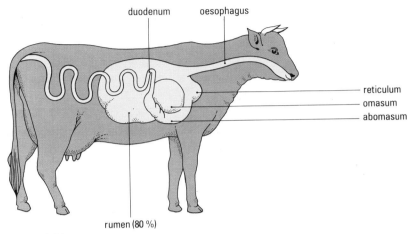

Figure 4.14
A cow's stomach.

Animals which chew cud, like sheep and cattle, have a very large stomach made up of four parts (see figure 4.14). When food is swallowed the first time it is formed into balls of *cud*. These are returned to the mouth and chewed over again, often while the animal is lying down. When the food is swallowed the second time it goes into the largest part of the stomach which is called the *rumen* (this is why cud-chewing animals are called ruminants). The rumen contains the bacteria that digest cellulose.

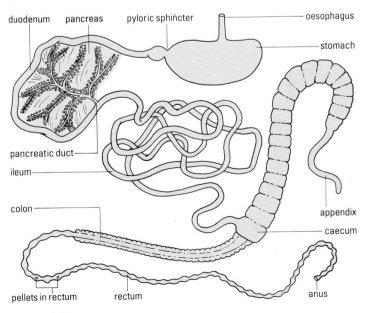

Figure 4.15
The gut of a rabbit. How does it differ from the human gut?

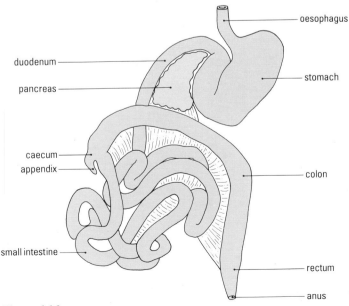

Figure 4.16
The gut of a cat. Compare this with the gut of a rabbit and the human gut.

Rabbits have a large but simple stomach. The cellulose-digesting bacteria are in other parts of the gut, the *caecum* and the *appendix* (see figure 4.15). The first time the food goes through the rabbit's gut, rather soft faecal pellets containing a lot of undigested food are produced. These are eaten again as soon as they are produced from the anus. Because the pellets have been through the gut once, cellulose-digesting bacteria are present. When they enter the stomach for the second time they stay there for a while and the undigested food has a second chance to be digested. The second time round, the familiar hard rabbit "droppings" are produced.

Carnivores may require a lot of energy to catch their prey but, having caught it, they do not chew it. They swallow it whole or in large pieces. They can then rest while the meal is digested. The stomach may have to be large but one meal will last a long time (figure 4.16).

OBSERVE   INTERPRET

11 What differences can you see between a carnivore's gut and that of a herbivore and an omnivore? How do you account for the differences?

Review

In this chapter we have seen that the structure of teeth and of guts can be related to the kind of diet an animal eats. In the next chapter we are going to look at what happens to food in the gut.

Why is my gut folded?

Chapter **B**5

The gut as a food processor

How would I do up my laces if it wasn't?

Figure 5.1

B5.1 Food on the move

In order to make use of food an animal has first to get it into its mouth. This is where the food processing starts, as you probably saw by looking at teeth in Chapter **B**4. After the food enters the mouth it may be swallowed whole or it may be ground up.

---

1 Which animals swallow their food without chewing it and which ones grind it up?

Your mouth is the beginning of a very long tube called by a variety of names, the simplest of which is "the gut". The food has to travel 10 metres through the gut before it reappears in quite a different form at the other end!

How much space does your gut take up?

M
MEASURE

The place where the gut lies is called the abdominal cavity. You can't break into it so you will have to measure this space from the outside. One way would be to use a tape measure or a ruler to measure

1 its height
2 its width
3 how deep it is from front to back (you may have to get someone to do that for you).

You may be able to think of a more accurate way.

P
PLAN

---

2 If you assume that your abdominal cavity is a box, what is its volume?

You will find that the abdominal cavity is not very large; perhaps it is about the size of a small suitcase. Even so, it contains ten metres of gut and somehow, all that you eat has to pass along it. Obviously your gut must be folded up.

---

3 Suggest how food might be moved through the gut.

You could be forgiven for suggesting that food slides slowly down the gut in the same way as Newton's apple fell from the tree – by gravity. That would only work if the gut wasn't folded very much (and if you stayed upright!).

4 If the food did move down the gut as a result of gravity, what would happen to people in spacecraft, in conditions of weightlessness?

Here's something a little messy you could try at home. Stand on your head with your feet against a wall. Take a glass of water and drink some of it with a straw. You'll probably need a friend to help you if you want to avoid making too much mess!

5 Can you drink any of the water?

You will realize that there must be a different way to explain how food moves through the gut. It is moved along by two sets of muscles in the gut wall and their activity is known as *peristalsis*.

People sometimes have things wrong with their gut and doctors need to find out what the problem is. They prefer not to operate unless it is essential. A technique has been developed which allows an X-ray photograph to be taken of the gut. (See Chapter **P15** in your Physics book.)

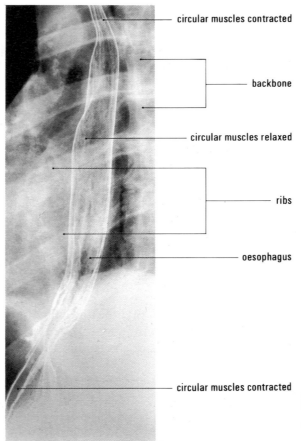

circular muscles contracted

backbone

circular muscles relaxed

ribs

oesophagus

circular muscles contracted

Figure 5.2
The patient has been given barium sulphate to drink. Peristalsis is taking place in the oesophagus.

6 Why is it difficult to take an X-ray photograph of features of the gut?

The patient is given a suspension of barium sulphate to drink. The barium sulphate blocks the passage of X-rays. While it is travelling through the gut, X-ray photographs are taken. Figure 5.2 shows the oesophagus while peristalsis is taking place.

7 Make a copy of figure 5.3b in your notebook. Draw in the position of the circular and longitudinal muscles.

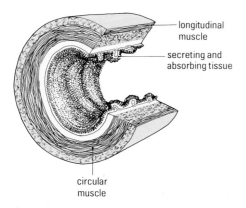

longitudinal muscle

secreting and absorbing tissue

circular muscle

a

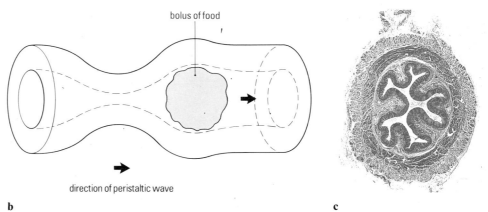

bolus of food

direction of peristaltic wave

b

c

Figure 5.3
a There are two layers of muscle around the gut. **b** Contraction of the longitudinal and circular muscles at different times enables peristalsis to take place. **c** A transverse section of the oesophagus.

8 On your diagram, label a place where you think the circular muscles would be contracted. Label a position where you think the circular muscles would be relaxed.

9 Where do you think the longitudinal muscles might be contracted?

10 Now try to explain, in your own words, how the two sets of muscles work so that food is moved along the gut.

If you watch a giraffe next time you visit the zoo, you may see movements as the food it has eaten travels down its neck. The giraffe chews the cud like a cow. So from time to time some partly digested food has to come from the stomach back to the mouth to be chewed once more. If you are patient and observant you may be able to see this too. But the food must be moistened.

11 Try eating two cream crackers quickly one after the other. You are not allowed a drink of water.

You can see how important saliva is in helping peristalsis to work.

There is more to the working of the gut than peristalsis, though. Once the food is in the gut, physical and chemical breakdown begins.

B5.2   Digestion

If you look at figure 5.4 you can see that if food is to be of any use to you it has to pass through the gut wall from the gut cavity into your bloodstream. The membranes of the cells lining the gut are *selectively permeable*, which means that only certain molecules can pass through them. (See Chapter **C**2 of your Chemistry book.) You can imagine the gut wall as a molecular sieve. In figure 5.4 the large molecules cannot move to the righthand side of the membrane, but the small ones can.

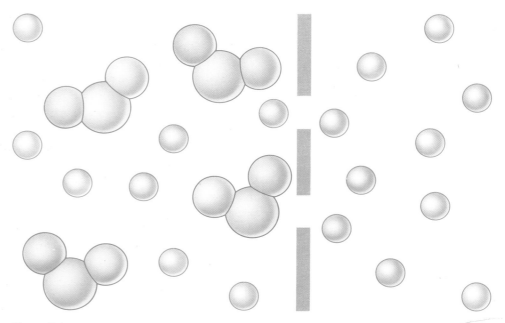

Figure 5.4
Only the small molecules can pass through the gaps in this membrane.

Worksheet **C**30 will demonstrate this effect.

It seems that we are faced with a problem. The food we eat is in the form of big chunks, but only small molecules can get through the gut wall into our bodies. Clearly, one of the main jobs of the gut must be to break the food down into small molecules. This process is called *digestion*.

Starch is a *carbohydrate* which is a large molecule formed from lots of smaller glucose molecules (See Chapter **C**2 in the Chemistry book.) Because it is so big it cannot pass through cell membranes, but it is possible for the glucose molecules to do so.

You probably know that biscuits and potatoes contain starch. Your mouth is the first part of the gut that the food enters so you would not be too surprised to find that some digestion of starch takes place there.

The saliva in the mouth contains something which can change starch to a sugar. You seldom eat just starch. Usually your mouth is full of a mixture of things when you are eating.

An experiment for you to design

It would be quite easy to modify the investigation in Worksheet **B**5A to try to find out whether the digestion of starch by amylase is affected by any of the following:

1 Common salt
2 Cigarette smoke
3 Diluting with distilled water
4 Various temperatures
5 Acids and alkalis.

You will need to write down how you are going to alter the instructions in Worksheet **B**5A.

B5.3   The faster the better

The substance in saliva which converts starch into sugar is called *salivary amylase*. (This is because the old name for starch was amylum.) Without this substance the starch would not change. Even if you boiled starch for a long while, it would hardly break down at all. If you boiled it with an acid there would be some breakdown, but it would be very little and very slow. If you think of how little time food spends in your mouth, and the rather low temperature of your body compared with boiling water, you will understand that amylase has some remarkable properties. It works best at body temperature and at a pH between 6 and 7, which is nearly neutral. (If you are not sure what pH is, see figure 5.6c.)

In chemistry the word *catalyst* is used to describe certain substances that can increase the rate of chemical reactions. Biological catalysts are called *enzymes*. They were given this name because they were first identified in yeast cells and zyme is an old name for yeast.

Enzymes are *proteins*. (You will meet protein molecules in Chapter **C**2 of the Chemistry book.) Proteins are large molecules, made up of long chains of smaller molecules called *amino acids*. These long chains can be folded up into all kinds of shapes. Each enzyme protein has a very special shape which is vital to its ability to act as a catalyst. The molecules on which it acts fit into the enzyme exactly, rather like a key fits a lock.

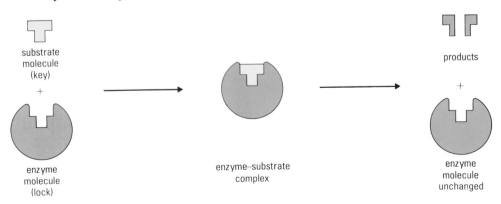

Figure 5.5
The molecules on which an enzyme acts are called substrate molecules. The enzyme and substrate molecules fit each other exactly, rather like the way a key fits a lock.

Only when the two molecules are as close to each other as a lock and key (figure 5.5) can a reaction take place. High temperatures or the wrong pH can change the shape of an enzyme and make it useless.

Consult your teacher before you go on to the next section.

The graphs in figure 5.6 show the effect of **a** pH and **b** temperature on the rate of an enzyme-controlled reaction. (Remember that rate always involves time – see Chapter **B**3.) A pH scale is given in figure 5.6c.

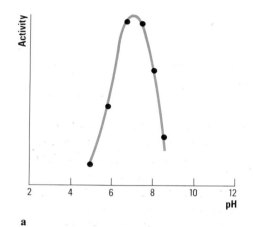

a

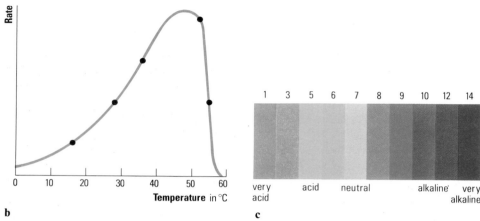

b   c

Figure 5.6
a and **b** These graphs show how fast an enzyme is reacting: its activity at different pH values (**a**) and at different temperatures (**b**).
c The pH scale. This is an indicator paper colour card for the full range pH 1–14.

INTERPRET

12 In graph **a** what is the pH at which the enzyme works fastest? (This is called the optimum pH.)

13 Explain why the reaction is slower both at very low and at very high temperatures (graph **b**).

Starch is not the only large molecule you eat. Proteins and fats, which are also large molecules, are important parts of your diet too and your gut produces enzymes which speed up their digestion as well.

Whatever food you eat, all the proteins that it contains will be broken down to one type of product – *amino acids*. All the carbohydrates will end up as a simple sugar – *glucose*. These are always produced when animals digest proteins and carbohydrates.

B5.4   A little more about enzymes

Many scientists have done a lot of research on enzymes. They are very complex molecules and the gut makes and uses many different ones. All organisms make enzymes, and not only in their guts. The potato plant uses enzymes to convert sugar into starch to store in the underground tuber. It uses a different enzyme to turn the starch back into sugar.

14 At what time of year will the potato plant produce and use the enzyme that changes starch to sugar?

Worksheet **B**5B will give you the opportunity to investigate the activity of a protein-digesting enzyme. Also see Chapter **C**10 of your Chemistry book for more about enzymes and washing powders. You can learn about the action of enzymes on carbohydrates in Chapter **C**3 (section 3.4).

B5.5   A matter of digestion

Figure 5.7

You may have seen a dissection of the gut of a small mammal. Even if you haven't, you are probably aware that the gut is very complicated. At the start of this chapter it became clear that it was not just a simple, straight tube. You can get some idea of what the human gut looks like from figure 4.13.

Between the mouth and anus there are several special regions, each doing a particular job. Once the food we have eaten has been digested, the resulting products must be *absorbed*. Any undigested or unabsorbed food will then leave the body as faeces. You can tell that the gut does a lot to the food if you compare what goes in with what comes out! (Figure 5.7.)

The first part of the gut inside your abdomen is the *stomach*. Its lining produces *gastric juice*. This contains hydrochloric acid (pH about 2) which kills most of the micro-organisms present in the food. Gastric juice also contains enzymes. The stomach wall is very muscular and churns and mixes the food; it is soon changed into a semi-fluid state.

INTERPRET

15 What is the optimum pH of the stomach enzymes likely to be?

16 How do you think the gastric juice will affect the activity of salivary amylase once it gets into the stomach?

As you have seen in Chapter **B**4, some animals such as cows and giraffes have a stomach which has many different chambers. The food is chewed, churned, rechewed, churned again and acted on by enzymes made by microorganisms in the stomach. In humans the stomach is simpler and merely acts as a temporary store of food where a little digestion takes place. The stomach has a valve which controls the release of its contents to the small intestine.

In the small intestine the food is mixed with:

pancreatic juice (a mixture of digestive enzymes from the pancreas); intestinal juice (a mixture of enzymes produced by the wall of the gut itself); and bile, an alkaline liquid, which does not contain enzymes, produced by the liver.

Bile emulsifies fats – this means that it breaks big fat droplets into lots of little ones. (See Chapter **C**9 in your Chemistry book.)

17 How might an alkaline fluid be useful in the small intestine?

18 How do you think making lots of small fat droplets from one big droplet helps with fat digestion?

B5.6　An absorbing activity

One function of the small intestine is digestion but it is also well designed to carry out the *absorption* of digested food products into the bloodstream.

INTERPRET

19 What features would you expect the small intestine to have in order to help with absorption?

The small intestine has about 5 million *villi* each about 1 mm long and less than 0.25 mm thick. It has been estimated that they provide up to 10 m² of surface area. That's the size of a small bedroom floor. This is increased by about 50 times by *microvilli*; there are 1000 microvilli, each 1 µm long, projecting from each cell on the surface of a villus. In figures 5.9 and 5.10 you can see a drawing of a villus and a highly magnified photograph of microvilli.

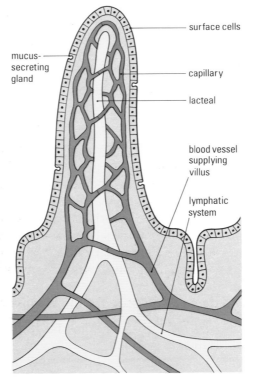

surface cells

mucus-secreting gland

capillary

lacteal

blood vessel supplying villus

lymphatic system

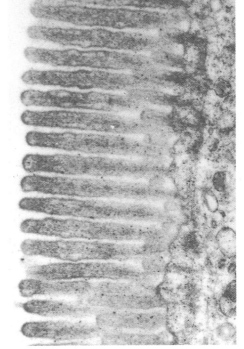

Figure 5.8
High magnification (× 53) enables us to see the villi on the lining of the human gut.

Figures 5.9 and 5.10
Each villus has a complicated internal structure, including many capillaries, and a highly folded outer surface. The photograph on the right (× 50 000) shows microvilli.

Most digested food passes through the walls of the villi into the small blood vessels called capillaries that are inside them (see Chapter **B**8). From here the blood carries away the food molecules and distributes them around the body.

See Worksheet **B**5C "The value of villi."

B5.7   The waste pipe

Undigested and unabsorbed food leaving the small intestine is called *faeces*. The faeces enter the large intestine where most of the water is reabsorbed into the blood during its passage along the intestine and what remains (now semi-solid) leaves the body.

In some herbivorous animals the *caecum* is a very important part of the gut where a lot of digestive activity takes place. However, in humans neither the caecum nor the appendix attached to it is of much use. If you have had appendicitis you know that this tiny part of your gut can cause a lot of trouble when it is inflamed!

When your gut becomes infected, one way in which it responds is to speed up peristalsis. As a result faeces pass through the *colon* much faster than usual and there is not time for the water to be reabsorbed. You can hear the effects of this and sometimes even feel them! And the unpleasant end result is *diarrhoea*.

---

20 Suggest what normally happens to faeces while they are in the colon.

The movement of faeces through the large intestine is made easier if it is full. Undigested material called *roughage* is very important in providing the bulk needed for muscles to squeeze against and keep faeces on the move. Too little roughage in the diet can lead to *constipation* (see Chapter **B**6).

---

21 Why do you think constipation is quite common in old people in the Western world and almost unheard of in African nations?

Faeces contain huge numbers of bacteria and these manufacture very important vitamins. Unfortunately, gases are a natural by-product of their activities and are released from the anus as *flatus*. A high proportion of flatus is atmospheric air swallowed when eating – the bacterial contribution creates the unpleasant smell.

Faeces are stored in the *colon* but when they are in the *rectum* or bowel they are normally pushed out of the body through the *anus* by peristalsis.

22 Identify the parts of the gut labelled X, Y and Z in figure 5.11.

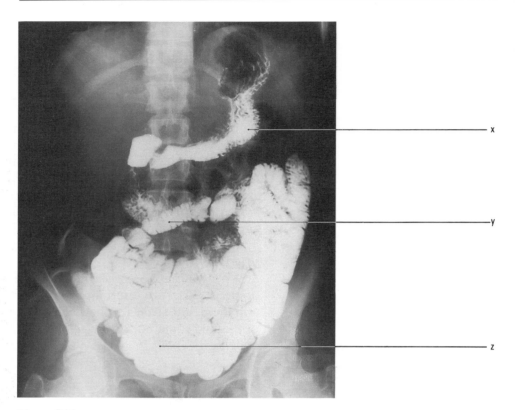

Figure 5.11
This X-ray photograph shows part of the human gut 18 hours
after the patient had drunk some barium sulphate.

You have now seen how the food is changed as it passes through the gut. It
is digested by enzymes, absorbed into the bloodstream and distributed
around the body to be used by the cells. The undigested remains are finally
expelled.

Chapter B6

Diet and good health

B6.1　What would you like for supper tonight?

Most people eat such a varied diet that it usually includes everything that is needed to keep the body healthy, without them having to think about it.

Figure 6.1
You are what you eat.

1 What things influence what you eat at any particular meal?

B6.2　Why do you need food — and what food do you need?

The food you eat supplies the raw materials for building the body and for making it work properly. These raw materials are *proteins*, *fats* and *carbohydrates*. But a healthy diet has to include other ingredients as well.

Vitamins are essential for health and they are found in so many foods that it is almost impossible to go short of any of them unless you eat a very poor diet indeed. Tiny amounts of some *minerals*, including calcium, phosphorus, sodium and iron, are needed too. The final ingredient of a healthy diet is *roughage* (vegetable fibre). A diet that gives you everything you need – but not more than you need – is called a *balanced diet*.

Proteins (see Chapter **C**3 of your Chemistry book) are the main building blocks which are essential for growth, replacement and repair of body tissues. Tiny quantities of fats are essential in every living cell, and many fats are rich in vitamins A, D and E. Both fats and carbohydrates (starchy and sugary foods) are a good source of energy. The body can store only a small amount of carbohydrate, although the amount of fat it can store is very much greater (see figure 6.3).

No one food contains all the essential ingredients, and no single food is essential for health. Figure 6.2 shows five groups of food. You can be sure of getting everything you need if you eat some foods from each of these groups every day.

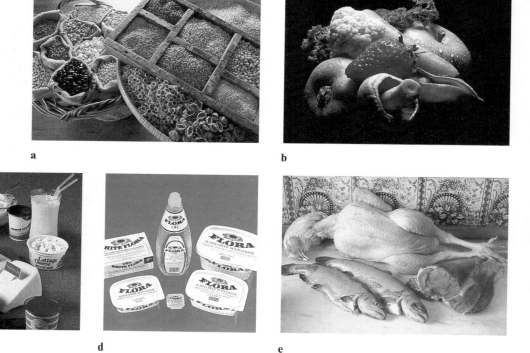

a

b

c

d

e

Figure 6.2
You will be sure of getting everything you need from your diet if, each day, you eat something from each of the five groups shown.

It doesn't matter if there are a few foods you never eat, because you will almost certainly eat others which will supply the same ingredients. Animals are the main source of protein in the Western diet and meat and fish are often said to be the "best" sources of protein. The reasoning behind this idea is that there are 20 amino acids which our bodies have to have in order to function. They are called essential amino acids and animal protein contains all of them. The body can use vegetable protein instead of animal protein, but some plants may lack one or other of the essential amino acids. So a wider variety of vegetable protein must be eaten in order to meet the body's needs.

> **2** **What other sources of protein are there besides meat?**

So long as you eat protein from other sources instead, meat is not essential. But the more limited your diet and the less variety of foods it includes, the more likely you are to have some dietary deficiency.

Vegetarianism and health

Being a vegetarian does not – or should not – consist simply of leaving the meat on the side of your plate. It should mean learning a little about vegetarian diets so that you can substitute other forms of protein (cereals, pulses or nuts) for the meat.

> **3** **Do you think vegetarians are likely to be healthier than other people – or not as healthy? Why?**

In fact, the term vegetarianism is used to describe several different kinds of diet. Some people call themselves vegetarians because they don't eat "red" meat or fowl although they do eat fish. Others eat no meat or fish, but will eat dairy products. The most extreme form of vegetarian is the vegan, who avoids all animal products.

Most vegetarian diets are very healthy. It is only the vegan who runs any real health risks. Vegans may suffer from deficiencies of particular vitamins (such as B12) or mineral salts (like calcium and iron) because some of these ingredients occur in plants in very small amounts or not at all.

Worksheet **B6A** will help you to analyse your daily diet.

B6.3   Getting the energy balance right

Although your diet is almost certainly balanced, in that it contains all the minerals and vitamins you need, it can still be unbalanced in terms of energy. The food that you eat provides energy – for warmth, building and repairing tissues, and carrying out all the physical and chemical processes by which the body functions.

Worksheet **B6B** will help you to look at the energy needs of different people and the energy values of different foods.

People's food needs vary

> **4** **Why do you think:**
> **a** **Inuit Indians (who used to be called Eskimos) eat large amounts of fat?**
> **b** **Doctors may recommend a diet high in protein after a patient's operation?**
> **c** **Women sometimes need extra iron?**

d Athletes sometimes take glucose tablets?
e Women who are strict vegans are always advised to take calcium and iron tablets during pregnancy?

B6.4   Too fat or too thin?

You probably know families in which nearly everyone is enviably slim, and others in which everyone is quite definitely fat. "Fatness just runs in our family" the fatties say, "there's nothing we can do about it". Or they may blame it on their "big bones", or their "glands". And yet "fatness" isn't an inherited characteristic like blue eyes, and only very seldom is it due to any disorder of the glands. In nearly every case there is one simple reason why people become fat. It is because they eat more food than they need.

If you take in a larger source of energy than you need the excess is stored as fat. This does not necessarily mean that someone who is fatter than you are eats more than you do.

5   What else might affect the rate at which a person stores fat?

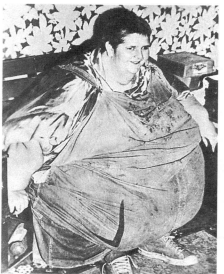

Figure 6.3
The world's fattest person, Robert Earl Hughes of the United States (1926–58). He weighed 485 kg.

Stay active – stay slim

Nearly always, fat people *do* eat more than thinner people. But everyone knows people who "eat like a horse" and are thin, and others who don't seem to eat as much as all that and are fat. The reason people are different is that the rate at which the chemical reactions in the cells of the body are carried out (*metabolic rate*) varies from person to person. Thinner people are often more active than fat people and they use up more of the food they eat as a source of energy. The less exercise you take, the less food you need.

When people blame their "glands" they really mean the *thyroid gland* because that is what controls the metabolic rate. So disorders of the thyroid gland can affect how fat you are. If the gland is overactive your metabolic rate will be speeded up; you will use more food as a source of energy and will become thinner. If the thyroid is underactive, the metabolic rate slows down and you will tend to get fat. But disorders of the thyroid gland are a rare cause of being too fat or too thin.

How much is too much?

How can you tell if you are fat? If you don't look fat you probably aren't. If you are not sure, measure your skinfold thickness. To do this lean forward slightly and pinch a fold of skin over your stomach just below the ribcage. If this is 2.5 cm thick or more, then you are probably too fat.

The chart in figure 6.5 will show you whether you are within the healthy or "desirable" range for someone of your height. One of the things you will notice from this chart is that your mass can vary by several kilograms and still be well within the desirable range. You needn't be a beanpole to be healthy!

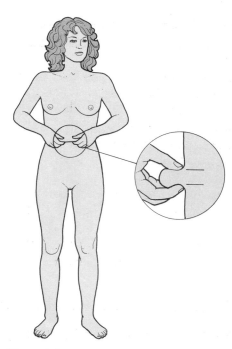

Figure 6.4
"Pinch an inch." If the fold is thicker than about 2.5 cm (1 inch), you are probably too fat. Fatness is often called *obesity*.

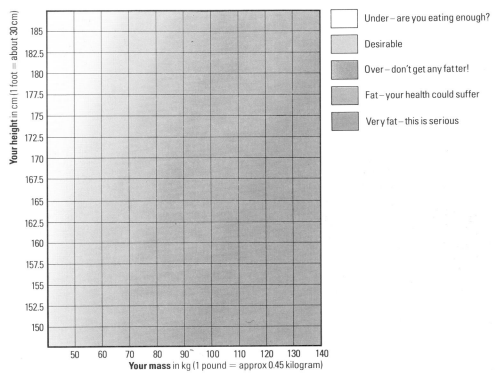

Figure 6.5
A chart of height and recommended body mass. Take a straight line up from your mass (without clothes) and a line across from your height (without shoes). The place where the two lines meet tells you how you rate.

6 Find your height in cm and mass in kg. Work out from the chart in figure 6.5 whether you are OK or not!

7 Fat people usually have to pay more to insure their lives. Why do you think this is?

It is a fact that fat people are much more likely than thinner people to have health problems. This is partly because of the extra bulk they have to carry around with them! It causes extra wear and tear on their joints and they are more likely to get arthritis. Being too fat may cause some people to develop diabetes (see Chapter **B**12) and fat people are more likely to develop gallstones. Unfortunately, having an operation is also a greater risk for fat people.

As well as this, fat people are more likely to develop high blood pressure and to suffer from heart disease. Exercise gives some protection against this but of course fat people tend to take less exercise. This in turn makes them still fatter and even more likely to develop heart disease. This is dealt with in Chapter **B**8 because you will find it easier to understand after you have learned about the heart and blood vessels.

8 What are the most important facts for a person to know about the dangers of being fat?

9 What advice would you give to a very fat person?

Too thin

Not surprisingly (because most people enjoy their food) it is easier to gain body mass than to lose it. If you are less than your desirable mass it is because you are eating less than you need to supply your body's energy requirements. And unless your natural appetite has decreased through illness, this isn't easy.

Normal slimming seldom leads to you becoming too thin, but a few people (about 1 in 100 teenage girls and a much smaller number of boys) become so worried about being too fat that their body mass drops dangerously low. This is a condition called *anorexia* (which means loss of appetite) *nervosa*.

Anorexia – a dangerous disease

The most noticeable thing about people who have anorexia nervosa is that even though it is obvious to everyone else that they are very thin they still claim that they are "too fat" and insist they need to slim. They will become vitamin-deficient and their skin will begin to look pale and papery. Because they are malnourished they are much less resistant to infections. Girls whose body mass has dropped to about 11 kg (24 lb) below normal may stop having periods, and their bodies may become more hairy. Without medical help, it is very difficult for people who have anorexia to start eating properly again and regain their normal body mass.

Sensible slimming

In order to reduce body mass, you must create what is called an "energy deficit". This means you must eat less food than your body requires as its daily source of energy. An ideal way is to exercise more as well as eat less.

"Crash diets"

The body does not store much carbohydrate although excess glucose is changed into a substance called *glycogen* which is stored in the liver and muscles. This can quickly be turned back into glucose to provide a source of energy when it is needed. During a short period of hunger, the body's glycogen stores are always the first to be used. So most of the body mass lost during a "crash diet" will be due to a loss of glycogen and water from the body. The glycogen will be replaced as soon as you start to eat again. Very little of what you wanted to lose – your body fat – will have disappeared. The fact that the diet has been so brief will mean that you won't have had time to learn new and healthier eating habits.

Altering your eating habits

Why do most people find it hard to stay slim when they have reduced their body mass after a diet?

If you really want to stay slim you have to learn a new pattern of eating. Otherwise, as soon as you stop dieting and go back to your old eating habits, back you will go to your old body mass. Most people can reduce their body mass for a few weeks. Less than 25 % of the people who try to slim by altering their eating habits succeed and stay permanently slim.

Figure 6.6 shows a number of different foods.

Figure 6.6
Eat yourself slim.

INTERPRET

10 Which of the foods in figure 6.6 would you give up if you wanted to become slimmer?

11 Why would you choose them?

Slow but sure

The best way to reduce your body mass is a "slow but sure" kind of diet that results in a loss of about 0.5 kg (1 lb) per week. It is best to work out a diet for yourself.

Here are some rules to follow:

1 Choose foods you enjoy
2 Include bulky foods
3 Avoid fatty or sugary foods
4 Don't give up bread or potatoes.

12 Give a reason for each of these rules.

B6.5   Controlling your appetite

Ideally your food intake should match your daily energy requirements, and there is a biological mechanism which controls your appetite. When you have not eaten for a while, the level of glucose circulating in your blood will be low, and a message is sent to the brain which tells you that you are hungry. When you have eaten, your stomach will be full and the message to stop eating is signalled to the brain.

Sometimes there is no food and if people cannot eat for any length of time they starve. First the body's supplies of glycogen are used up and then the fat stores. When these, too, are exhausted, the protein in the muscle has to be broken down to provide energy, so the starving person's muscles will become wasted. The real danger of starvation is this loss of protein. Protein deficiency lowers the body's resistance to infection, so starving people get diseases which may kill them.

Starving people can lose up to half their body mass but will recover and regain what they have lost when they are able to eat normally once more. But a loss of more than half their mass can be fatal.

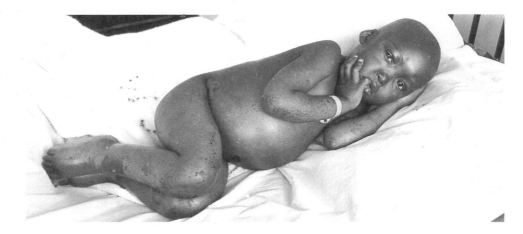

Figure 6.7
A starving child may look swollen because fluid is retained in the tissues.

B6.6 Everything you need to know about cholesterol

Cholesterol is a chemical found in some foods, particularly egg yolks and liver. Since it is an essential ingredient of some body tissues it is not in itself a "bad" thing but it has been found that some people have high levels of cholesterol in their blood. Figure 6.8 shows how the risk of heart attack increases with a rise in the cholesterol level in the blood. Figure 6.9 shows a transverse section of an artery with cholesterol deposited in its wall. Compare it with the healthy artery in figure 8.19 (page 98).

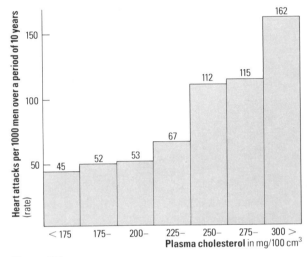

Figure 6.8
The risk of heart attack in relation to cholesterol in men aged 30 to 59 years.

Figure 6.9

13 By how many times does the risk of having a heart attack increase when the blood cholesterol level increases
a from 175 to 225 mg %; and
b from 200 to 250 mg %?

You might imagine that by reducing the amount of cholesterol in the diet you would also reduce the amount in the blood, and therefore the likelihood of heart attack, but it is unfortunately not quite as simple as that. There is no easy way of predicting which people will respond in this way to a decrease in dietary cholesterol. The safest solution is for everyone to aim for a reasonably low cholesterol diet. However, there is another, much more reliable way of lowering the cholesterol level in the blood, and that is to alter the amount and the type of fat in our diet.

The part played by fats

The food we eat contains three types of fats:

Saturated, which increase the blood cholesterol level and the build-up of cholesterol deposits on the inside of the arteries.

Mono-unsaturated, which have little effect on blood cholesterol.

Polyunsaturated, which decrease the blood cholesterol level.

Figure 6.10 shows the content of different sorts of fat in some common foods.

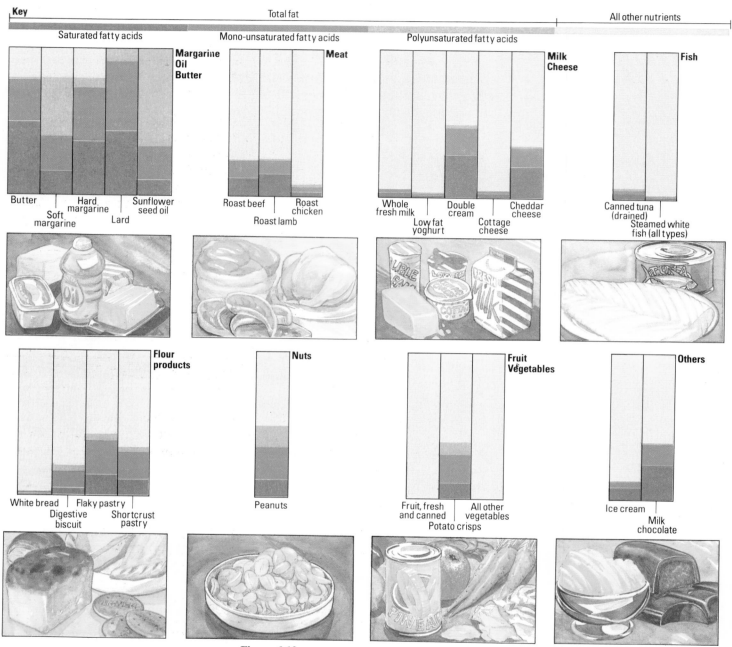

Figure 6.10

---

14 For a special lunch a family decided to have roast lamb with mint sauce, carrots and peas with melted butter, and boiled potatoes. For pudding they had apple pie made with flaky pastry, and ice cream and cream. This was followed by cheddar cheese and digestive biscuits. Finally they had coffee and cream and some milk chocolates. How would you change this menu to reduce its saturated fat content?

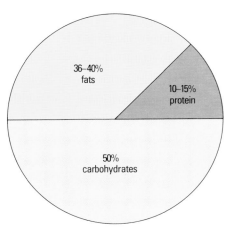

36–40%
fats

10–15%
protein

50%
carbohydrates

Figure 6.11
A Western, meat-based diet. In Japan, by contrast, fish forms a large part of the diet, and the Japanese derive only 20% of their energy from fats.

Japan has one of the lowest death rates from heart disease in the world.

15 Why do you think this is? (See also the graph in figure 6.11.)

B6.7   Cutting down on salt

In some people, too much salt can lead to increased blood pressure, which in turn increases the risk of a heart attack. Although only tiny quantities of salt are essential, most people eat about two teaspoonfuls of salt a day. This is largely because so many of the foods we buy ready to eat such as soups, baked beans, cornflakes, sauces and crisps have a high salt content. Since our bodies only need a pinch of salt a day, anything we can do to reduce our salt intake can only be good for our health.

16 Suggest two or three things you would do to cut down your daily salt intake.

B6.8   The importance of fibre in the diet

People who have no interest in eating sometimes maintain that food isn't really necessary – they could just as easily get all essential ingredients in the form of pills. They ignore the fact that an essential part of any diet is the part we cannot digest at all.

Bowels need bulk

The gut needs bulk if it is to function properly. In particular, if the colon contains only a small quantity of faeces, the bowel muscles literally cannot come to grips with them and propel them along. Undigested vegetable fibre (roughage) gives the faeces bulk. Fibre is the cellulose residue of vegetables, fruit, unrefined flour and cereals. Until the end of the nineteenth century the British diet contained plenty of it. Much of the energy in the diet was supplied by wholemeal bread and other wheat products. White bread, made from wheat flour from which most of the fibre had been removed, was not introduced until about 1880. It rapidly became a popular source of energy. Now the average Western diet contains a great many processed foods and very little fibre.

Low fibre – high risk

Constipation and piles (varicose veins – see Chapter **B**8 – in the rectum) are the most common results of a diet containing too little fibre. Lack of fibre is thought to be at least partly responsible for other digestive disorders too.

Diverticular disease, for example, is a disorder of the colon which is common in Western countries today. But it is rarely seen in underdeveloped parts of the world such as rural Africa, where a high-fibre diet is the rule. Some doctors also believe that a high-fibre diet protects the body against diabetes and cancer of the colon and rectum, and that it may lessen the risk of heart disease by lowering the level of cholesterol in the blood.

Eat more fibre – eat more bread

Most people only eat half as much high-fibre food as they need. Nutritional experts recommend that you should eat about 30 g of fibre a day. Bread contains a lot of it.

	Amount of fibre that is removed from the grain during processing	Fibre content
Wholemeal	none	9 %
Brown (wheatmeal)	about half	5 %
White	almost all	3 %

Figure 6.12
The fibre content of bread.

17 A slice of bread weighs about 60 g. How many slices of each of these types of bread would you need to eat in order to satisfy your daily requirement for fibre?

a

b

c

d

e

Figure 6.13
Fibre-rich foods.

B6.9   Food additives

So far we have been concerned only with the nutritional and energy value of food. Food often contains chemicals with no nutritional value called additives. Some have to be added to food to preserve it but many others are simply "cosmetic". They are not used to make food safer to eat but to "improve" its colour, texture or flavour. Although food additives are added in tiny quantities, their use is so widespread that the average person probably eats about 5 kg of them a year. There are many arguments for and against using them but we are not going to consider these here. However, some people are sensitive to certain additives. For example, about 10 % of people are allergic to tartrazine, a dye which is widely used to give a yellow colour to numerous foods, from smoked haddock to marzipan and orange squash. And about 5 % of people are susceptible to the "Chinese restaurant syndrome", developing feelings of burning or tightening in the neck, arms and chest as a reaction to the large quantities of monosodium glutamate often used to enhance the flavour of food in Chinese cooking. Proper labelling of foods would help people to avoid additives which they think have given them unpleasant symptoms in the past.

Your teacher may give you a worksheet which will give you more information about food additives and their uses.

Review

If you really did "Drink a pinta milka day", you would be taking almost a fifth of your day's energy requirements in milk alone. No single food is in itself especially "good" or especially "bad" for you, no matter what the food advertisers say. A healthy diet need not mean giving up anything you enjoy (except, perhaps, "chips with everything") or forcing yourself to eat anything you dislike.

But it may mean shifting the balance of what you eat, so that it includes rather more of some foods, rather less of others. It may mean adjusting your "energy balance" too, reducing the total energy you take in each day so that it more nearly matches your needs.

In talking about diet and health you will probably have noticed a common pattern emerging – the same advice given again and again for different, though related reasons. This means that you don't have to think about protecting yourself against any particular disease – heart attack or bowel disorders or obesity. The same four rules apply to anyone who wants to work out a new and healthier pattern of eating:

Cut down on sugar
Cut down on salt
Cut down on fats, especially saturated fats
Eat more high-fibre foods.

The Red, Amber and Green code is another way of remembering the rules for healthier eating.

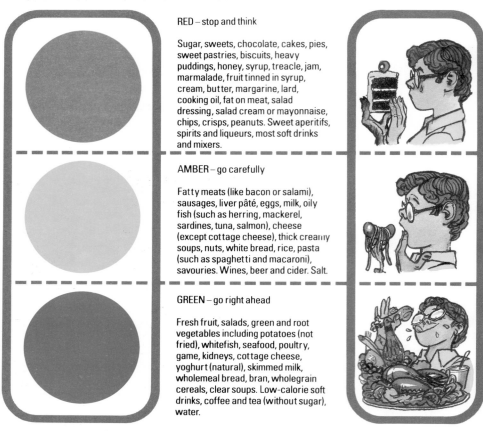

RED – stop and think

Sugar, sweets, chocolate, cakes, pies, sweet pastries, biscuits, heavy puddings, honey, syrup, treacle, jam, marmalade, fruit tinned in syrup, cream, butter, margarine, lard, cooking oil, fat on meat, salad dressing, salad cream or mayonnaise, chips, crisps, peanuts. Sweet aperitifs, spirits and liqueurs, most soft drinks and mixers.

AMBER – go carefully

Fatty meats (like bacon or salami), sausages, liver pâté, eggs, milk, oily fish (such as herring, mackerel, sardines, tuna, salmon), cheese (except cottage cheese), thick creamy soups, nuts, white bread, rice, pasta (such as spaghetti and macaroni), savouries. Wines, beer and cider. Salt.

GREEN – go right ahead

Fresh fruit, salads, green and root vegetables including potatoes (not fried), whitefish, seafood, poultry, game, kidneys, cottage cheese, yoghurt (natural), skimmed milk, wholemeal bread, bran, wholegrain cereals, clear soups. Low-calorie soft drinks, coffee and tea (without sugar), water.

Figure 6.14
The Red, Amber and Green code.

Chapter B7

The breath of life

B7.1   Holding your breath

If you tried holding your breath for as long as you could you would be doing very well to beat Robert Foster, who held his breath for 13 minutes and 42.7 seconds submerged in a Californian swimming pool!

Figure 7.1
Robert Foster held his breath for more than 13 minutes!

Some animals can hold their breath for considerably longer than this. Seals and whales, for instance, may dive for hours. But eventually they all have to come up to the surface for air. Clearly, breathing is essential to life and air must provide your bodies with something important. The main gases found in the air you breathe are:

Nitrogen (about 79 %)
Oxygen (about 20 %)
Carbon dioxide (about 0.03 %).

Air also contains some noble gases (see Chapter C17 in the Chemistry book).

a   b

Figure 7.2
Which of the gases in the atmosphere does your body need?

1 Which of the gases in the atmosphere does your body need? Figure 7.2 gives you a clue.

You can check your answer to question **1** by comparing the proportions of these gases found in the air you breathe in (*inhale*) and in the air you breathe out (*exhale*) shown in figure 7.3.

	Inhaled air (%)	Exhaled air (%)
Nitrogen	79.01	79.5
Oxygen	20.96	16.4
Carbon dioxide	0.03	4.1

Figure 7.3

2 Calculate by how much the percentage of each gas increases or decreases as a result of breathing.

3 Which gas is removed from the air and which is added to it in your lungs?

B7.2   Gas exchange

It is obvious that breathing changes the composition of inhaled air. This change takes place in your lungs and is called *gas exchange*.

4 What other differences do you think there are between inhaled and exhaled air?

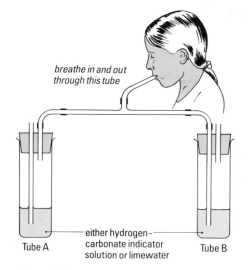

breathe in and out
through this tube

Tube A   either hydrogencarbonate indicator
solution or limewater   Tube B

Figure 7.4
A simple apparatus for detecting a difference in composition between inhaled and exhaled air.

You can use the apparatus shown in figure 7.4 to detect gas exchange. Breathe in and out of the apparatus through the mouthpiece until you notice a difference between the liquids in the tubes. You can use either limewater or hydrogencarbonate indicator in the tubes.

INTERPRET

5 Look carefully at the apparatus and work out which liquid is having inhaled air bubbled through it and which exhaled.

6 Which of the gases in the air is most likely to be causing the liquids to change?

A sensitive indicator

In this simple demonstration limewater reacts rather more slowly than the hydrogencarbonate indicator. Although this indicator is not specific (that is, does not **only** react with carbon dioxide), it is very sensitive. This means that it will react with rather small amounts of carbon dioxide and produce a colour change.

This property is useful if you want to see whether small organisms are producing carbon dioxide.

In Worksheet **B**7A, hydrogencarbonate indicator is used to investigate gas exchange on quite a small scale with a variety of organisms.

B7.3 Breathing in and breathing out

Gas exchange takes place in your *lungs*. These organs fill up most of the space inside your chest (*thorax*). They are protected by your ribs and breastbone and are separated from your *abdomen* by the *diaphragm*, a sheet of muscle and fibre. The position of your lungs and the diaphragm can be seen on an X-ray photograph. (Figure 7.5.)

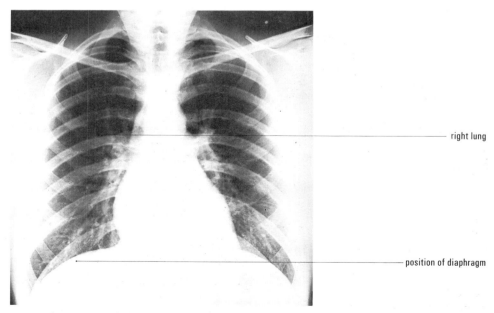

right lung

position of diaphragm

Figure 7.5
In this X-ray of a human thorax you can see the position of the lungs and the diaphragm.

What makes breathing happen?

We can think of the lungs as a container full of gas. The pressure exerted by any gas in a container will fall if the volume of the container increases. (See Chapter **P2** in the Physics book.) So any movements which increase the volume of your chest will decrease the pressure inside it. If the air pressure inside your lungs falls below atmospheric pressure, air from outside will enter them. This is what we call *inhaling*.

Worksheet **B**7B helps you to investigate how you breathe in and out.

Muscles can only *contract*; they are not capable of stretching themselves. The muscles occur in pairs and when one set of intercostal muscles contracts it causes the other set to be stretched. The two groups of muscles are said to be *antagonistic* to each other. You will meet this idea again when you consider how you use muscles to move your limbs.

The job of the pleural membranes

Since the lungs are constantly moving against the rib cage, it is essential that they are lubricated. The inside of the rib cage is lined by a thin sheet of tissue called the *pleural membrane*. Another pleural membrane is attached to the outside of each lung. The two membranes are separated by a thin layer of fluid called *pleural fluid*. This fluid is rather like lubricating oil and it stops the lungs from sticking to the chest wall. Sometimes people can get an infection of these membranes, called pleurisy. The two pleural membranes become roughened and their rubbing together causes pain. The patient has to take antibiotics to get rid of the infection. Worksheet **B**7C allows you to find out more about the job of the pleural membranes.

B7.4　From air to blood

Figure 7.6 shows an X-ray photograph of a lung after the person had been injected with oil that was opaque to X-rays.

> **7** How would you describe the pattern of air passages found in the lungs?

Suppose you were coming home in the car. You might leave a motorway and go along a main road. You would then probably turn off the main road into a side road and so on until you reached your house. The roads might branch repeatedly until the journey finished at your house in a road that did not lead anywhere – a "dead end".

The system of tubes in your lungs is rather like this. When you inhale, all the air passes down the windpipe or *trachea* which branches into two tubes (one to each lung) called *bronchi*. These branch into smaller bronchi which branch into even smaller tubes called *bronchioles*, finally ending in little sacs called *alveoli*. The alveoli are the "dead ends" where the gas exchange takes place (figure 7.7).

In the photograph in figure 7.8 you can see the trachea but all the other tubes are buried in the lung tissue. Worksheet **B**7D gives you a chance to examine lungs for yourself and to see this branching network of tubes.

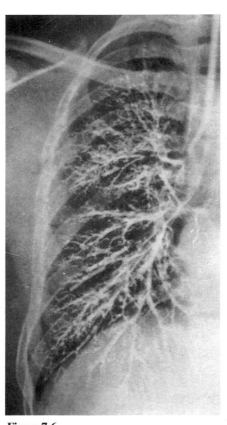

Figure 7.6
An X-ray photograph of human lungs after injection with oil that was opaque to X-rays. The air passages of the lungs show up white.

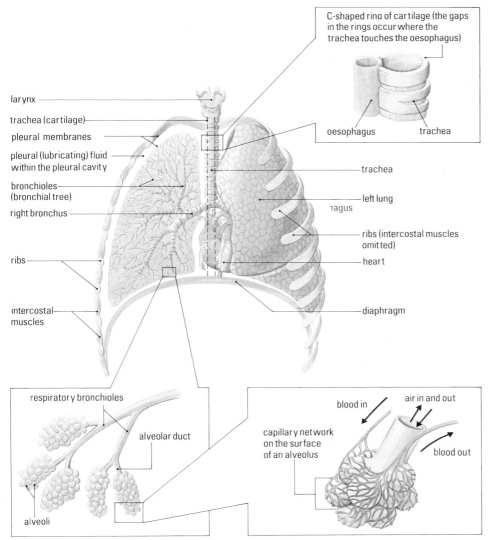

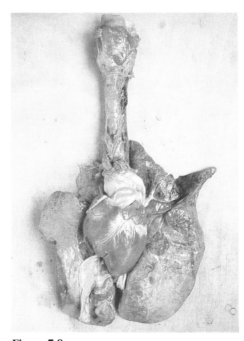

Figure 7.7
The air tubes in the lungs branch again and again, getting smaller all the time, until "dead ends" are reached. These are called *alveoli*.

Figure 7.8
A photograph of the trachea, lungs and heart of a sheep. What structures can you identify?

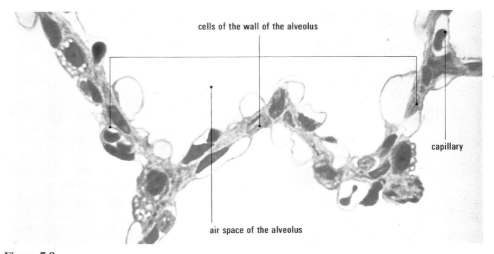

Figure 7.9
A photograph of a microscopic section through some alveoli in a lung. Notice how thin the alveolus wall is and how many capillaries there are.

Interpreting microscope slides is quite hard and you should consult your teacher before answering the next question.

The only way of seeing the alveoli is to make very thin slices of lung tissue which can be stained and looked at under a microscope. It is quite hard to interpret what you see under the microscope, but the photograph in figure 7.9 might help you.

Notice the thickness of the wall of the alveoli, and the blood capillaries.

8 From your observations suggest some ways in which the alveoli are suited to being the surface across which gas exchange takes place.

The process by which gas exchange takes place is called *diffusion*. This occurs in any liquid or gas when there are differences in the concentration of molecules. Diffusion of molecules takes place from where there is a higher concentration of a substance to where there is a lower concentration. Molecules will diffuse until they are evenly distributed.

There are many blood vessels in the lungs, bringing blood to and from the alveoli.

Let us look at how gas exchange takes place by diffusion in the alveoli.

	Concentration of gas in blood flowing to the alveoli	**Concentration of gas in air in the alveoli**
Oxygen	low	high
Carbon dioxide	high	low

Figure 7.10

9 Explain why
a oxygen will diffuse from the air in the alveoli into the blood and
b carbon dioxide will diffuse from the blood into the air in the alveoli.

You may think that when you breathe you replace all the air in your lungs with fresh air.

10 Breathe out as far as you possibly can. Do you think you have got rid of all the air in your lungs?

Some diving mammals like whales can in fact collapse their lungs so thoroughly that the alveoli contain no air.

11 This helps them to dive very deep; explain why this is.

12 Next time you are in the bath you could try doing this. Lie very still and breathe out as far as you can. Then breathe in as far as you can and hold your breath. What happens?

Each time you breathe, the air in the alveoli is not completely replaced. In fact, the composition of alveolar air remains remarkably constant. Figure 7.11 shows the percentages of oxygen and carbon dioxide in alveolar air, atmospheric air and the blood flowing to the alveoli.

	Atmospheric air (%)	Alveolar air (%)	Blood flowing to alveoli (%)
Oxygen	20.93	13.16	5.23
Carbon dioxide	0.03	5.26	5.90

Figure 7.11

13 Using these data, explain how oxygen gets from atmospheric air into our blood and how carbon dioxide gets from the blood in the lungs into the atmosphere.

Worksheets **B**7E and **B**7F will help you to investigate the effect of size on gas exchange and the effect of exercise on breathing rate.

B7.5   The pipe cleaners

In order to function efficiently the lungs must be kept clean. There are special cells lining the trachea and bronchi whose function it is to make sure that dust particles do not travel all the way to the delicate alveoli. Figures 7.12 and 7.13 show a section through a bronchus photographed through a microscope and a drawing of the same section.

Specialized cells called *goblet cells* are shown. These cells produce a substance called *mucus* on which dust particles get trapped. The tiny hairs

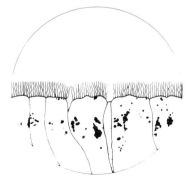

Figures 7.12 and **7.13**
A photograph and a diagram of a microscopic section through a bronchus.

(called *cilia*) which line the tube move the mucus upwards and out of the trachea into the throat. It is then swallowed. If a dust particle gets past this first line of defence it will enter the alveoli. Here it will be met by special cells called *phagocytes* ("cell eaters"). These cells move about gobbling up microbes and dust particles. There are serious consequences if any of the cleaning mechanisms of the lung are put out of action. That is exactly what smoking does, as we shall see later.

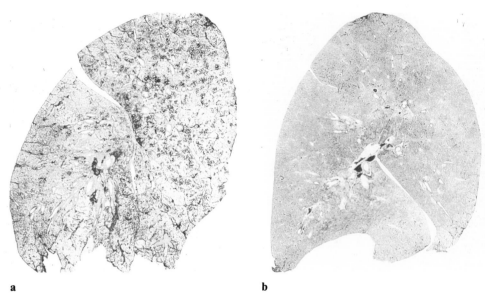

a   b

Figure 7.14
Photographs of sections through the lungs of two adult humans. The lungs of person (**a**) were full of tar deposits caused by cigarette smoking. Person (**b**) had healthy lungs.

The photographs in figure 7.14 show the differences between the lungs of two adult humans. The colour is due to a reaction of the lung tissue which resists damage to the delicate alveoli by smoke and dust particles. First, special cells wrap around the particles, trapping them. Then the alveolar cells release a fluid in which the irritating gases dissolve.

INTERPRET

14 This fluid tends to collect in the alveoli. What effect do you think this might have on gas exchange?

Obviously any build-up of particles in the lungs will damage them, and any damage will seriously reduce their effectiveness at gas exchange.

What is asthma?

People who suffer from asthma are particularly sensitive to certain chemicals to which they are said to be *allergic*. The bronchioles in the lungs have muscle in their walls. These chemicals cause the muscles to contract and the bronchioles become narrow. Inhalation is not a problem, but it is very difficult to exhale. As a result the concentration of carbon dioxide in the alveoli increases and the sufferer becomes short of oxygen. This can cause great distress. Inhalers contain chemical substances that can make the bronchiole muscles relax and help the breathing to return to normal.

B7.6 Smoking and health

The habit of smoking cigarettes is barely one hundred years old. Although tobacco was introduced by Sir Walter Raleigh and other explorers in the sixteenth century, it was smoked in pipes, and later, in the eighteenth century, taken in the form of snuff. It was only during the Crimean war that the British learned from the Turks how to hand roll and smoke cigarettes, and only towards the end of the nineteenth century that cigarettes started to be mass-produced.

Smoking can seriously damage your health ...

The table in figure 7.16 shows how many people in the United Kingdom died in 1983 from the **main** diseases associated with cigarette smoking (it can cause other diseases too).

		Number of deaths in 1983 from smoking-related diseases
Lung cancer	men	30 019
	women	10 257
	Total	40 276
Heart attack	men	102 574
	women	77 096
	Total	179 670
Bronchitis and emphysema	men	12 181
	women	4 680
	Total	16 861

Figure 7.16

Smoking is the cause of almost all *lung cancer* as well as *bronchitis* and *emphysema* (two diseases which result in increasing breathlessness and gradually destroy the lungs). And smokers are 2–3 times as likely to die from heart disease as non-smokers.

What does the damage?

Smokeless fuel has made Britain's cities clean. Imagine the difference that smokeless cigarettes would make to Britain's lungs. Most of the damage caused by smoking is due to harmful ingredients in the smoke – tar, carbon monoxide and nicotine. Cigarette smoke also contains substances that irritate the lungs and increase the production of mucus (*phlegm*) which is why smokers cough. Chemicals in the smoke may also gradually destroy the cilia which reduce the likelihood of infection by sweeping away the phlegm. So, in

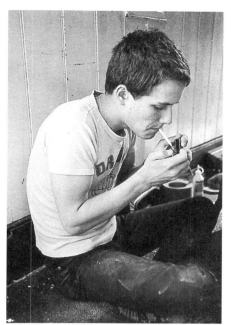

Figure 7.15
One quarter of all young smokers will have died 10 to 15 years before they should have done, just because they could not kick the smoking habit.

smokers, phlegm accumulates in the bronchi which often become infected, causing bronchitis.

Worksheet **B**7G is an investigation into some of the things that cigarette smoking may put into your lungs. Here are some details about them.

Tar is a dark brown, sticky substance, which collects in the lungs as the tobacco smoke cools. It contains *carcinogens* – chemical substances known to cause cancer.

Carbon monoxide is a gas which combines with haemoglobin, the oxygen-carrying substance in the red blood cells, even more readily than oxygen does (see Chapter **B**8). So it reduces the oxygen-carrying capacity of the blood by as much as 15 % in heavy smokers.

Nicotine is the addictive drug which makes smoking such a hard habit for many people to kick. It is also responsible for the yellow staining of a smoker's fingers and teeth. Nicotine can harm the heart and blood vessels too – it makes the heart beat faster, the blood pressure rise and the blood clot more easily.

Smoke from cigars and pipes contains more tar and nicotine than cigarette smoke, but cigar and pipe smokers are less likely to get lung cancer.

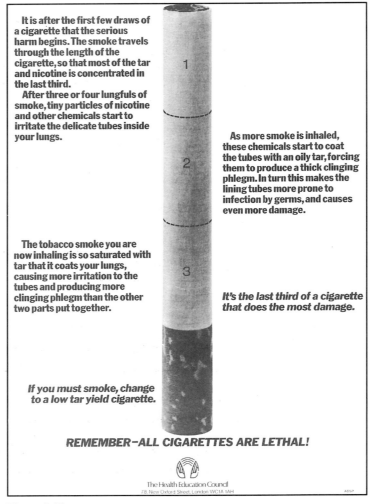

It is after the first few draws of a cigarette that the serious harm begins. The smoke travels through the length of the cigarette, so that most of the tar and nicotine is concentrated in the last third.

After three or four lungfuls of smoke, tiny particles of nicotine and other chemicals start to irritate the delicate tubes inside your lungs.

As more smoke is inhaled, these chemicals start to coat the tubes with an oily tar, forcing them to produce a thick clinging phlegm. In turn this makes the lining tubes more prone to infection by germs, and causes even more damage.

The tobacco smoke you are now inhaling is so saturated with tar that it coats your lungs, causing more irritation to the tubes and producing more clinging phlegm than the other two parts put together.

It's the last third of a cigarette that does the most damage.

If you must smoke, change to a low tar yield cigarette.

REMEMBER – ALL CIGARETTES ARE LETHAL!

The Health Education Council
78, New Oxford Street, London WC1A 1AH

Figure 7.17
There are many brands of cigarette, but there is no such thing as a "safe" cigarette.

15 Can you suggest a reason for this?

16 Do you think a campaign to convert cigarette smokers to other forms of smoking would help to reduce the health risks?

Getting off to a bad start

Pregnant women are always advised to give up smoking. One of the reasons for this is that babies born to women who smoke during pregnancy are smaller (on average 200 g lighter) and weaker than babies born to women who do not smoke. They evidently do not get the nourishment they need while they are developing in the uterus.

17 Why do you think this is?

18 Why is it that the husband, as well as the wife, is often advised to give up smoking when a baby is on the way?

19 Can you think of other groups of people for whom smoking might be especially dangerous or disadvantageous?

Reducing the number of cigarettes you smoke is the only thing that will significantly reduce your chances of developing lung cancer or heart disease. Changing to low tar or filter tip cigarettes will make very little difference. The only "safe" cigarette is the one that stays in the packet.

Giving up and cutting down

		1972	**1984**
Sales of packeted cigarettes in UK		130 500 million	99 000 million
Average weekly number of cigarettes smoked	men	120	115
	women	87	96

Figure 7.18

20 What do you deduce from the figures in this table?

The good news is that when smokers do give up, their risk of getting lung cancer stops increasing, and after 10–15 non-smoking years it is only slightly higher than that of someone who has never smoked at all.

Worksheet **B7H** will help you to carry out a survey into why people smoke and why some people go on smoking.

Chapter B8

Transport round the organism

B8.1 Delivering the goods

The word transport may conjure up an image of huge lorries, buses and trains. Vehicles like these play an important part in our lives. For example, lorries are used to carry food into our towns and to take rubbish away. If these transport services were to fail our towns would be thrown into chaos and life in them would grind to a halt.

Figure 8.1
Sights like this could become familiar if the transport system failed.

Just as human societies require transport services, so do most living organisms, and for many of the same reasons.

B8.2 Transport in plants

If a gardener wants to grow some potatoes, the easiest way is to plant a potato tuber. In the right conditions it will sprout, and a green shoot will appear above ground. At the same time a branching shoot system will spread

Figure 8.2
In potatoes, the transport system inside the plant connects the underground shoots and the leaves.

through the soil. By the summer many new potato tubers have been formed, each one attached to a shoot underground.

The potato tubers contain starch; in Chapter **B**3 you can see that starch is produced in plants as the main product of photosynthesis. The sugars from which starch is made are produced in the leaves above ground. So there must be a way for the sugars to be transported from the leaves to the tubers underground.

It is not a simple matter to discover how this transport takes place, and biologists have used a number of indirect ways to do so; one of these makes use of radioactive carbon dioxide.

If a plant is kept in an atmosphere which contains radioactive carbon dioxide, the sugars it makes will also be radioactive. This radioactivity can be detected if the plant is placed against a piece of photographic film in the dark, for a few days. Radioactivity makes the film go black. So a faint outline of the plant shows up, with some parts blacker than others.

Figure 8.3
In this photograph, the more radioactivity there is in the plant tissues, the blacker the film is. This bean plant photosynthesized in an atmosphere containing radioactive carbon dioxide.

1 Look at the photograph of the bean plant in figure 8.3. In which parts of the plant were the greatest concentrations of radioactivity?

Figure 8.3 gives us direct evidence that the products of photosynthesis are transported around a plant. Very often there is a greater concentration of radioactivity in the parts that are growing fast or where no photosynthesis is taking place.

---

2 Is this idea confirmed by the evidence in figure 8.3?

Figure 8.4
This plant is infested with aphids.

The plant suckers

You may have noticed that the leaves of plants infested with aphids are often rather sticky. If you look closely with a magnifying glass you will see drops of liquid on the tips of the abdomens of these insects. Aphids suck plant sap and they usually suck more than they need. The excess oozes from their bodies and is called honeydew. It is this that gets onto the leaves and makes them sticky.

Ants are often seen moving about aphid colonies on infested plants.

INTERPRET

---

3 Suggest a hypothesis to account for the presence of the ants.

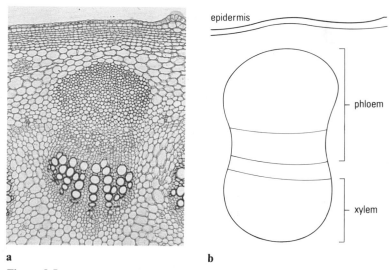

a   b

Figure 8.5
A photograph and a diagram of a section through the stem of a plant showing the phloem and xylem.

Aphids get the plant sap by piercing the tubes in the stem which are transporting the sugars around the plant. These tubes are called *phloem* and this tissue forms part of the transport system of a plant. Phloem tissue is living and its cells are not very strong. Their walls are thin and most phloem cells are renewed every year.

Plant cells also need a supply of other substances which are essential to life, such as water and minerals. These substances are in the soil so how do they get from the soil into a shoot or leaf cell?

You can go some way towards answering this question by doing a very simple experiment.

4 Take a piece of the leaf stalk of celery and put one end into water coloured with a red dye. Leave it in the dye for a while and observe what happens. Cut through the celery stalk in a number of places and look at the cut end.

5 Whereabouts in the stalk is the red dye?

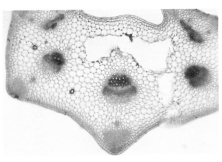

Figure 8.6
This section was cut through the stem of a celery plant after it had been put in a coloured dye for a while. The dye has stained certain parts of the stem.

Figure 8.6 shows the result of a similar investigation.

If you slowly break the celery and pull the two halves apart you will probably find that "strings" are exposed. You will also find that these are the coloured parts of the stalk.

Obviously there is some sort of conducting system for water in the stalk. It doesn't take much thought to work out that the water and mineral salts from the soil could be transported in such a system of tubes. (See figure 8.5.)

This system of tubes is called *xylem*. The xylem cells are arranged one on top of each other to form long columns. During development these cells lose their living contents and are therefore dead. Also the walls are made thicker by a substance called *lignin*. Xylem tissue is very tough and durable. Humans have found a use for it and a name. We call it *wood*. All of the wood you see around you is really xylem.

6 List the ways in which xylem is different from phloem.

The xylem stream

How water is carried from the roots to the top of the tallest tree is a question that puzzled early scientists. It is not an easy subject to study but it will tell us something if we find out which conditions speed up or slow down the rate at which this transport process takes place.

Worksheets **B8A** and **B8E** help you to investigate this.

It is known that water evaporates from the surfaces of plants by evaporation. This is called *transpiration*. Clearly, leaves play an important part in this. They not only provide a large surface area for evaporation to take place, but have specialized pores called *stomata* (see Chapter **B3**), which allow gas exchange between the leaf and the atmosphere. Unlike carbon dioxide and oxygen, which can move into and out of a leaf through stomata, water vapour can only leave the plant through these pores.

Worksheet **B8B** describes an experiment and gives some results on the rate at which water is lost from leaves.

The xylem tissue and phloem tissue together make up the transport system of plants. This system is very efficient, for it can carry water to the top of trees which are as much as 80 metres tall. (See figure 10.2, page 112.)

B8.3 Transport in animals

Like the cells in plants, our cells, too, need to be supplied with essential substances. In addition they produce wastes which have to be taken away.

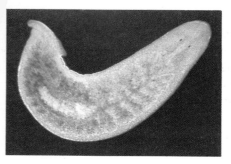

Figure 8.7
Gas exchange takes place over the
surface of organisms such as *Amoeba*
(figure 2.1, page 18), an earthworm –
Lumbricus (figure 2.7, page 22) and a
flatworm, *Planaria*, shown here.

Not all animals are like humans so we shall look at how substances are
transported in some other animals as well.

In Chapter **B**7 you can see that the time it takes to deliver oxygen by
diffusion is related to how far it has to diffuse. The greater the distance the
longer it will take.

Gas exchange takes place over the whole outer surface of *Amoeba*. See
figure 2.1, page 18.

7 Why is the delivery of sufficient oxygen not a problem for unicellular organisms like
Amoeba?

Gas exchange takes place over the whole outer surface of flatworms. They
have no way of transporting substances around their bodies.

8 Suggest how food and gases get to and from all parts of the flatworm.

9 Gas exchange takes place over the outer surface of earthworms too, but they have a
system for the transport of food and gases to all parts of their bodies. What features of
earthworms make such a transport system necessary?

Large animals have a transport system in which a whole fluid moves and
carries molecules to all the cells. Transporting molecules in this way is known
as *mass flow* because everything in the fluid moves. This is very much more
rapid and more effective than diffusion.

10 Can you think of any other examples of mass flow?

Worksheet **B8C** helps you to investigate the processes of diffusion and mass
flow.

All the vertebrates, and some other animals such as the annelids,
crustaceans and molluscs (see Chapter **B2**) have transport systems. They are
not identical but have a few things in common – the molecules are carried in a
specialized fluid usually called *blood*, which is kept moving by a *pump* called
the *heart*, and is contained in pipes called *blood vessels*.

B8.4   Looking at blood

You have probably fallen over at some time in your life and cut or grazed
your skin. What did you see? You immediately leaked – a liquid called blood
appeared.

Do you know what blood does besides carrying oxygen around your body?

At first sight it seems that blood is just a red liquid. But if a tube of blood is
spun in a machine called a centrifuge you will find it separates into two parts.
This is shown in figure 8.8.

Figure 8.8

Figure 8.9
A scanning electronmicrograph of
human red blood cells very highly
magnified.

Figure 8.10
Compare the colour of these two blood
samples. Which one is the more highly
oxygenated?

MEASURE   INTERPRET

The yellow liquid you can see at the top of the tube is called *plasma*. You
may have seen plasma if you have ever noticed what happens when a scab
forms. A short while after the red blood has stopped flowing you usually find
a yellowish fluid seeping from the wound. That is almost the same as plasma.
You probably know already that blood contains cells. These all go to the
bottom part of the tube when blood is centrifuged. The most common type of
cell in blood is the *red blood cell*.

Human red blood cells are unusual because they do not have a nucleus and
they have a quite distinctive shape which you can see in figure 8.9.

---

11 Take two pieces of Plasticine of the same mass. Carefully roll one into a sphere
and try to make the other one the same shape as a red blood cell from figure 8.9.

12 The two models you have made have the same mass and volume. In what way do
they differ from one another?

It is the red blood cells that carry the oxygen in your body so it is rather
important that you always have enough; and "enough" seems to be around 5
million in every cubic millimetre of blood in an adult human.

---

13 Assuming that an adult has about five litres of blood, how many red cells will there
be altogether? (There are 1 000 000 mm^3 in 1 L.)

The red blood cells contain a substance called *haemoglobin*. It is this
molecule which makes the blood red. Haemoglobin is a very complex protein
which contains iron. It can combine temporarily with oxygen to form
oxyhaemoglobin, which is what makes these cells very good carriers of oxygen
in your blood. The colour of the haemoglobin changes according to how
much oxygen it is carrying. Deoxygenated blood is dark red and oxygenated
blood is bright red. So it is possible to tell the difference between
deoxygenated and oxygenated blood by comparing their colours. (See
figure 8.10.)

You can get some idea of how much haemoglobin improves the ability of
the blood to carry oxygen by studying the table in figure 8.11. Each liquid had
been exposed to air which contained gases in the same concentrations as are
found in the alveoli of human lungs.

	cm^3 oxygen/ 100 cm^3 liquid
Water	0.3
Blood	19.0

Figure 8.11

---

14 How many times better is blood at carrying oxygen than water?

15 In your own words, explain why blood carries so much more oxygen than water can.

B8.5   More about red blood cells

The life span of a red blood cell is rather short. The cells are made in bone marrow from where they are released into the bloodstream. After 120 days of chemical and physical battering, during a journey of about 1100 km, they are broken up, mainly in your spleen. This means that if your red cell count is to remain constant the cells must be continually replaced. About 1 % are replaced daily. This represents about 25 g of cells every day or about three million each second!

Anaemia

Producing too many or too few red blood cells can cause problems. Too many red cells will make the blood more *viscous* which means it flows less easily. Too few red cells results in a condition called *anaemia*. If you are anaemic your blood is unable to transport enough oxygen to your cells. Anaemia has many different causes. Severe bleeding (haemorrhage) or a diet deficient in iron are two of them.

16 Why is the kind of anaemia which is caused by iron deficiency more likely to occur in women between 12 and 50 years old or in young infants?

Effect of high altitude

Many European athletes are worried when major events are held in countries at high altitude. The information in figure 8.12 provides you with a clue to the reason for their concern.

	Number of red blood cells/mm^3
At sea level	5 000 000
At 5333 m	7 370 000 (permanent residents)
At 5333 m	5 950 000 (temporary residents)

Figure 8.12

17 From the data in figure 8.12, what can you suggest about the body's response to altitude?

18 Can you suggest what the body gains from the response you have noticed?

19 If you had been the doctor to the World Cup football teams in Mexico in 1986 what advice would you have given to the manager about how long before the main tournament began the players should arrive?

Doping

Some athletes have misused what we know about red blood cells to give themselves an unfair advantage over their opponents. For example, seven members of the US cycling team in the 1984 Olympics – including four medallists – used blood doping. This process involves transfusing extra blood or red blood cells into the circulation. It is a technique now banned by the International Olympics Committee.

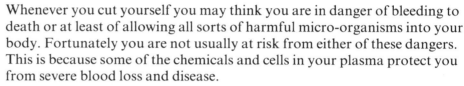

20 Explain how blood doping could improve athletic performance.

Carbon monoxide poisoning

Carbon monoxide is a poisonous gas found in cigarette smoke and car exhaust fumes. It is lethal in large amounts because it combines with haemoglobin much more readily than oxygen does. As a result, the blood carries less oxygen than it should and this can have serious consequences.

B8.6   Liquid protection

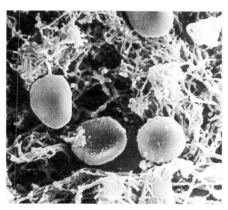

Figure 8.13
This is a highly magnified photograph of a blood clot. You can see the threads of fibrin trapping the red cells.

Whenever you cut yourself you may think you are in danger of bleeding to death or at least of allowing all sorts of harmful micro-organisms into your body. Fortunately you are not usually at risk from either of these dangers. This is because some of the chemicals and cells in your plasma protect you from severe blood loss and disease.

Any cut made in your skin is soon plugged. The plug is called a *clot* and it is this which stops the bleeding. Clotting is a very complicated process. A number of different chemical substances are needed, some of which you will have inherited; you obtain others from your diet.

Where your tissues are damaged, very small colourless structures called *platelets* burst open and release some of the chemical substances. These help to convert a soluble plasma protein called *fibrinogen* into a net of insoluble protein threads called *fibrin*. The fibrin net traps red blood cells, thus helping to plug the cut and prevent serious loss of blood. There are about 250 000 platelets in 1 cubic millimetre of blood.

In the meantime, any micro-organisms which may have entered the bloodstream are met by special defence cells called *white blood cells*. There are about 5000 white blood cells in 1 cubic millimetre of blood. They are larger than the red cells and have a nucleus. Some people have a blood disorder called leukaemia. One of the features of leukaemia is that the number of white cells circulating in the bloodstream increases dramatically.

There are several types of white blood cell. One kind, the phagocytes (which, as you can see in Chapter **B**7, means "cell eaters"), can consume invading micro-organisms. These white cells squeeze through the pores in the walls of the tiniest blood vessels, called *capillaries* (see section **B**8.9), and move to the site of the damage. Pus is the end result of the battle which takes place between the phagocytes and the invading micro-organisms.

There are other white blood cells which recognize the micro-organisms as foreign material and they construct special proteins, called *antibodies*, which help to destroy them. The antibodies cause the micro-organisms to clump together, which makes it easier for the cell-eating white blood cells to do their job.

Like the red blood cells, white blood cells are made in the bone marrow of the larger bones of the body. The cells which will eventually produce antibodies have to be specially prepared to do so in *lymph nodes*. Have you ever suffered from swollen glands? If you have you were probably feeling unwell at the time. The swellings occur at lymph nodes. Your largest lymph nodes are found under the angle of your jaw, in the armpits and in the groin.

21 Suggest a reason for the swelling of lymph nodes when you have an infection.

B8.7 Blood transfusions

Sometimes it is necessary to have a *blood transfusion*. Usually this is because a lot of blood has been lost, for example from a bleeding peptic ulcer, or as the result of a serious accident. There is a whole department of the National Health Service that exists simply to collect blood from donors and make it available for use.

You may have heard about long and difficult surgical operations such as heart transplants. These use a large volume of blood which comes from the "bank" of donated blood.

Of course not everyone can give blood. You must be over 18 and you must not be carrying any disease organisms in your bloodstream. The doctors at the blood transfusion centre check your blood very carefully before they use it to make sure that it is safe for the recipient.

Each of us belongs to a particular *blood group* – some you may have heard of are A, B, AB, or O; Rh + or Rh −. All of your red cells carry tiny marker proteins on their surface. There is quite a variety of types of these markers (called *antigens*) and your blood group is named after the type of antigen it carries. These antigens can stimulate the white blood cells in some people to make antibodies which can destroy red blood cells. Imagine what would

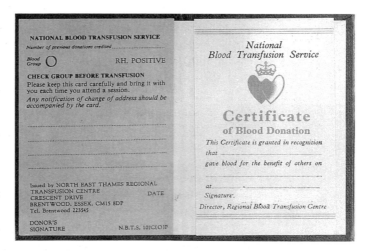

Figure 8.14
A card like this is given to every person who gives blood. The blood group of the donor in this case was O Rhesus positive. This is only one of several possible blood groups.

happen if you received a "life-saving" transfusion and then your body started to destroy all the new cells you had received. The result would kill you. So your blood is checked to see what antigens it carries – that is what blood group you belong to – and you will then be given a blood transfusion of a blood group that won't react with your group.

Blood donations are not just used to replace blood lost in an accident or operation. It is possible to separate from whole blood various components like white cells, red cells, plasma, clotting factors and others. Each of these components can then be used for people who need them.

B8.8   The perpetual pump

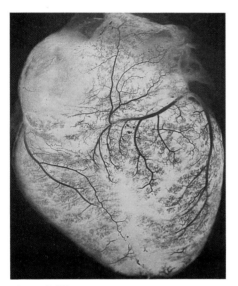

Figure 8.15
You can see the coronary arteries on the surface of this human heart.

The heart never rests. It is a muscle – the most active in the body. In an average lifetime, it will pump 225 million litres of blood through the body. In spite of the great capacity of your heart as a pump it is not moving an endless supply of blood from one place to another. It is pumping rather a small volume of blood round and round your body. That is why we talk of your blood *circulation*.

Every muscle needs a good blood supply to provide it with, among other things, oxygen. For the heart, with its ceaseless activity, an adequate and continuous blood supply is essential. The blood for the heart is supplied by two blood vessels (called coronary *arteries* – see section **B**8.9) which branch to form a network over its surface. And, as with any other muscle, the harder the heart has to beat – during vigorous exercise, for example – the more oxygen it will need.

22 **What other essential substance will be supplied by the blood?**

Sometimes the vessels which supply the heart become narrowed because cholesterol builds up on their walls (see figure 6.9, page 69). This is called *atheroma*. It means they will be able to carry less blood – probably enough if a person is resting quietly, but not enough during energetic exercise. Then it may cause a pain (called angina) but this will disappear if the person sits down and rests.

23 **Explain this observation.**

What is a heart attack?

Atheroma slows down the flow of blood through the vessels, and as a result it clots more readily. If a clot forms, then the vessel may be blocked completely. This results in a "heart attack". The muscle supplied by the vessel will be deprived altogether of oxygen, and will die. This will not be too serious if only a small branch of the blood supply to a small area of heart muscle is blocked. But if a major vessel becomes blocked, so that a large area of the heart muscle is affected, a heart attack can be fatal.

The causes of heart disease

Heart disease is extremely common. About one-third of all deaths in the UK are due to disease of the vessels supplying the heart muscle with blood (coronary artery disease). However, this was not always the case. Until about 1925, heart disease was rare.

24 Can you suggest why it has become so much more common since then?

In 1971, North Karelia, in Eastern Finland, had the highest death rate from heart disease in the world. All inhabitants were advised to stop smoking, eat less fat and more vegetables, avoid obesity, and have their blood pressure checked. By 1979 the death rate from heart disease had fallen by 24 % in men and 51 % in women – much more than the general fall in deaths from heart disease in the rest of the country during the same time.

25 What conclusions can be drawn from this study? How sure can you be about them?

Assessing the risks

26 Which factors seem to increase the risk of heart disease? (See also Chapter B6.)

You can see in Chapter **B**6 that the most important factor is almost certainly diet. The people most likely to have heart attacks are those who have a high level of cholesterol in their blood, and whose diet contains large amounts of animal fats. In countries where most people eat a diet that is low in cholesterol and animal fats, there is very little heart disease.

When a blood clot forms in blood vessels supplying blood to some part of the brain a *stroke* occurs. Brain cells need a continuous supply of oxygen and even a few minutes without it will kill them. People who suffer strokes can have difficulty in speaking, seeing or using a limb and can in some cases lose consciousness or die. Again, a clot is more likely to form if the normal smooth lining of your arteries has been narrowed by fat deposits.

To find out what a heart is really like it is best to look at the real thing. Worksheet **B**8D will give you a chance to look at and carefully examine a heart from the butcher's shop.

We said that the heart is a pump but in fact it is two pumps, side by side, which pump at exactly the same time. The right side of your heart receives blood which has been round the body. This blood has delivered oxygen to the cells of your body and is therefore **deoxygenated** (although it still contains a little oxygen). The right side of the heart pumps this blood to the lungs where it collects more oxygen, to become **oxygenated** once again. This newly oxygenated blood returns to the left side of the heart and is then pumped once again to all parts of your body.

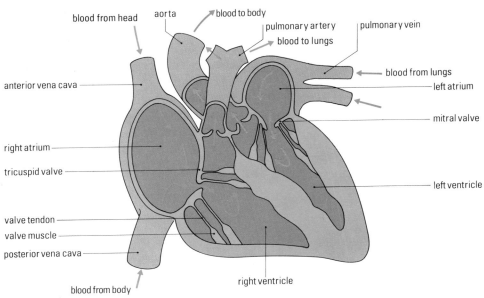

Figure 8.16
A diagram of a section through a mammal's heart. The arrows show the route taken by blood.

How fast does the heart beat?

You can find the answer to this by taking your pulse.

27 Find your pulse by putting your finger on the blood vessel found under your skin on the underside of your wrist near the base of your thumb. Use a stopwatch and count the beats for 30 seconds.

28 Why does counting your pulse tell you how fast your heart is beating?

29 How many times did your heart beat in a minute? (This is called your heart rate per minute.)

30 What is the average heart rate for your class?

31 Design an investigation which would enable you to find the effect of exercise on heart rate.

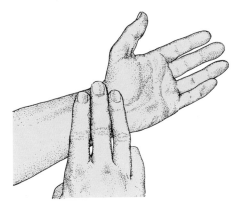

Figure 8.17
This is how to place your fingers if you want to find your pulse.

B8.9   The blood vessels

Blood leaving your heart delivers substances to all parts of your body. Other substances are collected from the tissues and the blood then returns to the heart. There are about 130 000 km of blood vessel inside you. Not all the vessels are identical and it is possible to recognize three main types. If you consider the job done by each type you may be able to understand their structure.

Arteries are the vessels which transport blood from the heart to the tissues. They have to withstand blood being forced into them at a high pressure by the pumping heart. Their walls are elastic and stretch when the heart beats.

While the heart is filling these stretched arteries return to their normal diameter once more. This movement of the artery walls helps to keep the blood flowing and it is also why your blood flows smoothly even though your heart beats in jerks.

The arteries branch repeatedly until eventually the smallest blood vessels arise; these are called *capillaries*. There are about 85 000 km of these tiny tubes inside your body, which gives you some idea of just how small they must be. Every cell in your body is close to a capillary. Blood flows very slowly through capillaries and their walls are very thin and porous. This makes it very easy for materials to be exchanged between the blood and the tissues.

32 Explain how the position of the capillaries and the nature of their walls is related to the exchange of substances between the blood and the tissues.

Figure 8.18 shows a capillary network in the foot of a young frog.

Capillaries join up to form larger and larger tubes until blood vessels called *veins* are formed. Veins are fairly easy to see if you look at your hands or wrists. They look like bluish lines. Sometimes they will be very swollen, at other times apparently quite empty.

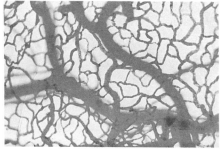

Figure 8.18
A capillary network.

33 Raise one arm in the air and hang the other down by your side. Keep them there like that for a minute or two. Then bring them both onto the bench in front of you and look at the difference between the veins on the back of your two hands.

34 Describe all the differences in appearance between your hands.

Veins are the thinner-walled blood vessels which take the blood from the tissues back to the heart. Blood inside them is at a low pressure and needs to be squeezed by your muscles to keep it moving. There are *valves* inside the veins to prevent the blood from going backwards, away from the heart.

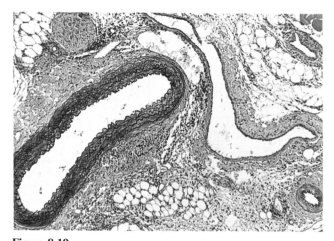
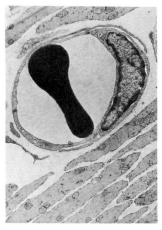

Figure 8.19
These photographs show sections of an artery, a vein and a capillary. Notice the differences between their sizes and the thickness of their walls. (Left × 120; right × 3400.)

Sometimes the elastic tissue in the walls of veins becomes flabby and the valves do not close properly. This condition is called varicose veins. These often occur in the legs, especially those of people who stand a great deal. Elastic stockings can help by giving some extra support. When varicose veins form in the rectum they are called piles (see Chapter **B**6).

Figure 8.19 shows actual transverse sections of the three main blood vessels.

35 In these photographs, decide which is an artery, which one a capillary and which a vein. Give reasons for your choice.

A diagram showing the names of some of the main arteries and veins in the circulation of blood in a human is shown in figure 8.20.

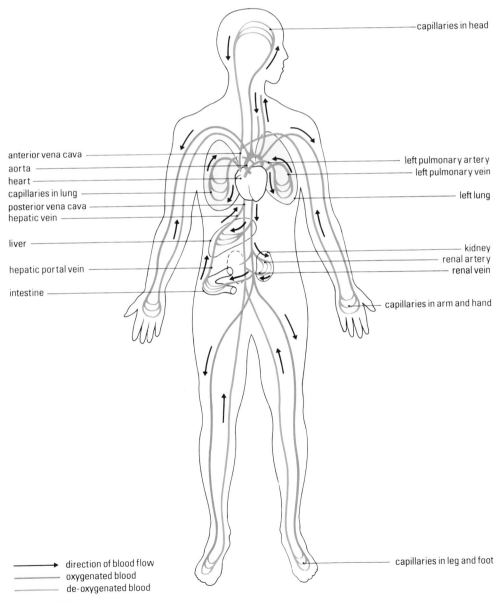

Figure 8.20
Some of the main arteries and veins in the human circulation.

B8.10   Severe bleeding

Our circulatory system normally contains about 5 L of blood which is being pumped round the body under pressure. Fluid (plasma) passes to and fro between the capillaries and the spaces in the body tissues and this keeps the volume of the blood constant.

If the body suddenly loses a large amount of fluid, the volume of circulating blood will be less and blood pressure will fall. *Shock* is the term used to describe what happens when a sudden fall in blood pressure deprives the body organs, especially the brain, of sufficient blood.

Causes of shock

Sudden severe external bleeding, from a cut artery for example, is one way in which enough body fluid can be lost to send the body into a state of shock. But it is not the only way.

36 What others can you think of?

What happens during shock?

An adult can lose up to just over 0.5 L of body fluid (the volume taken if you become a blood donor) without any ill effects. But if more than this is lost, blood pressure will start to fall.

The danger signs

The first one is a rapid pulse.

37 Why does the heart begin to beat faster?

A person suffering from shock will also become pale, cold and clammy and will feel weak. It is possible to see the explanation for this too. Because, as we have seen, it is vital to maintain an oxygen supply to the brain, the blood vessels in the skin and muscles are "shut down" so that less blood flows to these less important parts of the body.

This may stop the fall in blood pressure, but if it fails to do so the brain may then become short of oxygen. One of the first and most dangerous effects of this is that the brain's mechanism for maintaining blood pressure by controlling the volume of blood flowing in blood vessels will no longer operate. When this happens the blood pressure drops to a dangerously low level. The person becomes drowsy and confused and may lose consciousness altogether.

Someone in this dangerous state of shock cannot recover unless first aid is given and the lost fluid is replaced with a blood or plasma transfusion. If this is not done, both breathing and the heart may fail.

First aid for shock

Lie a patient who is conscious on his or her back with feet raised and head turned to one side.

DO NOT try to warm the patient by piling on blankets or giving hot water bottles. This will only draw blood back to the skin at the expense of more important organs.

INTERPRET

38 Can you work out why it does this?

It is better to try to stop further heat loss by putting a blanket under the patient, or lightly covering one who is shivering. DO NOT give anything (and especially not alcohol) to drink. But if the patient is thirsty you can moisten his or her lips with water.

Review

Unless an organism is extremely small or has a shape that gives it a relatively large surface area compared with its volume, it will require a transport system. Most transport systems consist of tube-like structures. In plants transport is achieved by a double system of phloem, carrying food, and xylem, carrying water and mineral ions. The cells from which the transport systems of plants are formed are fairly rigid and inactive. In animals a single fluid – often called blood – carries all the materials that are transported round the body and it is contained within flexible blood vessels of various types.

A plant's transport system simply contains the materials being transported. In animals, the blood is a tissue, consisting of different types of cell, each with its own function.

Human circulatory systems generally operate without fault for 70 years or more. But accident or unhealthy diet can cause blood loss or damage to the major blood vessels.

Chapter **B**9 — **Keeping going**

B9.1 The living engine

The invention of engines has greatly improved the quality of our lives. If they are supplied with a source of energy they seem to work tirelessly, day in, day out, for our benefit. (See Chapter **P**8, "Machines and engines", in the Physics book.)

Figure 9.1
All engines need a supply of energy.

You are an example of the most magnificent engine ever to have been made – the human being! Like all engines you too need a supply of energy. But you and other living organisms differ from all other engines in that without an energy supply you not only stop working, but you die. Food is the source of energy for the living engine. But how is the energy transferred from food to cells?

B9.2 Fuel for the living engine

Cooks are often warned not to let the chip pan get too hot, in case this causes a kitchen fire. Clearly, if food is burned a considerable amount of energy is transferred to the environment.

1 Give three ways by which you can tell that energy is being transferred to the surroundings when food burns.

However, as you will appreciate, we don't have little fires inside us burning up our corn flakes to provide us with energy.

In Chapter **B**3 you can learn about how food molecules like glucose can be built up from the small molecules, carbon dioxide and water, in the process of photosynthesis. For this to happen, energy is needed and comes from the sun. If living organisms could do something like the reverse of this process and could break up glucose molecules into smaller molecules, then energy might be transferred to the organism.

There are two parts to this idea – one is that the food is broken up; the other is that energy is transferred to the organism.

2 If glucose is broken up what might be formed again?

Another sign of food being "used" in this way in organisms would be that their mass would change.

3 Try to explain in your own words why their mass would change.

If energy is being transferred we would expect to see something happening – growth maybe, or a change in temperature.

One way to investigate these suggestions is to do some experiments for yourself. Another is to look at other people's results.

Four experiments and their results are described in Worksheet **B**9A.

The results from such experiments provide us with some evidence that

a living organisms can convert food molecules to carbon dioxide
b some energy contained in the food molecule is transferred to its surroundings, "warming them up", and
c at the same time, oxygen is removed from the surroundings.

This is a very important process and it is called *respiration*.

4 Which of the experiments provides evidence to support one or more of the conclusions **a, b** and **c**?

A simple shorthand way to write this process is:

Food + oxygen $\longrightarrow$ carbon dioxide + water + energy available for other purposes

B9.3   The power stations of the cell

If a little petrol is poured onto a bonfire the fire suddenly burns very fiercely for a short time. Petrol is also the fuel which is burned in the cylinders of a car engine. If you transferred all the energy in a litre of petrol to the car engine at once there might be one large explosion (you can find out more about petrol engines in Chapter **P8** in the Physics book). In fact there are a number of small controlled explosions and one litre of petrol will drive the car for quite a long way.

The energy in a food molecule must not be made available all at once to the human engine. This is where enzymes come into the story. The energy is transferred in small amounts under the control of enzymes. Each step of the gradual breakdown of the food molecules is controlled by a different enzyme. All these enzymes work together and ensure that energy transfer is gradual and controlled.

But where in a cell does respiration take place? The best way to answer this question is to look inside cells. Figure 9.2 is a highly magnified photograph of skeletal muscle tissue. The main parts are labelled for you. The muscle tissue does a lot of respiration because it does a lot of work.

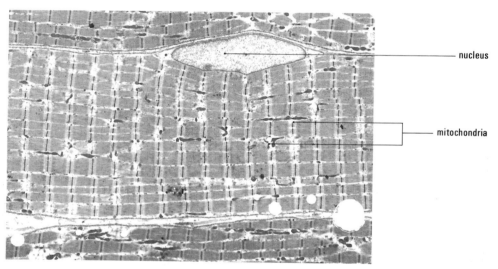

Figure 9.2
This highly magnified photograph shows skeletal muscle tissue.

5 In what structure in the cell do you think respiration takes place? Explain how you arrive at your answer.

Most of the energy transfer takes place inside the structures called *mitochondria* – which have been called the "powerhouses of the cell". The food molecule that is used by most organisms is glucose. The mitochondria contain nearly all the enzymes that are needed to break down glucose into carbon dioxide and water. In the process the energy is transferred, for instance to muscle fibres, enabling them to contract and enabling you to move about. However the transfer is not very efficient and much of the energy is transferred as heat.

Mitochondria are present in every living cell of all organisms larger than bacteria.

Figure 9.3
Root hairs on cress.

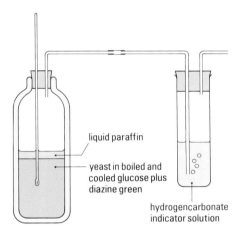

liquid paraffin

yeast in boiled and
cooled glucose plus
diazine green

hydrogencarbonate
indicator solution

Figure 9.4
The apparatus used to monitor the fermentation of glucose by yeast.

Temperature (°C)	Bubbles per minute
4	0
20	3
35	6
45	22
90	0

Figure 9.5

B9.4   Hard work

It is a bit easier to see examples of energy-requiring activities in animals than it is in plants. Animals and plants both grow – a process which requires energy – although this may happen quite slowly. However, animals move about, often very quickly, and they transfer energy to the surroundings, "warming them up" in the process. Both of these are easy for you to detect.

There are many other, less obvious examples of energy-requiring activities both in animals and in plants. A process in plants that is vital to their survival, and requires energy, is the uptake of mineral ions from the soil by the roots.

Water will move from where there is more of it to where there is less. Because there is usually more water in the soil than there is in root hairs, water moves into the root hairs from the soil.

This is not the case with mineral ions. There is, usually, far more of any particular ion inside the root cells than there is in the soil outside the root. The plant must have a constant supply of these ions, so work has to be done to move them **into** the roots.

When work is done, energy is transferred. There are plenty of mitochondria in the root cells. They transfer energy from sugars to what we might think of as "pumps" that can move ions into the roots. Because this movement of ions into roots requires energy it is called *active transport*.

There is some more information about active transport in Worksheet **B9B**.

B9.5   Respiring without oxygen

Respiration which uses oxygen is called *aerobic respiration*. However, some organisms can live in places where oxygen is scarce or even absent altogether. This suggests that they have a way of transferring energy from glucose without oxygen. It is called *anaerobic respiration*. Many of the organisms which can respire most successfully without oxygen are micro-organisms. Yeast is a fungus which we can use to demonstrate anaerobic respiration, or what is also called *fermentation*. See Worksheet **B9C**.

As an extension to the experiment in Worksheet **B9C**, a pupil set up the apparatus containing yeast and glucose at different temperatures and then counted the number of bubbles of carbon dioxide passing through the indicator every minute. Figure 9.4 shows the apparatus used and figure 9.5 shows the results.

6 Plot a line graph of these data.

7 State a conclusion you can draw from this graph.

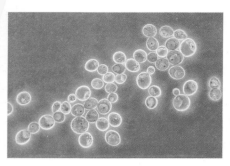

Figure 9.6
These are yeast organisms. Notice how small they are. (× 370)

Fermentation

Fermentation has different end products from aerobic respiration. Yeast produces ethanol and carbon dioxide during fermentation. If yeast has a supply of oxygen, then it will respire aerobically. When it does so it just produces carbon dioxide and water. It did not take humans very long to discover that fermented juices were quite pleasant to drink. It seems a fairly primitive thing to do – to squash fruits to extract the juices and sugars and then to allow a fungus to contaminate these and excrete its waste products into the liquid. The huge brewing industries of the world are based upon anaerobic respiration – that is, the fermentation of yeast.

In big breweries the whole process is carried out on a large scale. But no replacement for the microscopic fungus has been found, and yeast still provides the most important part of the process.

Brewing is probably one of the earliest examples of what we now call biotechnology – the use of organisms in industry.

Figure 9.7 gives you a recipe for making ginger beer.

---

8 Read the recipe and instructions for making ginger beer carefully and work out why it tastes different from other types of beer and why it will not make anyone drunk.

Ingredients:
Root ginger, 45 g
Cream of tartar, 30 g
Loaf sugar (granulated will do), 1.2 kg
Lemons, 2
Water, 9.6 litres
Brewing yeast, 30 g

Peel the lemons and squeeze them. Strain the juice into a large pan or bowl.
Pound up the ginger between two pieces of clean cloth until pulped.
Add the ginger, the cream of tartar and the sugar to the lemon juice.
Boil the water and pour it over these ingredients when it has just boiled.
Allow this mixture to stand until it is only just warm.
Add the yeast, which you should mix with a little water first to make it into a paste.
Stir the mixture very well, cover the bowl with a cloth and leave it in a warm place overnight.
In the morning, skim off all the yeast which will have risen to the top and bottle the beer immediately.
You can drink this at once although it improves a little if kept for two or three days.
(**Beware:** if you do keep it for more than a day, do not have the stoppers tightly on the bottles. They should be left loose enough for gas to escape.)

Figure 9.7
Recipe for ginger beer.

Anaerobic respiration in animals

It is simpler to investigate anaerobic respiration in yeasts than in animals because the end products are easier to detect. In animals anaerobic respiration also happens but we do not call it fermentation. It is a little harder to demonstrate and the end product is different.

However, if you can create a situation where your muscles need energy and oxygen is in short supply, you might be able to appreciate the effect that anaerobic respiration has.

0
OBSERVE

9 Try the following exercise.
a Raise one arm above the head and lower the other.
b Clench and unclench each fist at the same rate, preferably about twice every second.
c Notice the feeling in each arm as the exercise goes on.
d Continue doing this for as long as you can!
e When one arm becomes painful, rest both arms on the bench in front of you and notice what you feel in each.

10 In which arm did pain develop first?

11 What were the feelings of the painful arm when you rested it in a horizontal position?

The pain that developed in your arm was due to the build-up in the muscle of a chemical called *lactic acid*. If muscles (skeletal or heart) are made to contract when oxygen is in short supply then anaerobic respiration takes place in these muscles, producing lactic acid. The build-up of the level of this acid leads to the very unpleasant pain.

B9.6   Speed *versus* stamina

The ability of a hungry predator to catch its prey can mean the difference between life and death. Respiration, whether aerobic or anaerobic, plays a vital role in enabling the muscles of both predator and prey to contract in the race for survival.

Predators use a variety of chasing methods to catch their prey. For some, the race is a short fast event while for others it is a much more patient affair.

A cheetah, for example, can produce bursts of speed up to 147 km per hour to outpace a hare (see figure 9.8). Such magnificent sprints can only be kept up for a short time. If the quarry gets a good start, the cheetah drops out of the chase exhausted. Moreover, it seems odd to think that a cheetah running at top speed would outclass a human athlete in a 200 m sprint, but would be unlikely to complete a 1500 m race!

Figure 9.8
Cheetahs chasing a hare.

By contrast, an African hunting dog will jog along at about 14 km per hour until it sights its prey and only then will it hit its top speed of about 48 km per hour in the long chase which follows. This wears the prey down until it tires and the dog then pounces. Stamina appears to be the key to its success.

Fortunately, we no longer have to chase after our food, but we still take part in a variety of running events which test our athletic skill over a number of different distances from the 100 m to the marathon (figures 9.9 and 9.10). So how do our muscle cells obtain their energy during these different sorts of event?

Figure 9.9
The sprinter, Alan Wells of Great Britain, running in the 100 metres race in the Los Angeles Olympics, 1984.

Figure 9.10
The marathon runner, Charlie Spedding of Great Britain, winning a bronze medal in the 1984 Olympic Games.

Figure 9.11 shows the percentages of the energy needed which are obtained from aerobic and anaerobic respiration in races over different distances.

Event	Percentage of energy obtained from:	
	Aerobic respiration	**Anaerobic respiration**
100 m	0–5	95–100
800 m	35	65
1500 m	55	45
10 000 m	90	10
Marathon (42 186 m)	98	2

Figure 9.11

12 Why will an 800 m athlete have to retire from a race if he or she runs too fast in the first 400 m?

13 Why would it be rather silly to train for a 4 km rowing race by doing a series of short sprints up a hill until you were exhausted, every day for a week or two?

B9.7 Chemical reactions in cells

All the activities that we have mentioned in this chapter rely upon endless chemical activity going on in the cells of all living organisms. These chemical reactions are together called *metabolism* and they are under the direct control of enzymes. In the gut, enzymes digest food – they break big molecules into smaller ones (see Chapter **B**5) – but this is not the only sort of reaction that enzymes control. Many of the reactions going on inside cells are building-up reactions – big molecules are made from smaller, simpler ones. Other reactions involve rearrangements of the atoms in a molecule to change it slightly.

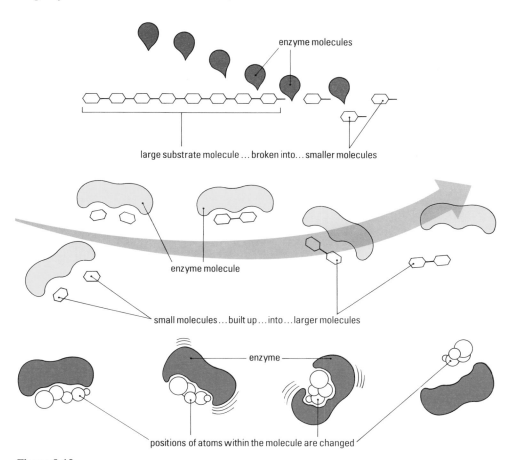

Figure 9.12
Enzymes do a variety of jobs.

14 What do Chapters **B**3 and **B**4 suggest you need to keep you going?

15 What is the gas that most organisms extract from the air? You can find out from Chapter **B**7.

Very simple questions perhaps, but the answers are very important. You may have begun to realize where the argument is leading. How much oxygen an organism uses up or how much food it eats could be a measure of its metabolism.

16 One of these two measurements would give a more accurate answer than the other. Which one do you think it is?

17 It will still probably be rather inaccurate; can you suggest why?

There are other signs of metabolism. Imagine you have just arrived from outer space and you have landed in the middle of your classroom. Look around you; listen to what is going on. What information can your sense organs pick up that indicates that human beings are metabolizing?

One suggestion may be that humans make a noise, or move about. They **do** things. They are **active**. Another is that they are **warm**. If you put some marble chips into hydrochloric acid in a flask and let them react for a while the flask will warm up. You can tell that a reaction is occurring because the temperature of the flask increases. If your temperature increased, an observer might suggest that it was because reactions were taking place inside you.

So from quite simple observations you could suggest that metabolism consumes food and oxygen and is able to make organisms active. It also causes some energy to be transferred to their surroundings. The rate at which an animal uses oxygen during a particular activity gives quite a good idea of how fast its metabolism is going during that activity – we call this its *metabolic rate*.

18 How do you think you could find out your body's metabolic rate?

19 Five statements follow. Look at each one and try to write down what it tells you about the factors that influence the rate of metabolism.
a Figure 9.14 suggests there is a relation between metabolic rate and body mass in shrews.
b A resting parakeet uses about 1900 mm³ of oxygen per g of body mass per hour but a flying parakeet uses about 22 000 mm³.
c You eat more food and use more oxygen in winter months than you do in summer.

Figure 9.13
A shrew.

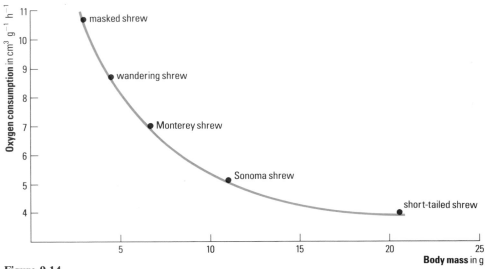

Figure 9.14
The graph shows the relation between oxygen consumption and body mass in shrews.

Figure 9.15
A humming bird, hovering before a flower.

d Hummingbirds have to feed almost constantly during the day. They use small, rapid wingbeats to stay airborne nearly the whole time. As darkness approaches they stop flying and feeding; their temperature falls and they remain inactive all through the night.

e Shrews eat the equivalent of 95 per cent of their body mass every day. They will die if they are deprived of food for longer than two or three hours.

20 Design an experiment to investigate how much oxygen a living organism consumes. Choose a suitable organism to investigate and remember to set up a control. In one of your containers you will need to use potassium hydroxide to absorb carbon dioxide from the air around the organism. Why? You should draw your apparatus and you should give simple step-by-step instructions on how to use it. At the end you should say what you will be measuring and what results you expect to see.

P
PLAN

Chapter **B10**   **Skeletons and muscles**

B10.1   Propping things up

If you have ever watched a live performance of motor cyclists making a pyramid you have probably held your breath and wondered how long it would be before they all toppled to the ground (figure 10.1).

Figure 10.1
A motor cycle pyramid of the "White Helmets" at Aldershot.

Figure 10.2
The giant sequoia named General Grant.

But have you ever thought about the mass of leaves and branches that there are in a mature tree?

The giant sequoia is the biggest tree we know. The one named "General Grant" is about 80 metres high and its mass is more than 2000 tonnes. Getting yourself balanced would be a major problem, and you would need to be very strong not to be blown over by the wind.

We can start to find out something about how plants are supported by looking at the structure of their stems. But first of all we must remind ourselves what material the stems are made of.

Plant cell walls are made from *cellulose* – a carbohydrate. In certain tissues there are some other substances deposited in the cell walls. One such material is *lignin* (see Chapter **B**8). You may be able to see this for yourself by putting a piece of matchstick in a solution which turns lignin bright red.

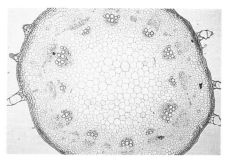

Figure 10.3
A transverse section through the stem of a sunflower, *Helianthus* sp.

Figure 10.5
The leaves of the water crowfoot are suspended in the stream water when it flows. If the flow were to stop the leaves would sink onto the mud.

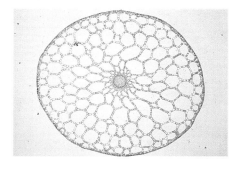

Figure 10.6
A section through the stem of a water plant.

1 Cellulose is a flexible material. What difference do you suppose the presence of lignin makes to the cell walls?

We can cut thin slices from plant stems, test them for lignin by staining and examine them under a microscope. Figures 10.3 and 10.4 show such sections from the stems of two different land plants.

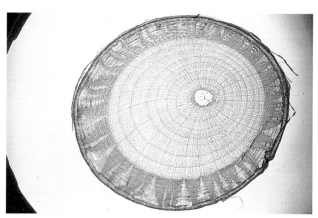

Figure 10.4
A transverse section through the stem of a lime, *Tilia* sp.

2 What can you conclude from the stem sections, about support in these two plant stems? Explain briefly in your own words.

You know that wood is tough and if you have broken the stalk of celery you will have seen that there are some tough "threads" in softer stemmed plants as well. In Chapter **B**8 we see that the water-conducting tissue – xylem – contains lignin in its walls.

If you have ever watched a field of grass or cereal in the wind you will have realized how important it is that the stems should be flexible rather than stiff. It takes quite strong winds to flatten cereal crops. If they were not flexible they would snap very easily.

Plants that live in water

Water plants are supported by the water they live in. Some of them have leaves which float on the surface of still water, like the water lily (see figure 14.12a, page 177). Other water plants are kept suspended by the flow of water in a stream (figure 10.5).

You might expect, therefore, to find that the stems of water plants have a different structure from the stems of land plants. Figure 10.6 shows a transverse section through the stem of a water plant.

3 Compare the stem of a water plant with the stem sections of land plants in figures 10.3 and 10.4. Write down all the differences you can see between them.

4 Suggest how these differences between stems may be related to their environments.

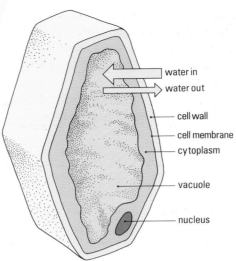

Figure 10.7
A plant cell. Water moves into the cell by osmosis.

Water does not only support plants by buoyancy from the outside. It is also important in keeping them supported from the inside.

In Chapter **B**9 we mention that water moves from the soil into plants through their root hairs. This happens because water will always move from where it is more concentrated to where it is less concentrated. We should now look at what happens in more detail. Plant cells, just like animal cells, have a membrane around them. Plant cells have a cell wall as well. Many substances with quite large molecules, like sugar, can pass through this wall, so we say it is *permeable*. Only smaller molecules like water pass through the cell membrane so it is described as being *differentially permeable*.

Now consider some plant cells. Their cytoplasm contains sugars, salts and proteins. When they are put in contact with water, it starts to move into the cells through the cell wall and cell membrane. This is because water is more concentrated outside the cells than inside.

Water will, of course, pass through the cell membrane in both directions but the overall movement is always from where it is more concentrated to where it is less concentrated. When water moves through a differentially permeable membrane in this way the process is called *osmosis*.

5 When will water stop moving into a plant cell?

If you put animal cells such as red blood cells into water (see Chapter **B**12), they will take in water and go on doing so until they burst. This cannot happen with plant cells.

6 What prevents plant cells from bursting?

a   b

Figure 10.8
The *Coleus* plant in (**a**) had been left without water for several days; (**b**) shows how it looked after watering.

As more water moves into the cell, the cytoplasm presses outwards on the cellulose cell wall. This starts to stretch. But it is very strong and cannot be broken in this way. Eventually the cell wall prevents any more water from moving into the cell. A cell in this state is described as being *turgid*.

Worksheet **B**10A gives you an opportunity to investigate osmosis and turgidity in a number of different tissues from different organisms.

Figure 10.8a shows a *Coleus* plant which was left without water. After several days, the leaves had wilted and looked floppy. After watering (10.8b) they were like leaves which had been in water all the time.

7 Use the information in this section to explain how water could help to support these plants.

B10.2 Limbs as props

The limbs of animals come in all shapes and sizes. Clearly, limbs have a variety of functions to perform in animals and one of the most important is support. This is particularly important for land animals. The limbs that help to prop them up are called legs. However, not all land animals have legs.

8 What are the disadvantages of having no legs?

Figure 10.9
Look at the different types of legs these animals have.

The legs of all land animals have to support the body mass whether the animal is big or small.

a Lizard

b Elephant

c Seal

d Giraffe

e Mole

9 Study the photographs in figure 10.9 and try to make one or two conclusions about how larger animals are able to support their mass.

The graph in figure 10.10 shows the shoulder heights of various mammals plotted against the body mass.

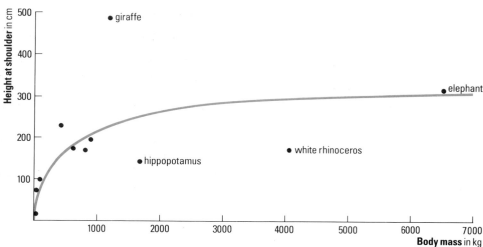

Figure 10.10
A graph of the heights of a number of mammals and their body mass.

10 What is the evidence in figure 10.10 to suggest that as mammals get bigger their legs do not increase in length in the same proportion as the body mass increases?

11 What do you think would happen if a mammal's legs did increase in length in proportion to the increase in its body mass?

Your observations should enable you to appreciate that larger animals have legs which are shorter and thicker than you would expect if they stayed in proportion to body mass. It appears that long, thin legs are not as effective as short, stout ones for supporting large masses.

12 If an animal does have long thin legs to support a large mass, like the giraffe, then what does it do which gives it added stability?

You do the same with the legs on a camera tripod. The camera isn't very heavy but if the tripod legs are too close together it can become very unstable.

Figure 10.11 shows the way the bones are arranged in two mammals. One is a heavy mammal and the other is a lighter one.

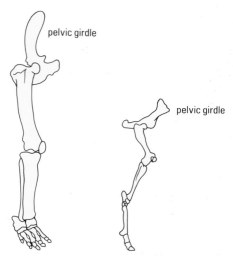

Figure 10.11
These are the hind limb bones of two mammals. How does the arrangement of bones in their legs differ?

13 Which leg belongs to the heavier mammal in figure 10.11? Explain how you made your decision.

Reptiles are constructed rather differently from mammals. If you looked at a lizard you might notice one feature about the way it was supported that must be quite a disadvantage. (See figure 10.9a, page 115.)

14 Why do you think that many lizards rest their bodies on the ground when they are not running about?

Birds are different again. They need bones to support their mass but they also need to be as light as possible. In many birds some of the bones are hollow with cross struts. This is a remarkable feature. It took human beings a long while to realize how stiff such structures are. You can learn more about such structures in Chapter **P**1 of the Physics book where you will see some man-made structures that employ this same principle in their support.

Figure 10.12
This section through the bone of a bird shows how the mass of the bone is reduced without lessening its strength.

B10.3   Joints and skeletons

Wherever two or more bones meet in your body you have a *joint*. There are many sorts of joints but we are only going to look at the most common type found in your body. This is the type of joint which allows quite a lot of movement. Because the space between the bones is filled with a liquid called *synovial fluid* it is called a *synovial joint*.

A diagram of a typical synovial joint is shown in figure 10.13.

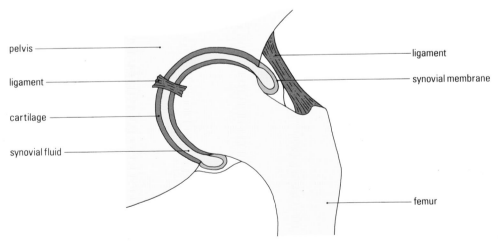

pelvis — ligament
ligament — synovial membrane
cartilage
synovial fluid
femur

Figure 10.13
A synovial joint. This is called a ball and socket joint. It is found at the hip.

INTERPRET

15 Which part of the synovial joint is likely to be responsible for:
reducing friction? (See Chapter **P**5 in your Physics book.)
holding the bones together?
holding the synovial fluid in place?
acting as a shock absorber?

Joints allow bones to move against each other, which is very important if locomotion is going to be possible.

16 Try this (and make sure no one is watching you!):
Stand up straight and keep your knees quite rigid and your legs straight.

17 How easy is it to walk?

18 Now try to prevent your legs from moving at the hip joint and see if you can walk at all.

19 What do you have to do with your body in order to move like this?

Different synovial joints in your body vary in the amount of movement they allow. It is fairly easy to identify two different types. They are called *ball and socket* joints and *hinge* joints. Ball and socket joints allow movement to take place in three planes. Your hip joint is an example of this type. Hinge joints allow movement in only one plane. Your elbow is an example.

20 Where in your body do you think there are other kinds of joint?

21 Why do you think the skull is made of many bones and joints rather than just one single bone?

B10.4   Muscles and movement

Figure 10.14
Without either muscles or bones you would be rather helpless!

Your legs are very important for lifting your body off the ground and in getting it moving. It is not just your bones which make this possible. Without the muscles which are attached to bones, your skeleton would be of very little use in helping you to move. In fact, both muscle and bone are needed to give support to your body, because without muscles to hold the bones still, even the strongest legs would quickly collapse under you. With lots of muscles, but without the bones you would be equally helpless.

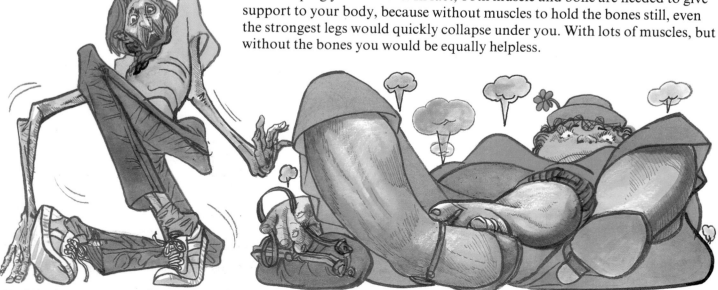

Muscles and bones not only provide the scaffolding needed to give your body support, but, with the nervous system, they provide the mechanism by which you move. Your muscles are connected to your bones by *tendons*. These connections act as tough non-elastic wires. When a muscle contracts and gets shorter it pulls on the tendon which in turn pulls on the bone. And, when your bones move, you move!

At this point it would be a good idea to try Worksheet **B**10B. It will show you the way in which a joint is constructed and you will be able to see not only the parts of a synovial joint but also the muscles and tendons that help it to move.

A number of requirements must be met if muscles are to be successful in getting you to move. One end must be anchored to a bone which doesn't move when the muscle contracts; the other end must be attached to a different bone which will move when the muscle contracts. And for this to happen there must be a movable joint between both bones. Contraction of the muscle will then swing the movable bone towards the stationary one.

There must also be a muscle to pull the bone back the other way. This is because muscles **pull** when they contract, but they can't push. They have to be stretched in order to get longer. So muscles are always found in pairs. One contracts while the other is stretched. This stretched muscle can then contract in its turn and stretch its counterpart. Because the two muscles oppose each other they are known as *antagonistic* pairs.

---

22 Where else have you met a pair of antagonistic muscles?

The muscle which straightens a limb is called the *extensor* and the one which bends a limb is called the *flexor*.

Figure 10.15 is a diagram of the antagonistic pair of muscles in your arm, which operate your elbow joint.

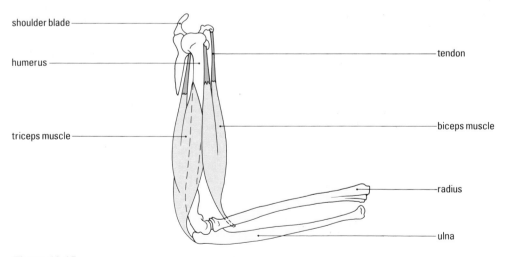

shoulder blade

humerus

triceps muscle

tendon

biceps muscle

radius

ulna

Figure 10.15
The chief muscles which move your arm at the elbow.

INTERPRET

23 Which muscle is the extensor (straightens the arm)?

The muscles in your arm are used to help you to lift things up. The muscles and bones in your arm are a machine. They enable you to do work. The muscle–bone machine of the arm is very useful; and it is quite efficient. It can do nearly all the things you want it to do – can't it?

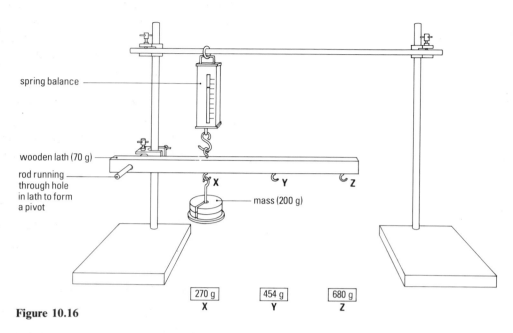

spring balance

wooden lath (70 g)

rod running through hole in lath to form a pivot

X   Y   Z

mass (200 g)

| 270 g | 454 g | 680 g |
| X | Y | Z |

Figure 10.16

Have a look at the model shown in figure 10.16. It resembles the muscle arrangement in your upper arm and the bones from your elbow to your hand. A mass was hooked onto the positions X, Y and Z in turn, and the reading on the spring balance was recorded. The results are shown in the boxes.

If you look at the figures in the boxes you will see that your muscle is really doing rather more work than it needs to. It would do less work if it was attached to your arm not near the elbow but at the wrist. Or things would improve if your arm was much shorter.

24 So what are you gaining from the arrangement of muscles and bones in your arms?

25 You can check all that has been said about the arm.
a Roll up your sleeve and put your hand, palm up, under a heavy object.
b Relax the muscles of your upper arm and feel them.
c Now try to lift the object and feel the muscles again.
d Put a finger into the crook of your elbow and feel the tendon.
e Now place your hand, palm up, on top of a table.
f Feel the muscles in your arm.
g Now press the back of your hand firmly down on the table and feel the biceps and the triceps.

26 Which one is contracted now?

The skeleton we possess is called an *endoskeleton* because it is inside our body. Our muscles are found outside our skeleton. There is one group of animals, the arthropods, which have an *exoskeleton* (see Chapter **B**2), that is, a skeleton found on the outside of their bodies.

B10.5 Damage may occur

Humans thrive on exercise provided that it does not strain the muscles, bones and joints beyond their limits. These tissues can bear increasing loads. This is really what training is about – putting greater and greater loads on the muscle–bone machine. But we can demand too much from the tissues. Overuse or misuse can result in injury.

Bones have to be rigid. This means that they cannot change their shape, or "give", if they are subjected to too much pressure. Instead they will break or split. Joints are much more flexible, but each one has only a limited range of movement and will be damaged or wrenched out of place if it is forced beyond that range, or in the wrong direction. Even muscles and tendons can be overstretched; this may damage the muscle fibres or tear them from their moorings.

27 What factors might make an athlete particularly "injury-prone"?

The importance of training

The body can adjust to the physical demands that are made upon it. Regular exercise increases the output of the heart; it also increases the amount of heart muscle.

28 Why are these changes a particular advantage to an athlete?

Injuries are most likely to occur if the individual takes strenuous exercise without a gradual period of training to build up strength and fitness. New recruits in the army sometimes suffer "march fractures" – small stress fractures in the bones of their feet. Athletes can be so anxious to improve their performance that they carry on exercising when the body is tired, so that tissues become inflamed and painful.

Injuries such as "tennis elbow", "housemaid's knee" and inflammation of the Achilles tendon which fastens the calf muscle to the heel bone are common in athletes who train too intensively or in long distance runners who run on a hard surface.

Warming up

Warming-up exercises can help to prevent injury and improve performance. When a muscle is at rest, most of the small blood vessels which supply the muscle are closed. As activity begins, the blood vessels open and the blood flow to the muscle increases. A muscle can only give its best performance when all its blood vessels are open and the blood flow to it is at its maximum. This is usually after about ten or twelve minutes of exercise.

Warm-up exercises increase the temperature of the muscles too and this makes injuries less likely. Cold muscles are less flexible and so more injury-prone.

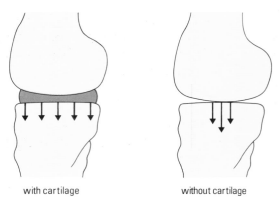

with cartilage   without cartilage

Figure 10.17
A knee joint. Can you see how important the cartilage is?

Thin ice will break if you stand on it. If you lie on it with your legs and arms outstretched it may bear your mass, because the total mass of your body is spread over a much larger area. The cartilage of the knee joint helps to spread the load evenly over the whole surface of the joint. As a result of aging or injury, the beautifully smooth surfaces of the cartilage may become roughened. Occasionally pieces of the cartilage can flake off. And if the cartilage, or one of the ligaments that hold the joint stable, is damaged, the mass will be unevenly distributed, increasing the wear and tear on one part of the joint.

Replacing damaged joints

Natural wear and tear on the mass-bearing joints, particularly the knee, hip and spine, can damage the cartilages. This is especially likely to happen if the joint has been over-used or injured, perhaps by excessive sporting activity. The bones can no longer slide freely over each other and the joint becomes increasingly painful and stiff. This condition is called *osteo-arthritis*, and it is an inevitable part of the aging process. Anyone who lives long enough will develop some degree of osteo-arthritis, though it may not be severe enough to cause any problems.

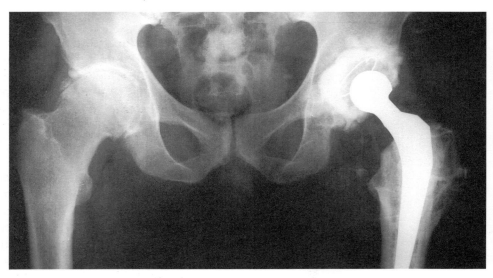

Figure 10.18
The hip joint you can see on the right has been replaced. The other is damaged and has not yet been repaired.

If a joint is badly damaged it can often be replaced by an artificial one made of metal or a combination of metal and plastic (figure 10.18). Hip joint replacements are nearly always successful. So are replacements of the elbow and finger joints.

B10.6   Moving through water

Land-dwellers and animals that move through air have to perform work in order to overcome the force of gravity. Water-dwellers do not have this problem to the same extent. Water gives them considerable support and takes this burden off their muscles. It is no surprise that the largest animal on Earth lives in water (figure 10.19).

Figure 10.19
At the top of the picture you see the smallest mammal in the world, the pygmy shrew, in relation to a horse's hoof.
At the bottom, you see the largest animal, the blue whale, in comparison with a horse.

Living in water has advantages and disadvantages. On the one hand, not so much energy needs to be provided to support the body. Many fish have a gas-filled bag called a swim bladder which reduces this need even further. On the other hand, water is much more viscous ("thicker") than air and offers more resistance to movement.

Have you ever tried walking through water? If you have you will have realized that it is much more difficult than walking through air. This is because of its greater viscosity. Fortunately, **you** don't have to put up with this problem; but the same cannot be said for the many animals that do live in water. They have no choice.

Having to push through water requires a considerable transfer of energy to muscles. In fact, much of the body mass of fish is made up of the muscles they use to propel themselves forwards through the water. Clearly, any way of reducing the amount of work that has to be done is going to be of immense value to the animals concerned.

When you swim you change your position from vertical to horizontal to help you move through water. Animals do the same – fish never swim sideways. Clearly, the shape of the animal is important. If you had to dive into water in an attempt to travel as far as possible when submerged you would do it with your arms up in a point. Not only do you travel further, but you are also spared a painful "belly flop". These observations suggest that the shape of an animal can be equally important when it moves through water.

Look at the fishes shown in figure 10.20.

Figure 10.20
What shape is common to all of these fishes?

29 Is there a shape which seems to be common to them all? If so draw it.

Your sketch has been made from your observations and so represents your idea of the shape which is most suitable for movement through water. The next step is to design and carry out an experiment to test your hypothesis.

Worksheet **B**10C helps you to do this.

Fish are shaped superbly to move through water. Their *streamlining* reduces the drag (or friction) of the water. (See Chapters **P**5 and **P**7 in the Physics book.) In this way less power is needed for locomotion. The more active the fish the more streamlined the shape.

Chapter **B11**   **Detecting changes**

B11.1   Well-behaved plants

1 Make a list of all the differences you can see between the seedlings grown in the dark, those grown in the light and those in light from one side.

2 What would happen to the seedlings if they never had any light?

Figure 11.1
Mustard seedlings grown in light (right), in the dark (top) and in light from one side.

On the whole green plants grow upwards. They do so even after being blown over.

It would appear that the growth of plants is somehow related to the nature of their surroundings. It would be correct to say that plants *respond* to them. And they respond in a way which increases their chance of survival. Environmental factors which bring about responses by living organisms are called *stimuli*. A fallen plant will respond by making its shoot bend upwards, away from the ground and into the air.

3 To what stimuli might the shoot of a fallen plant be responding?

The responses that organisms make to stimuli are called their *behaviour*. This seems to be triggered off by some happening in the environment which is picked up by the organism. As a result the organism or some part of it will make a response. For the moment the link between the input and output can be thought of as a kind of "message".

STIMULUS ⟶ RECEPTOR ⟶ (MESSAGE) ⟶ EFFECTOR ⟶ RESPONSE

Here are two new terms – *receptor* and *effector*.

The responses of some plants are rather more dramatic than the bending of the tip of a shoot. The Venus fly trap has modified leaves which have a kind of hinge in the middle. The upper surface of the leaf carries a few stout "hairs" and is covered with tiny glands that secrete a variety of chemicals. Some of these chemicals attract insects which come to the plant and wander about over the leaves. They only have to brush against some of the hairs and the leaf snaps shut by folding along its hinge. It does this so fast that the insect has very little chance of escaping.

a   b

Figure 11.2
A Venus fly trap catching a fly.

For every instance of behaviour by either a plant or an animal it should be possible to identify a receptor and an effector. The first is usually a cell, or group of cells, sensitive to changes in the environment. The second is a part of the organism which uses the instructions in the message to cause something to happen.

4 In the example of the Venus fly trap, what do you think is the receptor and what is the effector?

Because behaviour increases the chances of the organism staying alive we say that behaviour has *survival value*.

5 What could be the survival value to the Venus fly trap of the ability to catch insects?

6 What is the survival value to a fallen plant of bending to grow upwards once more?

B11.2   Light matters

The responses of plants to stimuli have fascinated scientists for many years. They have given particular attention to responses to light.

Despite many years of patient research by botanists it is still rather uncertain how these responses are brought about. Chemicals called *auxins* have been isolated from growing shoots and perhaps these are somehow involved. What is known is that the mechanisms are quite complex and that no one mechanism accounts fully for the plants' behaviour.

The responses of the fallen plant and of the mustard seedlings are not temporary changes but are the result of growth. We call responses of this type *tropisms*. A response to light is called a *phototropism*. Because a shoot responds to light by growing towards it, we call this a *positive* response. The way the shoot of a plant responds to gravity is called *negative gravitropism*.

7 How does this term suggest that the shoot of a plant responds to gravity?

Worksheet **B**11A gives you an opportunity to investigate tropisms for yourself.

B11.3   Animal responses

It is not only plants that respond to stimuli. Animals are also responsive and because the whole animal moves the responses are often easier to see.

Figures 11.3 and **11.4**
Animals respond in different ways.

8 What is the stimulus in the examples of the cat and the peacock shown in figures 11.3 and 11.4?

The data in figure 11.5 were obtained by a pupil using a trap to catch animals moving around on the soil surface at different times of the day.

Animal	Numbers caught 8 a.m. to 8 p.m.	Numbers caught 8 p.m. to 8 a.m.
Woodlice	10	36
Earthworms	1	3
Ants	22	30
Beetles	1	20
Slugs	0	2
Snails	1	4
Spiders	2	2

Figure 11.5

9 Suggest a hypothesis, related to the sensitivity of the animals to light, that might explain the difference between the two columns of data.

Most animals are sensitive to light. You will know that some animals are attracted to it if you have ever left your window open on a warm summer's night with the light on.

On the other hand, some animals move away from light. For example, blowfly maggots will crawl away from it. This helps to keep them buried in the moist tissues of whatever they are feeding on.

As with plants, animal behaviour also increases the chance of survival.

B11.4   Light for sight

Sight is one of your most useful senses. Think what life would be like without your eyes. Having **two** eyes is quite important too. Can you think of any animal that has only one eye?

10 Why are two eyes more useful than one? To get a clue, hold a 2p piece in one hand and a 1p piece in the other. Close one eye and move the coins until they appear to be the same size. Now open both your eyes.

11 What do you notice?

12 Now try to explain why two eyes are better than one.

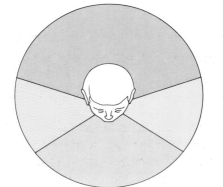

stereoscopic vision

vision with one eye

no vision

Figure 11.6
The field of vision of human eyes.

The ability to see things with two eyes at the same time is called *stereoscopic vision*. It is particularly useful in sport because judging the position of a ball is very difficult with only one eye. Two eyes enable you to appreciate objects in three dimensions. That is, they allow you to perceive distance.

13 By keeping your head facing forwards and not moving your eyes at all, work out the *field of vision* for both of your eyes. Close your left eye and ask someone to move an object in a fixed semi-circle one metre from your left around to your right. Repeat the procedure with your right eye closed.

14 Now produce a diagram showing how much stereoscopic vision you have.

B11.5   How the eye works

Figure 11.7 shows a vertical section through the eye of a mammal. All the main parts have been labelled. Worksheet **B**11B helps you to examine the eye of a mammal for yourself.

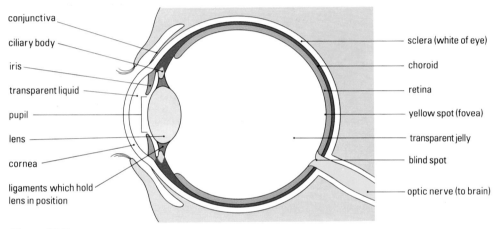

Figure 11.7

Your eye is a sphere divided into two fluid-filled chambers. The front chamber is filled with a liquid which helps to keep the transparent part of your eye bulging outwards.

15 Close your eyes and move them around as much as you can with your forefinger resting on the closed eyelid. What do you feel?

The bulge is called the *cornea* and it acts like a fixed lens. Since it is transparent, light entering your eye from an object is bent at the curved surface of your cornea. As a result an image appears upside down on the light-sensitive back wall of your eye. This back wall is called the *retina*.

If you own a camera you will know that you should protect its lens from dirt and dust. When you clean it you do so with great care so that you don't scratch it. Exactly the same precautions must be taken with your cornea. It must be kept moist by tear fluid otherwise it will dry up and become crinkled. A damaged cornea could make light bend in odd directions and make the image on the retina appear fuzzy. So it is good advice for motorbike riders to always wear their goggles.

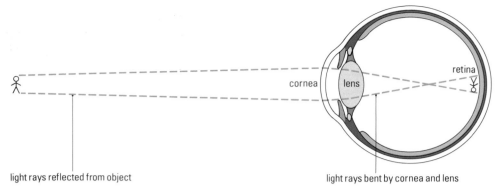

light rays reflected from object   light rays bent by cornea and lens

Figure 11.8
The cornea and lens refract the rays of light entering the eye.

Focusing

If you are to see clearly your eyes must be able to focus. To get a camera lens into focus, you have to move the lens until it is just the right distance away from the object you want to photograph. Your cornea is a fixed lens. So if an object moves closer or further away from you, its image on your retina will not remain clear unless there is another way to focus. The fine focusing you need is provided by the *lens* of the eye.

The lens is able to change shape. As it does so it can focus objects near or far exactly onto your retina. So you are able to see clearly over a range of distances without having to move your eyes forwards and backwards!

The lens is suspended from a ring of muscle called the *ciliary body* by threads known as *suspensory ligaments*. When the ciliary muscles contract the cables are slackened. This allows the flexible lens to become more curved.

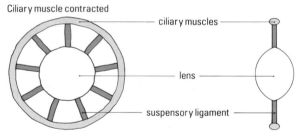

Figure 11.9
When the ciliary muscles contract the lens becomes fat. Where does this focus the light?

16 Draw a diagram similar to the one in figure 11.9 but show the ciliary muscles relaxed and the effect this will have on the lens.

Looking at things which are very close to your eyes can be tiring. For example, some people complain that their eyes ache when they have done a lot of reading or sewing.

17 Bearing this information in mind, do you think your lens is less curved or more curved when you are doing close work?

As you get older the cells in the centre of your lens start to die from lack of oxygen and nutrients. The dead cells harden and this makes the lens stiffer and less able to change shape. Figure 11.10 shows how the ability to focus properly falls off with age.

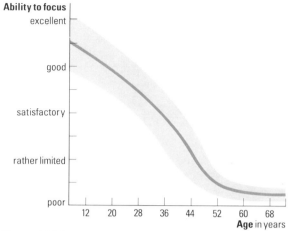

Figure 11.10
This graph shows how the ability to focus properly decreases, the older you become.

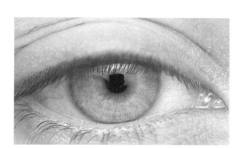

Figure 11.11
A contracted pupil.

Figure 11.12
A dilated pupil.

Sensing light for human sight

To get into the back chamber of your eye, light has to pass through a hole called the *pupil*. This hole is surrounded by the coloured part of your eye which is called the *iris*. This contains two sets of muscles. They control the size of your pupil, and thus the amount of light getting into your eye. Contraction of one set of muscles causes the pupil to get smaller, while contraction of the other set will make the pupil bigger. Figures 11.11 and 11.12 show the end result of each type of muscle contraction.

INTERPRET

18 Draw a diagram of the iris and pupil and use it to indicate the most likely arrangement of the two sets of muscles.

The outer coat of the eye is very tough indeed. This tough coat is called the *sclerotic* and the muscles which you use to swivel your eye in its socket are attached to it.

The light-sensitive retina is made up of two types of sensory cells – *rods* and *cones*. There are about 125 000 000 rods in your retina. They are sensitive at low levels of light but only allow you to see in black and white. The retina contains around 6 000 000 cones. They are sensitive at relatively high light intensities and allow you to see in colour. Most of the light entering your eyes is focused onto one spot on the retina called the *yellow spot* (or fovea).

Seeing in colour

It is the cones which enable us to see colour. There are three kinds of cone, each with a different pigment. One is sensitive to red light, one to green light and the other to blue light. Just as any colour can be produced from red, blue and green light, all the colours we perceive are the result of the combined response of the cones to these different wavelengths of light.

The nerves which take the messages from the retina all leave the eyeball at the same point. It is called the *blind spot*.

19 Why do you think it is given this name?

20 You can demonstrate the blind spot by following these instructions, using figure 11.13.

Figure 11.13

a Hold the book in front of you and look at the batsman with your right eye.

b Close your left eye and slowly move the book away from you.

21 What happens to the image of the ball?

B11.6   Other senses

There are, however, other ways besides sight by which we detect stimuli in our environment.

Hearing and the ears

Where are your ears? No, not on the outside of your head but inside your skull. The business end of the ear is a coiled tube containing sensitive cells.

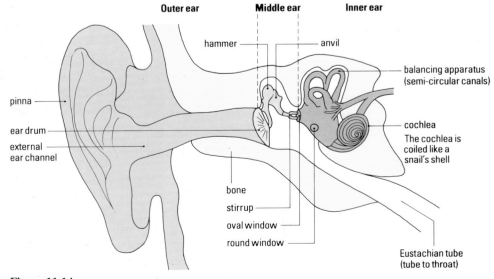

Figure 11.14
Some of the structures of the ear.

The outer part of the ear funnels the air vibrations we call sound down to the ear drum. The ear drum and tiny bones in the middle ear transmit and amplify the air vibrations and these vibrations stimulate the sensitive cells. Your ear drum needs to have the same air pressure on each side of it so there is a small canal (called the *Eustachian tube*) leading from the middle ear to the back of your throat. Every time you swallow, air can travel up or down the tube, making the air pressure on both sides of the ear drum the same.

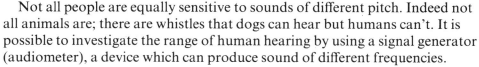

22 When are you aware that the pressure is different on the two sides of your ear drum? What do you usually do to make it the same on each side again?

23 Why do you sometimes "feel deaf" when you have a cold or throat infection?

Not all people are equally sensitive to sounds of different pitch. Indeed not all animals are; there are whistles that dogs can hear but humans can't. It is possible to investigate the range of human hearing by using a signal generator (audiometer), a device which can produce sound of different frequencies.

A group of young people were played sounds of different pitches and asked to indicate whether they could hear them. For each sound the number who said they could hear it was converted to a percentage of the whole group. The results from this investigation are shown in figure 11.15.
Answer the questions that follow by referring to the data in the table.

M

MEASURE

Frequency used in Hz	% sensitive
1 000	100
15 000	100
20	33
18 000	78
0	10
2 000	100
20 000	56
21 000	44
14 000	100
19	33
17	22
0	20
6 000	100
16	0
14 000	100
22 000	0

Figure 11.15

24 What is the range of hearing in this group of young people?

25 What was the purpose of using zero Hz during the sequence of frequencies played to the young people?

The range of human hearing is rather poor when compared with some other animals'. Cats can hear up to 50 000 Hz and bats up to 150 000 Hz. The range for mice extends up to 100 000 Hz; the squeaky sound we hear from them represents their "deep voice"! When you next take a peaceful walk through the countryside be thankful that you are unaware of the absolute bedlam that other animals have to put up with!

Some of the other parts of your inner ear enable you to know the position of your body when you are absolutely still. You know, for instance, which way up you are. This may seem obvious to you, but without the special sense cells found in your inner ear you would **not** know.

A sense of touch

Touch plays a very important part in your life. This is reflected in the fact that many of the words you use every day relate to your sense of touch: smooth, rough, prickly, hard, soft and so on.

Touch is a truly remarkable sense. Blind people learn to "read" through their finger tips. This is a very difficult skill but competent readers of Braille are able to read as fast as sighted people.

Worksheet **B11C** uses a simple finger maze to see how good you are at using your sense of touch.

Pressure, pain, temperature and texture can all be detected by an assortment of receptor cells found in your skin. Scientists have investigated how far apart two pin points touched on the skin at the same time must be, in order to be detected as two separate points. You can try this for yourself, using Worksheet **B**11D.

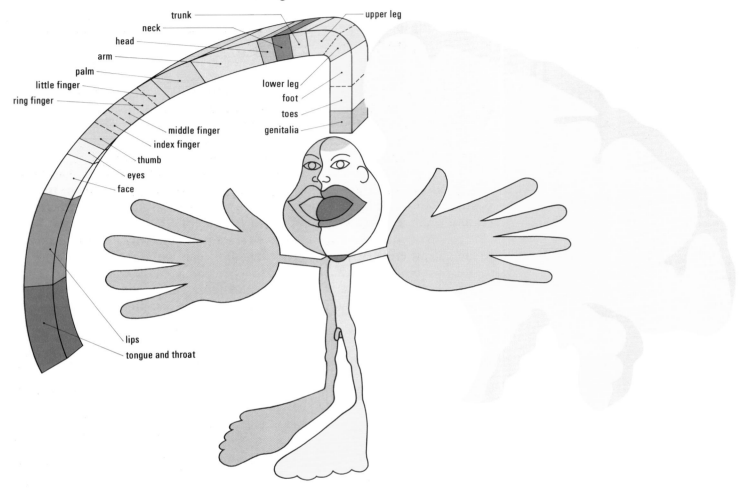

Figure 11.16
The size of the parts of this man's body represents how sensitive they are to touch.

If we research carefully the distribution of touch receptors all over the body, we can build up a picture of the sensitivity of the different parts of the body. In figure 11.16 an artist has drawn a man with the size of the parts of his body proportional to their sensitivity to touch.

Taste and smell

There is obvious survival value in being able to detect the bitter taste of many poisonous berries, and the scent marking of territories by many mammals would be a waste of time if potential intruders couldn't detect the scents.

Both taste and smell are chemical senses and the receptors in the nose and mouth are very sensitive to chemical molecules in the air or dissolved in your food. The so-called taste receptors are found on your tongue. About 9000 receptors enable you to distinguish four different sensations – salt, sweet, bitter and sour. These receptors are not evenly distributed on your tongue. Figure 11.17 shows the pattern of distribution.

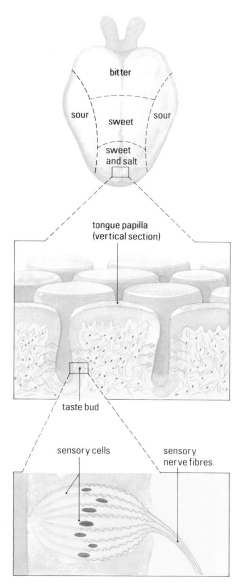

Figure 11.17
Different parts of the tongue contain receptors for different sensations.

Your sense of smell is about 10 000 times more acute than your sense of taste. In fact, the sensations you get when you think you are tasting food are more often than not from its smell. Have you ever noticed how you can sometimes lose the ability to taste your food when you have a severe cold?

B11.7 The faster the better

There are times when it is very important to respond to a stimulus as fast as possible as, for example, when you touch the hot plate on a cooker. If you took a long time to think about taking your hand away you would get burned. The time taken for you to respond to such a stimulus is very short and thus the minimum of damage is done, even if it is still quite painful.

There is obviously a connection between the sense cells in your skin and the muscle cells in your arm and fingers. This all-important link is made up of *nerve cells*. These cells specialize in passing messages from one part of your body to another at considerable speed.

Figure 11.18 shows the routes taken by the message and the nerve cells involved in withdrawing your hand from a sharp pain.

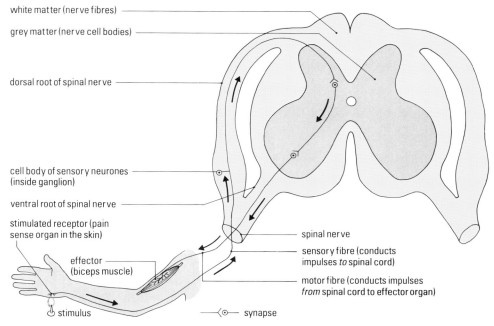

Figure 11.18
A section through the spinal cord and the reflex arc responsible for the rapid removal of your hand from a sharp pain.

One type of nerve cell carries the message from the receptor cell in your skin to the nervous tissue of the *spinal cord*. It is passed to another nerve cell inside the spinal cord and then a message leaves the spinal cord and travels to a muscle (effector) in your finger. The whole process takes very little time and is known as a *reflex action*. The pathway from receptor to effector is a *reflex arc*. The cells and organs involved make up the *nervous system*. The central parts are obviously the brain and spinal cord, so they are called the *central nervous system*.

One of the first things a doctor will do on seeing someone who has been involved in an accident is to test the patient's reflexes. For example, a bright light is shone into the eyes, or the tendon below the kneecap is tapped with a hammer. If the reflexes take place the doctor can be fairly confident that little damage has been done to the patient's nervous system.

In section **B**11.1 you read about the Venus fly trap. In spite of the speed of its response, it seems quite clear that neither it nor any other plant has a nervous system. That does not mean to say that co-ordination is impossible in organisms other than animals. But the range and type of activities that animals can do is very much greater than (and different from) those of plants.

B11.8   Nerves and nerve cells

There are about 28 billion nerve cells in your body, each able to carry messages from one part of your body to another part as quickly as possible. The speed of the message varies in different types of nerve cell, but the biggest one could pass a message from the top to the bottom of this page in $\frac{1}{1500}$ s.

Figure 11.19 shows a diagram of a nerve cell.

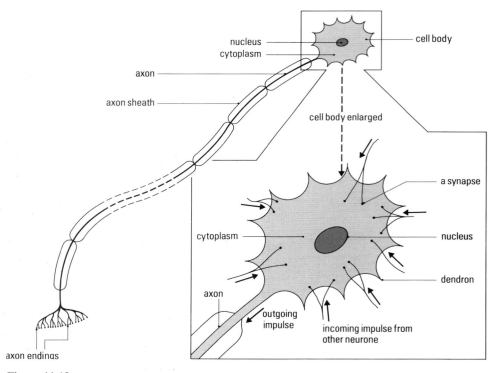

Figure 11.19
A motor nerve cell.

Nerve cells are in close contact with each other but there is always a small gap between them, and they never touch. The gap is called a *synapse*. When a message reaches the end of an axon chemicals are released into the gap which cause the message to start another journey along the next nerve cell. Only one end of a nerve cell can make and release these chemicals, so synapses are important because they ensure that nerve messages can only travel in one direction.

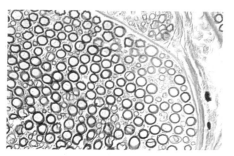

Figure 11.20
This is a highly magnified photograph of the interior of a nerve.

A *nerve* is a collection of axons all wrapped up into a living communication cable. It is rather like a very complex telephone cable that carries many individual wires in it. Figure 11.20 shows a transverse section through a nerve. The chemical used to stain the tissue turns fatty material black. (See Chapter **P21**, "Communication", in the Physics book.)

---

26 What is the evidence in the transverse section to support the statement that a nerve is made up of many individual axons?

27 What job do you think the fatty material in the nerves does?

B11.9   The brain

At the front of a London underground train you find the driver with his hands on the controls for the whole train. When the train reaches a terminus the driver gets out and goes to the other end of the train. When it sets out on the return journey the driver is once more at the front with all the controls.

---

28 What does the driver have to do during the journey that makes it wiser for him to be at the front rather than the back?

You have probably heard of "back-seat drivers"; you may even have one in your family! It would be difficult to drive a car safely if you were in the back seat. The car usually travels forwards and the best place for the driver is in the front.

Most animals move in one direction only for most of the time.

29 By looking at an animal, how can you tell which direction it moves in?

We usually say that an animal moves "forwards" and the "front" end of the animal is the part that goes first. Whether you are looking at a spider (see figure 2.5, page 21) or a seal (see figure 10.9, page 115), the front of the animal has a head which contains organs for feeding and many sense organs. In all organisms with a well developed nervous system the head also contains a great concentration of nerve cells with very many synapses between them. In invertebrates this group of nerve cells is relatively small, but in vertebrates, particularly in mammals and most especially in humans, the *brain* – as this collection of nerve cells is always called – is relatively large.

30 Make a list of all the other structures there are in your head as well as your brain.

You can probably see from your list that most of the volume of your head is concerned with the brain and its protection.

What's under my hair?

If you feel the top of your head it is obvious that the skin and muscle of the scalp are not very thick. Under them is very hard bone. The bony *skull* is, in fact, made of many different bones fitting into each other at immovable joints called sutures. The part of your skull that encloses and protects the brain is called the *cranium*.

31 In babies, part of the cranium is not bony at birth. Can you suggest why this is?

There are holes through the bone of the skull to allow blood vessels and nerves to enter and leave the brain. Inside the cranium there are two very tough membranes called the *meninges* which surround the brain and help it to keep its shape. Between these two membranes there is a fluid, called cerebro-spinal fluid, which both cushions the brain against shock as well as helping to nourish it.

In the mid 1980s many cases of an infection called *meningitis* were reported in the national newspapers. This disease is the result of infection of the meninges by bacteria or viruses.

32 Why is meningitis a serious disease and why can treating it be difficult?

Meningitis caused by bacteria can be treated with antibiotics but it is very hard to treat meningitis when it is caused by a virus. If the infection reaches the brain, then death may be the result.

The brain is actually very well protected from damage and infection. You may often have banged your head quite hard and the only damage has been a bruise. If you bang your head very hard indeed – as may happen in a road accident or on the sports field – you may suffer from *concussion*.

33 What are the signs and symptoms of concussion?

If you are concussed on the sports field, the referee or umpire may ask you some apparently silly questions like "How many fingers am I holding up?" or "What day is it today?". You may be asked if you remember what happened to you. If you appear to be confused or if you can't remember what happened, you may have to leave the field. If you have been concussed, a very large number of the nerve cells in your brain may have been put permanently out of action. Indeed, if you have banged your head very hard, some of the tiny blood vessels inside your head may have broken open and there may be bleeding. This is why you are put under observation for as much as 24 hours after being concussed.

---

34 Why are you in danger if bleeding occurs inside the cranium?

The largest part of the brain is divided into two halves – the right and left *cerebral hemispheres*. If a brain is cut vertically, it is possible to see the main features of the brain. Figure 11.21 shows a section like this.

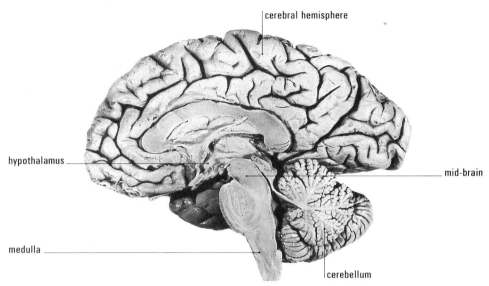

Figure 11.21
The human brain.

Almost all of the tissue that you can see in this section is nervous tissue and it is made up of two types of cell – the nerve cells and "connective tissue" cells which pack, protect and insulate the nerve cells. There are about 10 000 000 000 nerve cells and each one makes connections (synapses) with thousands of other nerve cells. Messages (nerve impulses) travel from one nerve cell to another across these synapses. So there are many millions of different paths by which nerve messages may travel in the brain. When a nerve impulse reaches the brain from a receptor, it is possible for it to generate many more impulses within the brain, which could lead to many different responses being made to the incoming information. The brain co-ordinates incoming and outgoing impulses and makes the body produce the appropriate response to every stimulus.

---

35 Look at figure 11.21. Which is the largest area of the brain?

The very large cerebral hemispheres are often referred to as your "*grey matter*". This is because the nerve cells in the surface layers look greyish. The nerve fibres which are in the middle part of the brain are called *white matter*. This is because they have lots of fatty material around them which makes them look white. This part of your brain is very active at the moment. It is where your thinking goes on and where your memory is centred. That is not all, though. If you are in the middle of an argument with a friend in the corridor and the bell for lessons goes, you **may** stop your argument, collect up your books and go to your next class! Without the correct working of your cerebral hemispheres you could not do any of those things – you would not realize that the bell had gone nor would you be able to decide what to do next.

36 Suggest some of the signs and symptoms that might occur if your cerebral hemispheres were injured.

Other parts of the brain control other functions in your body: the *medulla* controls the vital functions of breathing and heartbeat, for example. If this part of the brain is injured, death follows almost immediately.

37 Read the following true short story and then try to suggest what the function of the *cerebellum* is.

A man was once found lying face down on the floor of a church eating a banana. When asked what he thought he was doing he replied "Eating a banana". "What are you doing lying on the floor then?" asked the priest. "It's the only way I can catch it" said the man. He was suffering from the severely damaging effects of syphilis (see page 266). In his case, the bacteria causing the disease had infected the cerebellum. When he got to his feet, the man staggered off down the church as though drunk – slowing down and then speeding up, veering to one side and then to the other.

There are many other important parts of the brain, most of them quite small in size. The hypothalamus is mentioned in Chapter **B**12 and the pituitary gland in Chapter **B**21. Although these parts of the brain are tiny, you can see that their activity is vital to your survival.

B11.10   Altering things

Your sense organs and your brain together tell you something about the environment in which you live. Your brain interprets information received from the sense organs and in this way you respond to stimuli present in the environment.

Not much can be done to change the outside world, but centuries ago people discovered that this real world would **look** quite different if they ate or drank or smoked certain substances which altered the way the nervous system worked. These substances are called *drugs* and all of them are **dangerous**. Of course, many drugs are used by doctors to relieve pain and to treat diseases.

Who takes drugs?

38 Suggest some of the reasons for which people might take drugs. Why do you think young people are especially likely to take drugs?

Getting hooked

It is the pleasant effects produced by drugs that are the problem because they may cause people to want to take the drug more and more often. Someone who tries to stop taking a drug may feel very unhappy or anxious. When this happens the user is said to be *emotionally dependent* on the drug, and will find it hard to give up.

Under some circumstances a person who stops taking the drug may have very unpleasant physical symptoms such as severe headaches and sickness. If this is the case, we say that this person is *physically dependent* on the drug.

Another danger of regular drug taking is that the body may become *tolerant* of the drug. Tolerance means that you have to take more and more of the drug to get the same effect, and you become even more dependent upon it and suffer more and more physical damage.

The problems of dependence

Someone whose whole world revolves around a particular drug is bound to find that this restricts other areas of his or her life. Drug dependence – especially on heroin and alcohol – can destroy people's health, but it can also alter the personality, destroy family life and maybe cost people their jobs too. The cost of buying drugs may also be so enormous that they are then forced to get money dishonestly.

The table shows how likely various drugs are to cause dependence. Notice that although most addictive drugs are illegal, two of the most damaging and addictive drugs of all – tobacco and alcohol – are legal and easy to obtain.

	Physical dependence	**Emotional dependence**
Illegal drugs		
Cannabis	*	**
Cocaine		***
Heroin	***	***
LSD		*
Amphetamines	*	***
Solvents		*
Legal, medical drugs		
Barbiturates	***	**
Benzodiazepines	**	**
Legal, non-medical drugs		
Alcohol	**	***
Tobacco	**	***

Figure 11.22
*slight or variable dependence   **moderate dependence   ***severe dependence

Some of these drugs, for example the benzodiazepines, which are used as tranquillizers and sleeping pills, are useful medicines.

39 How can doctors make sure that their patients don't get "hooked" on these drugs?

What happens when you drink alcohol?

Alcohol was probably the first drug to be discovered, and it is almost certainly the most widely used. It is easy to forget that alcohol is an addictive drug that can be just as physically harmful and personally destructive as heroin. It may take many years for the regular drinker to become dependent on alcohol – much longer than it takes to become dependent on heroin. But far more people take alcohol than any other drug and so the total number of addicts is far greater. So it is worth looking at this particular drug in more detail. If you understand its dangers it is easier to avoid them.

How alcohol affects you

Alcohol is absorbed from the gut into the blood, then broken down by the liver and excreted in the urine. A small amount of alcohol is also excreted in the breath (and can be detected by the "breathalyser" test given to drivers). It takes several hours for all the alcohol to be excreted from the body.

Tolerance to alcohol develops quickly. Heavy drinkers are often proud of the way they can "hold their drink", taking far more than an inexperienced drinker without showing any effects. But they may be taking dangerously large amounts without realizing the physical damage the drug is doing to their brain and heart and liver.

Drinking sensibly

It is only when the alcohol reaches the brain that its effects are felt. How "drunk" someone becomes depends on the concentration of alcohol in the blood (measured in mg of alcohol per 100 ml of blood). The more slowly alcohol is absorbed, the lower will be its concentration in the blood – and the less marked its effects. So the first rule of sensible drinking is to make sure that the alcohol is absorbed as slowly as possible.

This can be done if people:

1 *Eat with their drink*. Food, especially hot food, slows down the rate at which alcohol is absorbed into the bloodstream, and therefore the rate at which it reaches the brain.
2 *Sip slowly*. A drink that is gulped down quickly will be quickly absorbed, with a "rush" of alcohol into the bloodstream.

½ pint beer

1 glass sherry

1 glass wine

1 whisky

Figure 11.23
Each of these glasses contains one unit of alcohol.

INTERPRET

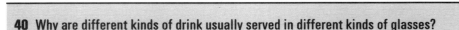

40 Why are different kinds of drink usually served in different kinds of glasses?

Keeping within the limit

The blood alcohol level obviously depends not only on how much, but also on exactly what, a person has drunk. Some drinks affect people more because they contain more alcohol. A useful way to keep track of what has been drunk is to measure it in "units of alcohol". All the glasses shown in figure 11.23 contain one unit of alcohol. As a general rule, if more than 5 units of alcohol are consumed, the blood alcohol level will be above the legal limit for drivers (80 mg of alcohol per 100 ml of blood).

However, most doctors agree that it is not enough just to keep below the legal limit. Someone who regularly drinks 5 units of alcohol a day may not be

Figure 12.3
If you are cold the hairs on your skin stand on end and you get goose pimples.

Figure 12.4
a Penguins often huddle together, and those on the edge change places with those in the middle from time to time.
b After a good run in the park, a dog will often hang out its tongue and will pant quite hard for a few minutes.
c Elephants often stand in the shade and flap their ears.

people you know so that the necessary action can be taken before their condition becomes too serious.

When furry mammals are cold, contraction of the erector muscles makes their hairs stand up. (In you, the same process produces goose pimples.) As a result a layer of air is trapped between the skin surface and the atmosphere.

---

11 How is this movement of body hair of benefit to a mammal in cold air?

Your skin also has a layer of fat just underneath the surface. This fat is a very good insulating layer for your body and it prevents energy from being transferred to your surroundings. Some mammals with little body hair, such as dolphins, have a particularly thick layer of fat just underneath their skin. It is called *blubber*.

Behaviour and body temperature

No doubt you have taken your jumper off when you have got hot or have curled up in bed on a cold winter's night. These are behavioural methods of regulating your body temperature. Figure 12.4 shows some other examples of animals behaving in a way that helps them to regulate their body temperature.

a

b

c

---

12 Suggest how each example of behaviour shown in figure 12.4 may help to regulate the body temperature.

We have already mentioned that not all animals have a constant body temperature. The graph in figure 12.5 shows the results obtained when the body temperatures of two different animals were measured at a variety of different air temperatures.

---

13 Describe in your own words what the graph shows about the difference between the two animals.

14 A cat is a mammal, and a lizard is a reptile. Which line on the graph would represent the cat, and which the lizard?

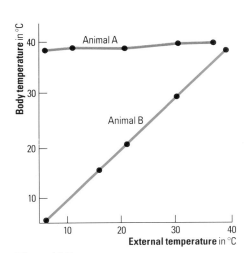

Figure 12.5

15 Here are three observations. Use the terms and the information in this section to suggest in each case what the behaviour may have to do with body temperature.
a Crocodiles lie on river banks in the hot sun with their mouths open.
b On a cool day butterflies spread their wings out and vibrate them for several minutes before attempting to take off.
c Desert lizards are most active in the early morning and evening.

The process of keeping anything at a constant level inside you is called *homeostasis*. Nerves play an important part in homeostasis. By carrying messages quickly they help your body to adjust as rapidly as possible to changing circumstances. (For more about control systems, see Chapter **P20**, "Control", in your Physics book.)

Not surprisingly there are lots of other things besides temperature which need to be kept at constant levels inside you.

16 Can you think of anything else which might need to be kept at a fairly steady level?

B12.3   Control of blood sugar level

Have you ever felt faint with hunger? If it's a long time since you've eaten, or you have perhaps missed a meal altogether, you may feel slightly faint or sick or giddy. This is because the level of sugar in your blood is very low – if you eat something sweet or starchy you will rapidly feel better.

You can see in Chapter **B6** that glucose is the sugar which is the body's source of energy. Someone's blood sugar concentration was measured over a 12-hour period. The results are shown in figure 12.6.

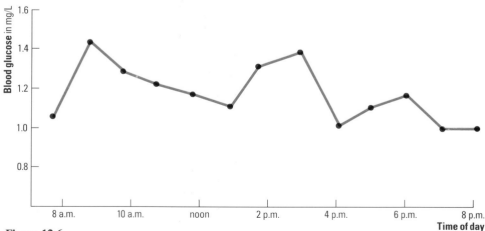

Figure 12.6

17 Suggest an explanation of the changes you can see in the graph.

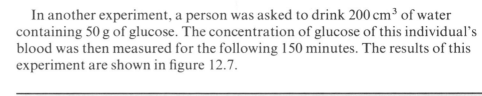

18 What evidence is there in the graph that there is a mechanism in your body that keeps the blood sugar level constant?

In another experiment, a person was asked to drink $200 \, cm^3$ of water containing 50 g of glucose. The concentration of glucose of this individual's blood was then measured for the following 150 minutes. The results of this experiment are shown in figure 12.7.

19 What do these results suggest about the control of blood sugar level in the blood?

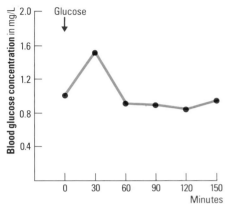

Figure 12.7

The *pancreas* (figure 4.16, page 49) makes enzymes which take part in the digestion of food in the gut; but it also makes another chemical that is secreted directly into the bloodstream. It is called *insulin* and it is a protein. Chemicals such as insulin which are released directly into your bloodstream are called *hormones*. They are carried around your body in the blood and can reach every part of you. Hormones are, in effect, chemical messengers.

The level of glucose in the blood is controlled by the action of insulin. Normally just enough insulin is produced to keep the glucose concentration fairly constant. It seems that insulin is released by the pancreas in response to a rise in the blood glucose level, which is why more is produced after a meal. Insulin enables glucose to be taken up by body cells where it can be used as a source of energy. In the liver, the extra glucose available after a meal is stored as *glycogen*, an insoluble carbohydrate. Glycogen can be quickly broken down into glucose again and released from the liver when it is needed.

Figure 12.8 summarizes the action of insulin in controlling blood sugar level.

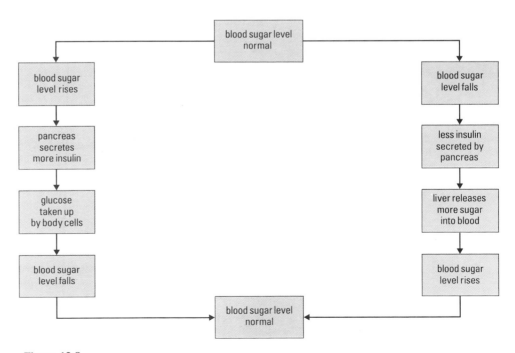

Figure 12.8
This diagram should help you to learn how insulin controls the blood sugar level.

20 Explain in your own words why glucose is quite useless to the body unless insulin is present.

Diabetes

If the pancreas produces too little insulin, glucose is "trapped" in the blood. The glucose level in the blood builds up until it reaches about twice the normal level, when it will start to appear in the urine. When this happens, large amounts of water are drawn out of the body with the glucose, so large volumes of urine are produced.

This condition is called *diabetes*.

21 Can you explain why people who have diabetes may become thin and feel weak?

22 Can you explain why they get very thirsty?

Figure 12.9
Insulin is injected under the skin. It hurts very little and even quite young children can soon learn to inject themselves.

Some people develop diabetes because the pancreas does not work properly – it produces very little insulin, or even none at all. This is usually the case in young people who have diabetes. This kind of diabetes can be treated by giving regular injections of insulin.

23 Why must insulin be injected rather than taken by mouth?

Sometimes people develop diabetes when they are older – usually over forty. Like most body organs the pancreas becomes less efficient with advancing age.

24 Some people develop diabetes after they have become fat. Can you explain why this might happen?

Many people who develop diabetes late in life do not need to take extra insulin – if they get slimmer and cut sugary foods out of their diet, the insulin the pancreas produces is often enough.

Engineering insulin

When insulin was first made available for the treatment of diabetes it was extracted from the pancreases of slaughtered pigs and cattle. During the 1980s techniques of *genetic engineering* became available and now bacteria can be "instructed" to make insulin which is identical to human insulin. This is therefore likely to be more effective and safer than the insulin from pigs or cattle.

People with diabetes have to try to keep their own blood glucose level as steady as possible since they cannot easily vary the amount of insulin in their bodies hour by hour to match their needs as the normal person does. Therefore they have to eat fixed amounts of carbohydrates at regular times during the day; if they are going to take some extra exercise they will need to eat extra carbohydrate to provide for this.

B12.4   **What goes in must come out**

Have you ever drunk a lot of liquid in one go? That bloated feeling you get is the body's way of telling you that you don't need to drink any more. In fact, if you drink more liquid than you need your body will soon get rid of the extra amount. On the other hand, activities which cause you to lose a lot of water because you sweat a lot, for example, make you feel very thirsty.

It appears that there is a mechanism in your body which keeps the amount of water inside it within certain limits, not too high and not too low.

Scientists have measured the daily intake and output of water in an average resting adult in order to investigate this idea. The results are shown in figure 12.10.

		Volume in cm^3
Input	drink	1200
	food	1000
	metabolism	300
Output	urine	1500
	exhaled air	350
	skin	500
	faeces	150

Figure 12.10b

Water gain

food 1000 cm^3

drink 1200 cm^3

respiration in all cells 300 cm^3

total 2500 cm^3

Water loss

exhaled air 350 cm^3

skin 500 cm^3

urine 1500 cm^3

faeces 150 cm^3

total 2500 cm^3

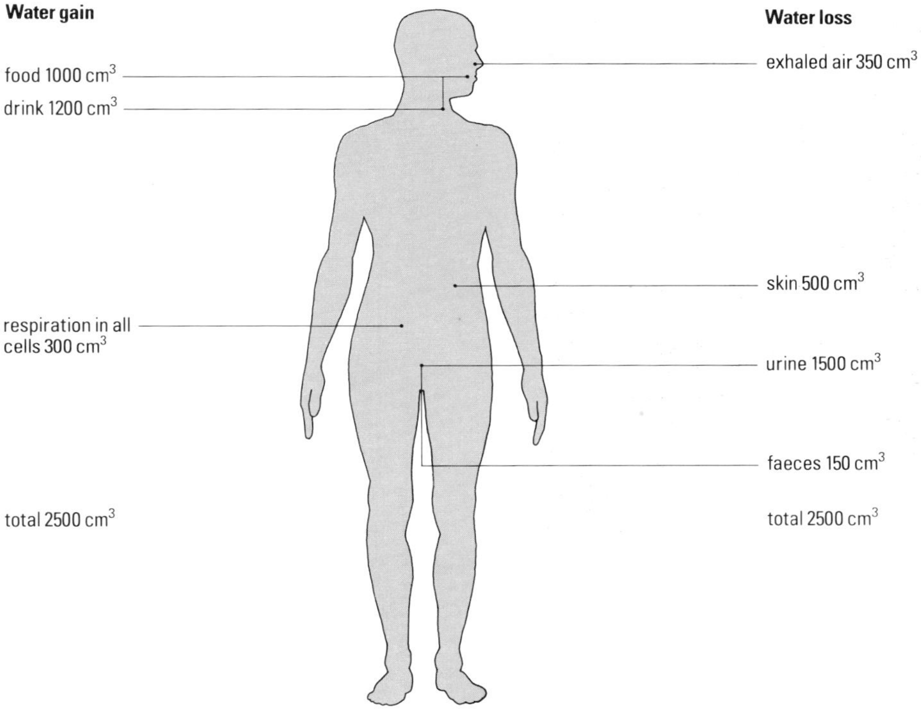

Figure 12.10
The daily intake and output of water by an average resting adult human.

25 How does the water input compare with the water output?

Have you ever thought what would happen to your body if excess water were not removed? Shrivelling up because of lack of water seems just as undesirable. The experiment described in Worksheet **B**12C shows what would happen.

Red blood cells which have burst or crinkled are of no use to you. So it is important to keep the water level of the plasma fairly constant if you are to avoid damage to your cells. Water absorbed by your gut enters your blood which would become very dilute unless the water were removed. The reverse would be the effect if you lost too much water without replacing it. In this case the plasma would become more salty and more viscous.

So it seems that the amount of water in our bodies is controlled. Two organs are especially concerned with this – the *kidneys*. The position of these bean-shaped organs is shown in figure 12.11. See also Worksheet **B**12D.

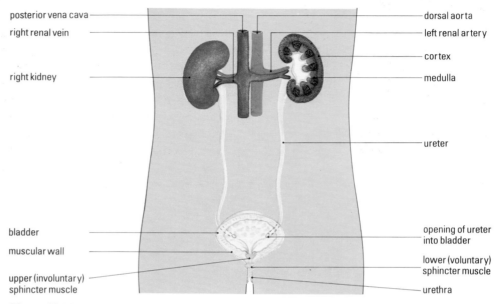

Figure 12.11
The kidneys are positioned towards the back wall of the abdominal cavity, just above the waist.

One of the main function of the kidneys is to regulate the amount of water removed from the body. The control mechanism is very effective. Of the 180 litres of water which filter into your nephrons every day, only 1.5 litres will trickle down your ureters to be expelled from your bladder when you urinate.

But your kidneys have another function. They not only regulate the level of water in your body so it stays within reasonable limits – they also get rid of, or *excrete* poisonous substances from your blood. The most important excretory substance they remove is *urea*. This is the waste substance produced by the breakdown of excess amino acids in your liver. The kidney controls the level of some mineral salts in the body fluids as well.

B12.5   What happens when a kidney fails?

Sometimes a kidney stops working altogether, because it is diseased or damaged. If only one kidney fails, the other can usually do the job of two. But if both stop working, waste products start to build up in the body. Unless these waste products can be removed the person will die. Until the 1960s several thousand such people died each year. Nowadays their lives can usually be saved.

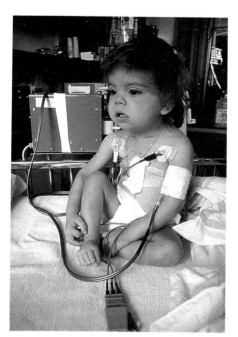

Figure 12.12
A patient undergoing dialysis.

There are two ways of treating someone with kidney failure. The first is to use an "artificial kidney". The patient's blood is led through a tube from an artery in an arm or leg and passed through a special machine which cleans it. The blood is then fed back into the patient's body through a vein. This process is called *dialysis*. Within the kidney machine the blood is separated by a very thin membrane from a watery fluid called the dialysate. Waste products like urea pass from the blood across the membrane into the dialysate.

If it is to work effectively, the artificial kidney must allow waste products to pass through the membrane to the dialysate, but not useful substances such as glucose and some salts. It must also not allow too little or too much water to be lost.

The patient on dialysis has to be connected to the machine two or three times a week for about ten hours at a time to filter out all the waste products in the blood. As you can imagine dialysis is an uncomfortable, tedious and time-consuming procedure. But it can keep the patient alive.

The second way of treating kidney failure is by a *kidney transplant*. A better solution for the patient is to replace a damaged or non-functioning kidney by a healthy one donated by another person. The kidney may be taken from someone who has just died or from a living donor – who will be able to survive very well with his or her one remaining kidney. It is usual for a living donor to be a close blood relative, not just because only a relative is likely to care enough about the person to give the kidney, but because the body tissues of close relatives are more likely to match each other. Sometimes a donated kidney is "rejected" by the body which tries to destroy this "foreign" tissue just as it would try to destroy invading bacteria.

26 Why do you think a kidney transplant between identical twins is nearly always successful?

Many people now carry donor cards which say that when they die they wish their kidneys to be used for transplants. Even so it is difficult for surgeons to get as many donated kidneys as they need and most patients have to wait a long time before a kidney which is a good match for them becomes available.

Donor Card

I would like to help someone to live after my death Keep the card with you at all times in a place where it will be found quickly

Figure 12.13
People who are willing, when they die, to donate their kidneys to someone else carry donor cards like this one.

B12.6 **Other adjustments**

In this chapter, so far, you have seen how important it is that body temperature, blood sugar and the level of water and excretory products in the body are kept fairly constant. Earlier on the term homeostasis was used and you should now have more idea of what it means and why it is vital to life. It really means "keeping the internal environment (that is the surroundings of the cells) in a near steady state".

There are many other examples of control mechanisms besides the ones in this chapter. Two of them are referred to in Chapters **B**7 and **B**8.

An experiment on breathing rate is suggested in Chapter **B**7.

Quite a long time ago scientists interested in the control of breathing

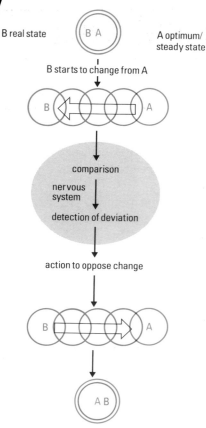

B real state   A optimum/
                      steady state

B starts to change from A

comparison

ner vous
system

detection of deviation

action to oppose change

Figure 12.14
Negative feedback control.

discovered that if you breathe in and out of a sealed bag it increases the depth and rate of breathing. Obviously the oxygen gets used up and the carbon dioxide content of the bag increases, and it is not a safe thing to do. This is because it lowers the oxygen content of your blood and increases the carbon dioxide. Either of the changes could provide the stimulus to increase your breathing rate.

In fact, it is the carbon dioxide level in your blood to which your body mainly responds. There is a part of your brain called the *medulla oblongata* which is sensitive to carbon dioxide levels. Depending on the levels detected, nerve messages are sent to your diaphragm and intercostal muscles which change the rate and depth of your breathing (see Chapter **B**7).

The example referred to in Chapter **B**8 is the control of heart beat; you may have investigated the effect of exercise on your pulse rate. In this example the messages are sent to the "pacemaker" of your heart which will cause the heart rate to change according to the needs of the body. Worksheet **B**12E will enable you to investigate how the pulse rate varies under different conditions.

Review

Whatever example of homeostasis we look at, the principle is always the same. A change in the internal environment brings about a correcting process which restores things to normal again – the correcting process then stops. This is called feedback. Figure 12.14 summarizes the principle of what is called *negative feedback control*.

INTERPRET

27 Can you see why it is called "negative" feedback control?

Topic B3

Living organisms and their environment

The people in this family are having a picnic. They are enjoying conditions of life that make them feel comfortable and happy.

Chapter B13

Making sense of any environment

B13.1 Conditions of life

We all know what conditions we like best and are comfortable in. We like warm and dry surroundings, light, good food and the company of other people. The photograph on the preceding page shows one way of enjoying these conditions.

Biologists call our surroundings our *environment*. The features of our environment, such as light intensity, temperature and food supply are called *environmental factors*. It is these that make up the "conditions of life" for an organism. Humans are unusual because, unlike most other living organisms, we are able to control the environment we live in. We have not always done this – for example, our early ancestors did not make clothes or build houses. They stayed in their natural environment, which was probably tropical grasslands in Africa (see also Chapter **B**23). The conditions of life elsewhere were unsuitable for them and they were not able to change them. Perhaps the reason we like warm, dry conditions is that we are still in some ways tropical animals. However, we now live all over the world, often in natural environments which are quite different from each other and from our ancestors' environment.

Figure 13.1 shows people who live in two different environments.

Figure 13.1
These two groups of people live in different parts of the world where conditions of life are very different.
a Masai women and children in front of their huts in the Rift valley in Kenya.
b In Norway, Lapps have camped for the night during their spring migration.

a

b

---

1 For each photograph in figure 13.1, say how the environment is different from the original African grasslands.

The houses that people build help to control certain environmental factors.

Figure 13.2
A typical part of a shore where limpets live.

> **2 Suggest three factors that are controlled in a European house.**

If you find it hard to believe that we really are tropical animals, think what it would be like to live in England with no clothing or shelter. Most organisms have no control over their environment. If we find an organism living in a particular place, then the environment of that place must be providing everything necessary for the organism to remain alive.

To take one example, limpets are molluscs (see Chapter **B2**) which live on rocks on the seashore. When the tide is in they are covered by sea water. Part of the reason for the survival of limpets on a rocky shore is that this environment provides suitable conditions for life. (Figure 13.2.)

INTERPRET

> **3 Which environmental factors would you think are essential for the survival of limpets?**

The conditions of warmth and dryness that humans enjoy would soon kill the limpet. To understand more about environmental factors we can list them and then think what effect each will have on the life of the limpet.

Tides – limpets become inactive as the rocks dry once the tide has gone out (ebbed).

Temperature – there may be a great difference between the body temperature of a limpet under water and its body temperature when it is exposed to the air during low tide.

Food and space – limpets spend their lives on the surface of rocks on which they move around, grazing on the green protists (See Chapter **B2**) that grow there. So for two reasons, no rocks mean no limpets.

Predators – these will eat limpets. If there are more predators such as seagulls, there will be fewer limpets.

Other limpets – if limpets are to reproduce and give rise to new individuals, both sexes must be present.

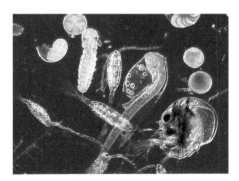
Figure 13.3
The young form of a limpet, called a larva, floats in the sea eating single-celled protists.

These factors only apply to the adult limpets. Limpet larvae (young limpets) are microscopic and are not attached to rocks. They drift and swim in the water along with many other tiny organisms. (This drifting population of very small organisms is called the *plankton*.) At this stage, different environmental factors are important, and for the limpet larvae to survive a different set of conditions for life is necessary. (See figure 13.3.)

A place to live

The place where an organism lives is called its *habitat*. Each habitat has a set of environmental factors associated with it. These factors are not constant; many of them, like temperature, vary during the year. But the variation is about the same every year. Many species of organism can only survive in one kind of habitat because they or their young are only able to tolerate the conditions in that habitat.

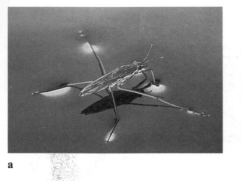
a

b

c

d

e

Figure 13.4
A range of organisms in their natural habitats. **a** A pond skater, *Gerris* sp. **b** Yellow iris, *Iris pseudodacorus*. **c** Roof lichen. **d** Ox-eye daisies – *Chrysanthemum* sp. **e** A tiger, *Felis tigris*.

4 Describe the habitat of each organism in figure 13.4 and also of the following:
>   blackbird (figure 1.11, Section 1.4)
>   penguin (figure 12.4, page 147)
>   coconut palm (figure 2.1, page 19)
>   woodlouse (figure 1.2, page 9)
>   earthworm (figure 2.7, page 22)

Very seldom will you find only one species of organism in a habitat. Some of the photographs referred to in question **4** show more than one species. The group of organisms that share a habitat is called a *community*.

B13.2   Some natural communities

There are thousands of different natural communities, and very often each has its own special assortment of animals and plants. Wherever you live there will be examples of natural communities nearby – you may recognize some familiar examples from the photographs in figure 13.5. You can see others in figure 4.1, page 42, and figure 3.15, page 40.

a

b

c

d

Figure 13.5
A range of communities. **a** Deciduous wood. **b** A rocky shore. **c** A village pond in summer.
d A piece of waste ground in August.

In fact, these communities are found in what we call *ecosystems*. An ecosystem consists of different habitats next to each other; although they share the same weather, they provide different conditions of life. The pond in figure 13.5c is a good example. Different habitats like the water surface, submerged clumps of plants and the mud at the bottom all have different conditions of life, and different organisms live in each. But they all live in the same pond water and the same weather "happens" to all parts of the pond. Therefore, ecosystems are, of course, larger than the habitats they contain, and also they are often most easily identified by the organisms that live in them. For example, the most obvious difference between coniferous forest and deciduous forest ecosystems is the kind of trees that live in them.

5 Give the names of two species of animal and two species of plant that you would expect to find in each of the communities in figure 13.5.

Sometimes, a "natural" community will develop in an area which is man-made, such as a wall, a breakwater or cleared ground.

6 The plants are usually the most obvious living parts of a community such as a forest. Why is this?

Of course, the best way to find out more about any natural community is to study it for yourself. Most communities are so complex that it is difficult to know where to start in order to try and understand them. Worksheet **B13A** gives you some information on how to do this. One of the things you will discover is that, even in the simplest community, there are many different kinds of organisms and only a few are large enough to be seen with the naked eye. However, some communities have a small number of different species and few organisms of each kind. Very cold or dry habitats have communities like this.

7 Suggest two examples of habitats that support small communities with only a few different species in them.

At the other extreme, coral reefs and tropical rain forests have a large variety of different species and are very crowded. Figure 13.6 shows the contrast between these two sorts of community.

Figure 13.6
"Rich" and "poor" communities.
a A deep ocean floor.
b A coral reef in the Red Sea.
  Note that the corals are not flowers but predatory animals that will paralyse and eat any small animal that touches them. A coral reef has millions of these coral polyps, busily eating such things as crab and fish larvae. But there are still plenty of crabs and fish living in coral reefs.
c The Namib desert in Namibia.
d The tropical rain forest of Monteverde in Costa Rica.

a

b

c

d

INTERPRET

8 From what you have read so far, suggest an explanation for the differences between the communities
a in the depths of the ocean and in a coral reef, and
b in desert and in a rain forest.

B13.3   Changes – weather, season and tide

The environment in a particular habitat does not always stay the same. The seasons, the weather and tides change, altering the conditions for life in many habitats. Winter always follows summer, low tide always follows high tide and day follows night. These changes are so predictable that many organisms have a pattern of behaviour that matches them. They may behave in different ways at different times of the day or year when the conditions alter. Figure 13.7 gives some examples of the way that organisms respond to regular patterns of change. See also Worksheet **B**13C.

Environmental change	Behaviour	Example
Decreasing temperature	Hibernation Dormancy Migration to warmer regions	Bat, hedgehog Seeds, frog, most insects Some birds, *e.g.* swift and osprey
Increasing temperature	Reproduction	Grass snake, many insects
Drought	Early shedding of leaves	Oak
Ebbing tide	Starting feeding	Shore birds, *e.g.* oyster catcher
Dawn	Starting to sing	Many song birds
Nightfall	Beginning to hunt	Owl, fox

Figure 13.7

Many birds migrate further south from Europe before the start of winter.

9 What advantages do birds gain by going south for the winter?

10 Think of some examples of animals and plants that only give birth to their young in the spring. What are the advantages of reproducing then rather than at some other time of year?

11 What changes might a lobster living on the floor of the sea experience
a daily and,
b yearly? (See figure 1.7, page 11.)

Animals which have a pattern of behaviour that matches regular changes in their environment have been studied to see what happens if the conditions do not change. Figures 13.8 and 13.9 show the results of an investigation in which the activity of two large African lizards was recorded for a number of days. At first the animals were kept in alternating periods of light and dark. Then the environment was changed artificially so that it was light all the time.

12 In what ways did the activity of the lizards change between light and dark conditions? Which of these changes continued to be seen when the animals were kept in constant light?

Changing the body clock

Humans, too, show daily patterns of behaviour which are called *diurnal* rhythms. Newborn babies do not have these rhythms. They are gradually established as the brain matures during the first few months of life. Any parent of a new baby will tell you that – unfortunately – babies do not seem to realize that they are meant to switch off all unnecessary activity and sleep quietly through the night, and to eat, cry and excrete only during the day! Once these rhythms have become established, it is difficult to alter them. For example, when shift workers change from a day to a night shift they find it

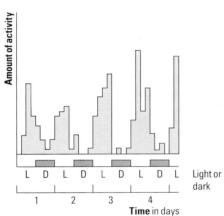

Figure 13.8
The activity of two African monitor lizards kept together over four days in alternating 12 hours' light and 12 hours' darkness.

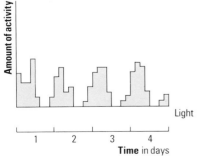

Figure 13.9
The activity of the same two African monitor lizards kept together over four days in constant artificial light.

INTERPRET

difficult at first to sleep during the day. It seems as though there is something in the human body that acts rather like a clock – a "body clock". It is probably the result of brain activity. It takes a while for the "body clock" to adjust when we change our normal pattern.

Why do people get jet lag?

People who travel east or west into a different time zone find that for several days, if their body clock says "bedtime", they feel sleepy, even if it is bright daylight outside. Someone who travels westward to America, with a time difference of 5 to 8 hours, will find that it takes 2 to 4 days for sleep patterns to adjust.

A time change like this upsets not only your sleep patterns, but all the daily rhythms of the body. Body temperature, heart activity, the ability to concentrate, appetite, and even certain hormone levels, are all affected. It takes most people about one day for every hour's time change to adjust completely to the new time.

> **13** In humans the disturbance of diurnal rhythms can have quite a serious effect on both mental and physical performance. What advice would you give athletes travelling from Britain to Los Angeles, for example, for a major athletics event?

Rapid changes in weather do not have constant patterns like the changing seasons, and when they happen, some organisms behave in a way that seems to take advantage of a good opportunity!

If you have ever carried out some field work on a habitat, you may remember it well because the weather was very hot, or cold, or perhaps very wet. You should remember, though, that the habitat does not always have the weather that you had on your visit. Whatever changes may take place in the environment, the organisms that are in a particular habitat are able to live there quite successfully.

Worksheet **B**13B looks at the effect of weather conditions on the growth of a tree year by year.

B13.4   Changes – competition, succession and climax communities

Competition

You have probably seen mustard seedlings growing in plastic boxes in greengrocers' shops and supermarkets. You will notice that they are crowded together and they are easily cut for use in salads. Figure 13.10a shows what happens to the same plants if the seeds are sown in soil and left to grow for a week. Ten seeds were grown in one seed tray, one thousand in the other. Figure 13.10b shows what had happened to the same plants after four weeks, while figure 13.10c shows what the flower heads of the plants were like eight weeks after sowing.

Figure 13.10
Competition among mustard plants.
10 seeds were sown in one seed tray,
1000 in the other. The seed trays were
photographed (**a**) after one week and
(**b**) again after another four weeks.
Photographs in **c(i)** and **c(ii)** show the
differences between two typical flower
heads eight weeks after sowing; **c(i)** is
from the tray with 10 seeds and **c(ii)**
from the one with 1000 seeds.

a

b

c(i)   c(ii)

OBSERVE   INTERPRET

14 What results of competition can you see in figure 13.10a and b? How has
competition affected reproduction in the two plants shown in figure 13.10c?

If the presence of other plants reduces the amount of an essential resource
that a plant requires then the plants are *competing* against each other. The
limited resource becomes a limiting factor. (See Chapter **B**3.) The plants are
said to be in *competition* with each other. Competition affects every living
organism. Any gardener will tell you how "weeds" will soon cover a patch of
cleared ground if they are not controlled. The "weed" seeds germinate and
"weed" seedlings grow up close together and begin to compete with each
other and with any crops that may have been planted as well. Forest trees also
compete with each other.

15 List the resources for which forest trees might compete.

It is not only plants that compete. Farmyard hens compete with each other
for food and build up a "pecking order" where the top-ranking hen can feed
unchallenged by any of the other birds. The bird at the bottom of the pecking
order has to compete against all the others in the flock.

Lemmings, which are rather like large hamsters (figure 13.11), live in the
regions surrounding the North Pole called tundra, where few different kinds
of plants grow and those that do are rather small. Sometimes lemmings go on
mass migrations and this behaviour seems to be connected with competition.

Figure 13.11
A lemming in its natural habitat, the
tundra.

16 What are the lemmings most likely to be competing for?

17 What explanation can you suggest for these mass migrations?

There are many resources for which organisms may compete.

18 Name two organisms that might compete for each of the following resources:
a light
b water
c nesting sites
d settling sites
e mineral salts
f mates
g territory

You may often observe animals competing directly and actively with each other: for example, two puppies scrapping over a bone or two small children fighting over a toy. It may surprise you to learn that some plants can compete "actively". They may do this by releasing a chemical that will deter competitors – or even kill them.

Worksheet **B**13E gives you an opportunity to investigate some of the ways in which plants compete.

Succession

When organisms in an environment compete they can bring about important biological changes in the habitat or ecosystem in which they live. Wherever you live, the area is probably quite different from what it was like 8000 years ago. When people first arrived in Britain after the last Ice Age, much of England was covered in forest. Most of the forest was cut down long ago. However, if a patch of ground is cleared so that it is bare soil, and then left completely alone, it will very slowly change back into forest. Figure 13.12 shows the various stages of this change. On the same piece of land one

Figure 13.12
Succession from cleared ground to deciduous forest in an oak-hornbeam forest in southern Poland.
a Cleared ground.
b After 7 years.

(Continued)

a

b   After 7 years

c   After 15 years

d   After 30 years

e   After 95 years

f   After 150 years

Figure 13.12 (continued)
c After 15 years, the low-growing plants compete for light with taller plants.
d After 30 years, young trees appear– as they grow larger they shade out the thistles and grasses, which slowly disappear.
e A woodland develops after about 95 years, but at first the trees are smaller and close together, causing dense shading of the ground. So the ground cover of herbaceous plants (those that are not trees) also disappears.
f After 150 years, the young woodland slowly ages and as it does so, some of the trees die. The remaining ones are not so crowded. They grow larger and taller. By the time the forest is mature, enough light falls between the well-spaced trees for herbaceous plants to grow once again on the forest floor.

ecosystem will follow or succeed an earlier one. So the changes that occur are known as *succession*.

Climax communities

Succession does not go on forever. In all communities a stage is reached which does not seem to develop any further as time goes by. Obviously organisms die and are replaced; but they are replaced by the same sorts of organisms. The community does not change any more – it is a mature community, or what we call a *climax community*. Communities are usually at this stage, unless something has damaged them or unless humans have interrupted the succession. These communities are very *stable* – this means that organisms that live in a climax community have conditions of life that

a

b

c

Figure 13.13
Some climax communities that occur in Britain. **a** Deciduous woodland: Wistman's Wood in Devonshire. **b** Upland moor in Perthshire. **c** A saltmarsh at low tide. **d** A Caledonian pine forest in the Cairngorms.

d

were there long ago, and are likely to be there in the future. The most famous and complex climax communities, coral reefs and tropical rain forests, have in some cases been where they are now for millions of years. (Figure 13.6.)

To explore a climax community you have to find somewhere that hasn't been affected by people for a long time. In Britain this can be difficult – towns and farmland are obviously unsuitable. Some climax communities that can be found are shown in figure 13.13.

Chapter **B14**

The webs of life

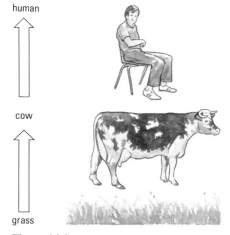

Figure 14.1
A simple food chain.

B14.1   Food chains and food webs

What did you have for your last meal? Whatever your diet, your meal probably included vegetables, or some sort of food made from plants – like bread or something else made from flour – and perhaps some meat, fish, eggs or dairy produce (milk, butter, cheese or yoghurt). It might be useful to revise what each of these foods provides for you (see Chapter **B**6).

1 Which of the other foods you eat come from animals?

When you look at any list of animals that humans eat you may notice that apart from fish the animals are nearly all herbivores (see Chapter **B**4). A cow feeds on grass, and uses the proteins in the plants in making proteins for itself. So, when we eat beef, we are eating proteins that have originally been made by plants. This is a simple example of what is called a *food chain* and figure 14.1 shows an easy way to write it down.

If you had fish such as cod for lunch you can still build up a food chain (figure 14.2). It just has more links in it because a cod eats other animals – in other words it is a carnivore, not a herbivore.

The arrows in a food chain are always drawn to show the direction in which the food goes – they point from the food to the feeder. For example, when we eat cod the proteins, carbohydrates and fats pass from the fish and become part of us. But food is also a source of energy and so the arrows also show the direction in which the energy is transferred through a food chain.

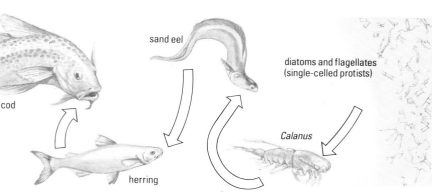

Figure 14.2
A longer food chain.

Figure 14.3 shows three organisms which make up a very simple food chain from a pond.

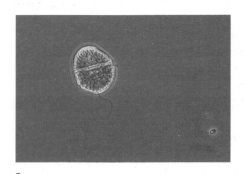

a

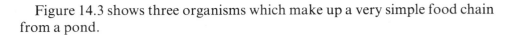

b

c

Figure 14.3
These three kinds of common pond organism are often linked in a food chain.
a *Gyrodinium*, a green single-celled protist; see also figure 14.12b.
b *Daphnia*, the water flea.
c Several *Hydra* attached to a water plant. Some of them are feeding on the water flea.

Figure 14.4
A community that lives in the Arctic tundra of Alaska provides one example of a food web. The thickness of the arrow gives an idea of the relative importance of the different routes through the web. Notice how important the lemmings are.

2 Using the information given in figure 14.3, write down the food chain which you think is formed by the organisms shown.

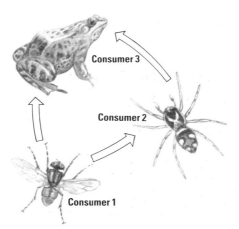

Figure 14.5
A food web for a pond community. Notice how sometimes a link between two organisms may "jump" one level of consumer (sometimes two levels are "jumped").

It is very easy to over-simplify what really happens in a community. A farmer's field does not have just one kind of plant (grass) growing in it with one kind of herbivore (cow) eating it. There will be other plants; and there will be many different herbivores such as slugs and caterpillars, as well as larger ones like rabbits, feeding on them. The small herbivores in turn will become food for carnivores like robins, blackbirds and hedgehogs, while hawks or foxes may eat the rabbits. Several food chains will exist in a community found in a natural ecosystem. They link up with each other into what is known as a *food web*. In figure 14.4 you can see an example of a food web in a natural habitat.

It is possible to classify all the organisms in food web into one of two categories – *producers* and *consumers.*

A producer is an organism that makes organic chemicals such as proteins and carbohydrates from simple substances like water, carbon dioxide and mineral salts. It uses light as a source of energy (see Chapter **B**3). In nearly all cases these organisms are green protists or plants and they produce the food for all other organisms in the food web.

A consumer is an organism that obtains all the chemicals it needs from the food it eats. Such organisms can be bacteria, fungi or animals.

There may be several "levels" of consumer. For example:

Primary consumers (C_1) are always herbivores – they eat the producers.
Secondary consumers (C_2) are always carnivores that eat herbivores.
Tertiary consumers (C_3) eat secondary consumers, but they may eat the primary consumers as well. (See figure 14.5.)

In some food webs there may also be higher levels of consumer. All these different "levels" in a food web are called *trophic levels* – from the Greek word *trophos* which means "a feeder".

A
APPLY

3 Try and work out food chains that include you and all the food items in your last meal. This will be easy for any food made out of plants or plant products!

Humans, pigs and badgers are all omnivores. You may remember from Chapter **B**6 that an omnivore is an animal that eats plants as well as animals.

I
INTERPRET

4 What "level" of consumer would you say a human is?

You or your friends probably have pets. All pets are descended from animals that were once wild.

A
APPLY

5 Try to find out where the wild relatives or ancestors of our domestic pets live or lived in their natural habitat. Work out a food chain for your pet or its ancestor in the natural habitat. (You may have to get some help from your teacher or a book!)

6 How does the food chain you have worked out differ from the food chain to which the animal belongs today?

A permanently manned Moon base would need to produce its own food to save the cost of transporting it from the Earth. If you were in charge of food production for the base you might want to set up a food web.

7 What would you have to include in your food web and what would you want to leave out? Give the reasons for what you decide to do.

Agricultural pests often eat some of the food we produce for ourselves (we say they are competing with us for our food).

8 Make a food web that might exist on a farm. Include humans, the organisms which are food for humans and one or more of the organisms which are pests.

Take a look at all of the food webs you have made.

9 What do you notice about:
a the kind of organism that is always at the very beginning of a food web?
b the numbers of ''links'' in any single food chain?

How is a food web constructed?

If you have studied a habitat, you might well wonder how it is possible to construct a food web of the community that lives there. It contains so many different kinds of organism, most of which cannot even be named easily. This need not worry you! Ecologists (scientists who study ecology) have exactly the same problems, and an enormous amount of work has to go into unravelling even fairly straightforward food webs. Many have not been studied at all, and we can only guess at what is happening.

Here are some guidelines about how to produce a food web.

How do I know what each organism is?

Finding out the exact name of each organism you come across is not really very important. You can learn about food webs without detailed knowledge of animal and plant names. However, you can use a key (such as the ones provided for you to use with Worksheet **B**1B) which will help you find the group to which the more common animals belong.

What do I include and what do I leave out?

Find out which are the most common plants, herbivores and carnivores – include these and leave out the rest. Different types of carnivore are very different sizes. What they eat often depends on how big they are.

a

b

Figure 14.6
a The centipede has large fangs which inject poison.
b The grasshopper, *Gastrimargus flavipes*, has mouthparts that are good at cutting. Here, it is eating a blade of grass.

It would be as unlikely for a fox to eat greenfly as it would be for a spider to eat deer! Food webs that include small herbivores often contain many more organisms (and many more links) than those which contain only large herbivores. If you find large numbers of greenfly in the ecosystem you are studying, but few other herbivores, then you ought to look for the small carnivores that may be eating them. Then you must look for the larger carnivores that eat the smaller ones, and so on.

How do I know if an animal is a herbivore or a carnivore?

In many cases you may already know without needing to check or ask. In mammals the kind of teeth will give a clue (see Chapter **B**4) and so will the mouth parts of some other animals (see figure 14.6).
Perhaps the easiest and quickest way to find out if an animal is a herbivore or a carnivore is to find out what it is, using a key; this may give brief notes on what each animal eats.

How do I know what an organism feeds on?

The most reliable way to find out would be to examine the contents of the animal's gut but it is not a good idea to kill an animal in order to do this. Some animals advertise what they eat either by letting large indigestible pieces pass out of their gut in the faeces, or by regurgitating the parts of their prey that they cannot digest. Birds of prey commonly do this by parcelling up the undigested parts in pellets. These can be dissected under water and the teeth and jaws of the small mammals that form a major part of these birds' diet can easily be seen. Animals that eat fruits may often pass out the seeds of the fruit in their faeces. It is not too difficult to compare the seeds from the faeces with the seeds you find inside living fruits and in this way to identify what the animal has been eating. During a short practical exercise, you will be very fortunate if you see one organism actually eating another! Of course if you do, this is positive evidence of the predator's diet and you can then put a proved link in your food web. This is a good opportunity for you to use your powers of observation. Worksheet **B**14A gives you some instructions for working out a food web.

B14.2   Parasites and food webs

Almost every food web contains at least one *parasite*. A parasite is an organism that usually lives upon or within another organism (the *host*) and uses the host or the host's food supply as its own food source. Because the food for the parasite comes from the host, the parasite gains and the host loses. Think back to the last time you were ill because of an infection. A parasitic organism such as a bacterium had invaded your body and lived there as a parasite. You perhaps felt awful, but finally your body produced a chemical substance called an *antibody* which killed the bacteria, or you took an antibiotic drug which killed them and you recovered. Some parasites are much larger than bacteria but even so, they may not cause so many unwelcome signs of their presence. Some examples of parasites on humans are shown in figure 14.7.

Figure 14.7
Uninvited guests on the human body.

a Head louse
This small insect is quite common and lives on the scalp, feeding on hair. Its egg cases attached to hairs are known as nits.

b Common cold virus
Cells become inflamed as they are invaded by the virus. Many more viruses are made and these break out of the dying cells, ready to invade other ones.

c Trypanosome
This tiny single-celled organism causes sleeping sickness and lives in the blood.

d *Salmonella* bacterium
Salmonella bacteria may be found in undercooked meat, and are a main cause of "food poisoning".

e *Schistosoma*, a flatworm (male and female)
These small flatworms live in blood vessels associated with the intestine. They cause *bilharzia*, a serious disease producing sickness and weakness, which is fatal if untreated. It is not found in Britain but millions of people suffer from it in the tropics, especially people such as rice field workers, who have to spend much of their time in water, where *Schistosoma* begins its life cycle. (See also figure 14.8.)

f Pin worm or thread worm (a nematode)
This lives in the intestine and at night the female lays her eggs around the anus. The rather unhygienic habits of small children mean that the eggs get caught in the fingernails and find their way to the child's mouth, or someone else's mouth, spreading the worms. These are surprisingly common, and many people are infected without realizing it.

g Gonorrhoea bacterium
This causes a sexually transmitted disease. The bacteria live in the reproductive systems of men and women. In this photograph, they are the cluster of dots.

h Athlete's foot fungus
This parasite lives in the skin between the toes, causing itching and soreness.

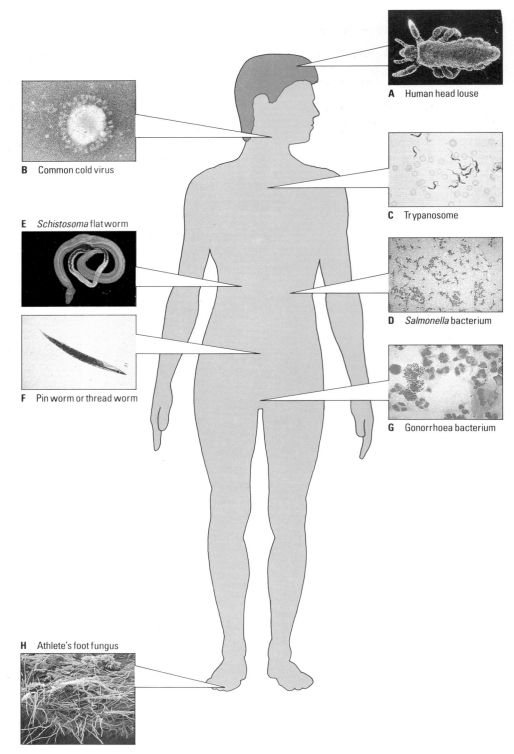

B   Common cold virus

E   *Schistosoma* flatworm

F   Pin worm or thread worm

H   Athlete's foot fungus

A   Human head louse

C   Trypanosome

D   *Salmonella* bacterium

G   Gonorrhoea bacterium

Parasites are consumers and may occur in plants as well as in animals. There is a constant struggle between parasites and their hosts; the parasites have to feed, although the host organism is not **usually** killed.

In order to understand more about how parasites fit into food webs, we shall look in a little more detail at the ways in which some parasites live and the effects that they can have on other organisms.

Some parasites may cause such violent symptoms in their hosts, or may be present in such large numbers, that the hosts die. This can happen to humans

Figure 14.8

a The protein consumed per person in different parts of the world.

b The gross national product (GNP) in different parts of the world. GNP means the average amount of wealth produced per person per year.

c The world distribution of *Schistosoma* – an intestinal worm parasite of people which causes *bilharzia*. (See also figure 14.7.)

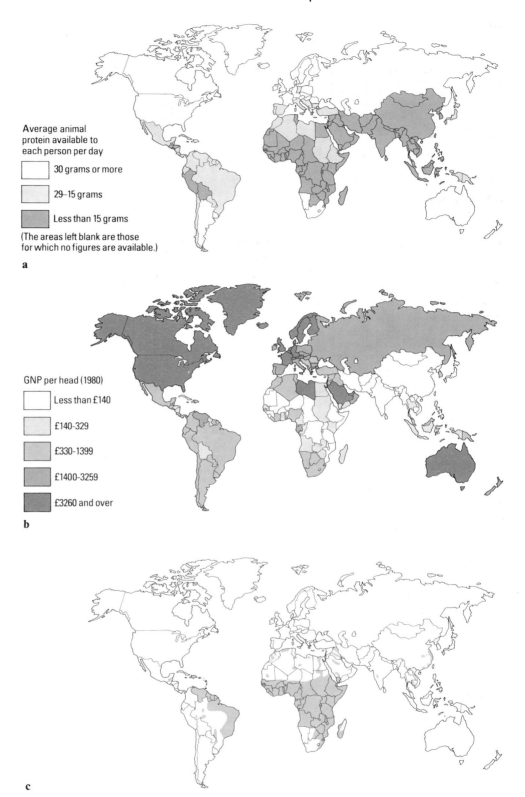

Average animal protein available to each person per day

☐ 30 grams or more

☐ 29–15 grams

☐ Less than 15 grams

(The areas left blank are those for which no figures are available.)

a

GNP per head (1980)

☐ Less than £140

☐ £140–329

☐ £330–1399

☐ £1400–3259

☐ £3260 and over

b

c

too, especially in parts of the world where the people are poor and do not have enough food.

The maps in figure 14.8 show the parts of the world where people are undernourished, the degree of poverty or affluence in different parts and those places where a parasitic worm is found. Figure 23.21 (page 309) shows where there is malaria.

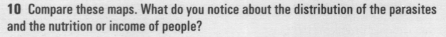

10 Compare these maps. What do you notice about the distribution of the parasites and the nutrition or income of people?

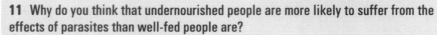

11 Why do you think that undernourished people are more likely to suffer from the effects of parasites than well-fed people are?

Parasites are very common and wild organisms have them. Most organisms survive with their parasites, in many cases without appearing to suffer any harm. If the parasite causes so much harm to its host that the host dies, then the parasite dies with it. What is more, even parasites can have parasites.

Parasites often have special ways of surviving and many possess features which are of advantage in a parasitic way of life.

Parasite adaptation

Parasites that live on the body surface are called *ectoparasites*. Figure 14.9 shows some of their special features.

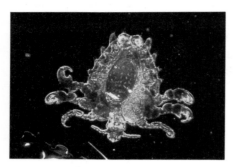

Figure 14.9
This insect is the crab louse – a parasite on humans. It lives in the hairs of the pubic region.

12 What features can you see in figure 14.9 which may be those of an ectoparasite?

Endoparasites live **inside** their host. They too have special features. The adult beef tapeworm lives in the small intestine of humans.

13 Suggest two ways in which the intestine is a favourable place for a parasite to live and two ways in which it is not.

Many of the special features seen in parasites are related to reproduction. The flatworms which cause bilharzia live in pairs – male and female – in their host; they are permanently mated and the eggs are fertilized inside the female. (Figure 14.7.)

Worksheet **B**14B gives you information about a common parasite of plants, and instructions about how to investigate its life history.

B14.3   The flow of energy through food webs

Have you ever been travelling in a car when it has run out of petrol? Even if you haven't, it is not difficult to work out what happens – the engine splutters, then stops running altogether, and soon, the car comes to a standstill. The petrol is the car's source of energy and its engine can only keep running for as long as petrol is available from the tank.

Animals, including humans, depend on plants in many ways but it is as a source of energy that plants are the base of all food webs.

14 List the activities for which organisms require energy.

15 What determines how much energy an ecosystem will receive? Give examples of some habitats which receive a lot of energy and some which receive less energy.

In almost every ecosystem the community that lives there will contain some plants, but some ecosystems support more or larger plants than others. Equatorial rain forest supports many more plants per hectare than does desert; in temperate countries such as Britain, high moorland (figure 13.13b, page 166) supports a smaller quantity of plant material per hectare than oak woodland does (figure 13.12, page 165).

16 Suggest why the amounts of vegetation in ecosystems such as these are so different.

In any environment all the green plants photosynthesize. The greater the number of plants, the more photosynthesis will take place. The more photosynthesis there is, the more carbohydrates will be produced. In other words, any environment which supports a lot of plant life will be able to "harvest" more of the light energy from the sun than one with fewer plants (see Chapter **B**3). Then more energy is available for the primary consumers and, in turn, for the secondary consumers and so on.

Worksheet **B**14C gives you a method for working out approximately the energy content of some food **you** might eat.

B14.4   Pyramids in ecology

Think of a large grassy field that has not been mown or ploughed for three or four years. No grazing farm animals like cows or sheep have entered the field during that time. There will be no trees, but there will be plenty of long grass and other herbaceous plants. Rabbits are also living in the field, feeding on the plants growing there. There are foxes living around the edges of the field and they eat the rabbits.

17 At a guess, which would you say there were more of, plants or rabbits?

18 Would you expect there to be more rabbits than foxes, or more foxes than rabbits?

Whether you are familiar with rabbits and foxes in fields or not, you probably thought that there would be more plants than rabbits, and more rabbits than foxes – and you would have been right. This illustrates a general rule that applies to most habitats and it can be summarized as shown in figure 14.10. The size of the "bars" in the pyramid represent relative numbers of organisms at each trophic level.

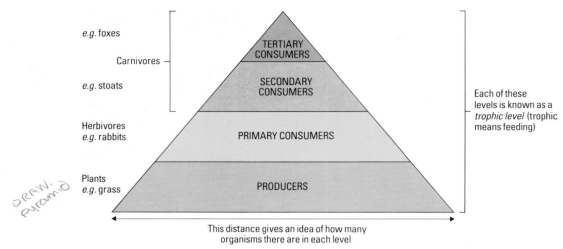

DRAW PYRAMID

Figure 14.10
A theoretical pyramid of numbers.

This sort of diagram is known as a *pyramid of numbers*. Figure 14.11 shows a real example that ecologists have produced.

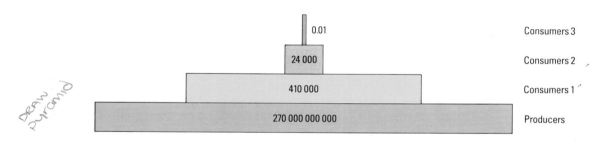

DRAW PYRAMID

Figures show numbers of organisms under 1 m² of water surface

Figure 14.11
A real pyramid of numbers for a community in a Florida river.

INTERPRET

19 What could the enormous number of producers in the Florida river be?

20 Construct your own pyramid from the following numbers of organisms in 0.1 hectare of a grassland area in America. Draw the different trophic levels to scale (the single consumer 3 should be represented by a single vertical line).

Primary producers	1 500 000
Consumers 1	200 000
Consumers 2	90 000
Consumers 3	1

A pyramid of numbers is a model to show how much food is available for each trophic level in a measured area of a habitat. This model is used because sometimes (but by no means always!) it is quite easy to count the number of organisms present. However, it can be misleading, because each organism will count as one, no matter how large or small it is. This means that a unicellular organism like a diatom, found in a pond, would count the same as a multicellular waterlily in the same pond. Obviously, there is more food in one waterlily than in one microscopic diatom (see figure 14.12 and figure 14.3a, page 168).

Figure 14.12
a A waterlily, *Nymphaea* hybrid.
b Freshwater diatoms (green single-celled protists), *Ceratium* spp.

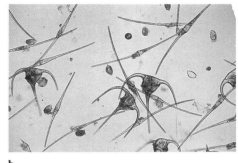

a   **b**

If we made a pyramid of numbers for an area of oak woodland it would be a rather odd shape for a pyramid!

draw Pyramid

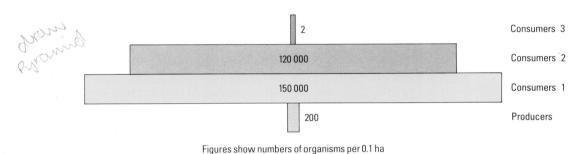

2	Consumers 3
120 000	Consumers 2
150 000	Consumers 1
200	Producers

Figures show numbers of organisms per 0.1 ha

Figure 14.13
A pyramid of numbers for a community in an English oakwood.

A APPLY

21 What do you think the 200 producers in figure 14.13 could be?

Pyramids of biomass

Ecologists have overcome the problems of using numbers to show how much food there is in each trophic level of a habitat. Instead of counting the number of individual organisms, they estimate the total **mass** of all the organisms at each level. (They dry them first so that water is not included.) The mass of the living parts of each trophic level is known as *biomass*. When pyramids are constructed, using biomass instead of numbers, they are known as *pyramids of biomass*.

Using biomass makes much more sense out of the food webs, as we can see by comparing the two pyramids for the same English oak forest in figures 14.13 and 14.14.

draw Pyramid

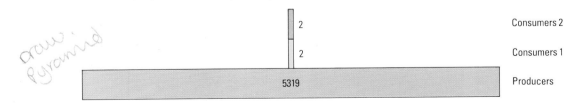

2	Consumers 2
2	Consumers 1
5319	Producers

Figures show biomass in g/m²

Figure 14.14
A pyramid of biomass for the same English oakwood as in figure 14.13.

Another kind of pyramid

There is still one problem in using pyramids of biomass or numbers to represent quantities of organisms at different trophic levels in a food web. The biomass and numbers of any organism may vary during the year.

22 Give a reason why the biomass of the oak trees in a forest will be different in November from what it is in June.

23 Give a reason why the biomass of green protists in a pond will be low in February, very much higher in May and low again in July.

Some organisms may grow or reproduce very much faster than others. So although an oak tree has a much greater biomass than 10 000 000 green protists, the protists reproduce so fast that in one year they may produce as much food for consumers as an oak tree does.

The most accurate way to model the food web in an ecosystem is to construct a *pyramid of energy* for a whole year. Pyramids of energy for different habitats can be compared. This method can, for example, be used to show how much human food is produced by different farming methods. It would not be very helpful to compare different pyramids of numbers or biomass. Figure 14.15 is a pyramid of energy for the same Florida river as is shown in figure 14.11.

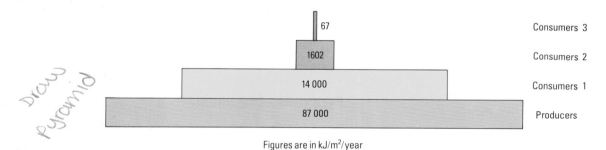

67	Consumers 3
1602	Consumers 2
14 000	Consumers 1
87 000	Producers

Figures are in kJ/m²/year

Figure 14.15
A pyramid of energy for the same Florida river as in figure 14.11.

Notice how much less energy each trophic level appears to "contain" compared with the energy content of the level below it.

24 Use the information and ideas in this chapter to explain why the large carnivores at the tops of food webs are relatively rare in nature.

25 Explain why the territories of top predators are usually very large.

26 Explain why the number of "links" in a food chain rarely exceeds five.

Chapter **B**15   **Salts and cycles**

B15.1   Plant mineral requirements

If you drive through the countryside during the summer you may notice two agricultural activities. You may see crops being harvested and you may be aware that the farmers have spread manure or fertilizer on the harvested fields before they plough them. (See figures 15.1 and 15.2.)

Figure 15.1
Harvest time for barley.

Figure 15.2
Fertilizer being spread over a field before ploughing.

This cycle of activity takes place regularly, year after year, and it suggests that the manure or fertilizer will put back into the soil something that the crops have taken out. One of the things removed from the soil by plants is *mineral salts*.

1 What else, apart from mineral salts, do plants remove from the soil as they grow?

2 Whatever you gave as your answer to question **1**, it is very unlikely that farmers have to go to the trouble of replenishing the soil's supply of this substance after each harvest. Explain why not.

Adding manure to a field does not just replace mineral salts. It adds *humus* – the plant remains that are in the manure as well.

3 Find out what benefit there is in adding humus to the soil.

In Chapter **B**3 we look in some detail at the way green plants make carbohydrates by photosynthesis, using the energy of sunlight and absorbing the raw materials carbon dioxide and water from their environment. But these two raw materials alone will not keep plants alive for long. Each plant must have the correct balance of different mineral salts. One thing to remember is that each salt consists of two kinds of *ion* (see Chapter **C**5 in the Chemistry book). These ions are absorbed separately by plant roots. (See Chapter **B**9.) Figure 15.3 gives you an idea of how much of different ions plants need. A plant could obtain nitrate ions either from ammonium nitrate or from sodium nitrate. For this reason the salts in figure 15.4 are shown as the separate ions. See also Chapters **C**15 and **C**16 in the Chemistry book.

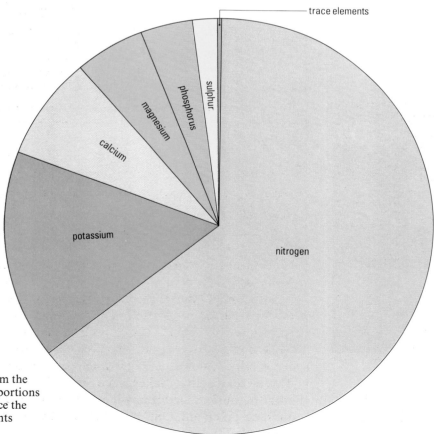

Figure 15.3
The elements that plants need from the soil. This pie chart shows the proportions of the most important ones. Notice the tiny proportion of all trace elements shown together.

Some ions are only needed by plants in very small amounts. These are the ions of *trace elements*. If a plant does not have enough of a particular ion it will show signs of a deficiency disease. Animals also suffer from deficiency diseases if they lack certain ions.

4 Animals do not absorb ions from the soil. Where do they get them from?

5 Name one deficiency disease that animals suffer from. What ion does this mean they lack?

Figure 15.4 names some ions that plants absorb from the soil and says what each is used for in the plant.

	Element	Ion	Function of ion in plant
Major elements	Nitrogen	NO_3^-	Provides the nitrogen that is an essential raw material in the manufacture of amino acids
	Potassium	K^+	Makes many enzymes active; used in the operation of stomata
	Phosphorus	PO_4^{3-}	Essential in every energy transfer within the cell
	Calcium	Ca^{2+}	Raw material for cell walls
	Magnesium	Mg^{2+}	Raw material needed for making chlorophyll
	Sulphur	SO_4^{2-}	Raw material for making certain amino acids
Trace elements	Copper	Cu^{2+}	Involved in cell respiration and photosynthesis
	Manganese	Mn^{2+}	Necessary for some cell enzymes to work

Figure 15.4

6 What would you expect to be the signs of magnesium deficiency in a plant? Explain your answer.

Figure 15.5
Fertilizer production is big business. Millions of pounds are spent each year on fertilizers, so that farm land can continue to be used to grow crops for food. The fertilizer must be spread evenly over the ground to make sure that all plants in the field can obtain adequate amounts. It is also important not to apply too much, as this would be wasteful and could cause problems if it were washed by rain into a lake (see Chapter **B**17).

Worksheet **B**15A investigates the effect of mineral ions on the growth of *Lemna* plants.

A farmer might find that a crop gives a poor harvest one year, or that the plants in a field do not look as healthy as they should, even though there have been no pests or disease. It could well be that the concentration in the soil of one of the mineral ions that the plants need is too low. A soil test will quickly show which one is in short supply, and the farmer can put things right by adding *fertilizer* of the right kind to his soil.

In 1985, world production of just one type of fertilizer was 78 000 000 tonnes. The UK used 1 600 000 tonnes of this, costing Britain's farmers a total of £400 000 000.

Wild plants must be able to get all the ions they require, in the correct quantities, from the soil where they are growing. If not, they will die. Not all plants require the same amounts of all the different mineral salts. So the types of plants that will be able to grow in a particular habitat will depend on the relative concentrations of the different ions in the soil. This, in turn, will be related to the type of rock from which the soil was formed. Thus, the distribution of plants is affected very much by the nature of the soil.

7 Many plants, including most house plants, garden plants and crops, would die if you watered them with sea water. Suggest reasons why this would happen.

B15.2   Decomposition

From time to time you may have come across the corpse of a hedgehog or small bird that has been hit by a car. Each autumn you see leaves falling from trees and forming thick layers on the ground (figure 15.6). This is happening all over the world where there is life, and yet these dead remains seem to disappear.

Where does all this dead material go?

Some of it may be eaten. There are many animals which eat dead material. You can probably think of some yourself.

Figure 15.6
Where does it all go? This photograph shows leaves on the ground after the autumn fall.

Figure 15.7
Organisms that feed on dead remains.
(*Continued*)

i Termite

ii Furniture beetle

iii Maggots of blowfly

iv Hyena

v Vulture

a Wood

b Zebra carcass

c Dead rat

Figure 15.7 (continued)
Dead remains.

d Wood

e Decayed elephant carcass

8 Match up the two sets of photographs in figure 15.7 of animals and the dead material they eat.

Not all dead organisms are eaten by animals. Dead remains will slowly disappear even without any animals eating them.

Decomposer organisms, especially bacteria and fungi, feed upon the remains which then get used up as shown in figure 15.8.

Figure 15.8
This diagram shows where the materials in dead remains go during decomposition.

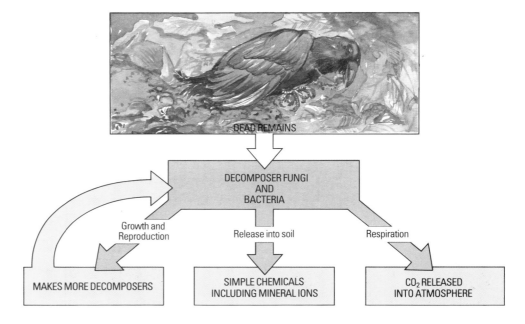

Figure 15.9
The soil mite, a common decomposer;
here it is among the leaf litter of the
forest floor.

Worksheet **B**15B gives you some opportunities to make hypotheses about decomposition and to test them for yourself.

There are many different kinds of small animals that are decomposers – like the soil mite in figure 15.9. Worksheet **B**15C tells you how you can extract such organisms from soil or leaf litter.

In natural communities, all faeces and dead organisms eventually fall to the ground. Thus the soil constantly has more material added to it. Decomposer organisms therefore have an abundant supply of food and there are huge numbers of them in the soil. If the amount of dead material (organic matter) is increased, as it is in a compost heap, then there are even greater numbers of decomposers present. With all these organisms decomposing the organic matter, it should be no surprise to learn that many of the soil animals are in fact not decomposers, but carnivores that eat the decomposers. Two examples are shown in figure 15.10. Others are the centipede (figure 14.6, page 171) and the mole (figure 10.9e, page 115).

a

b

Figure 15.10
Two carnivores that eat decomposers. **a** The carabid beetle, *Carabus arvensis*.
b The false scorpion, *Dinocheirus* sp.

There are complete food webs linking organisms in the soil, all seeming to start with dead organic matter as food rather than with the green plants in the food webs dealt with in Chapter **B**14. In most habitats there are both sorts of food web.

Chapter **B**14 probably suggests to you that all food webs start with green plants, and the energy that maintains all communities comes, in the first place, from the sun via photosynthesis.

INTERPRET

9 Does the existence in the soil of food webs which seem to start with dead organic remains contradict this conclusion? Explain your answer.

In a few examples the only food web in a habitat is the decomposer food web. In such cases there has to be a source of food (wastes or dead remains) coming into the habitat. An example is shown in figure 15.11.

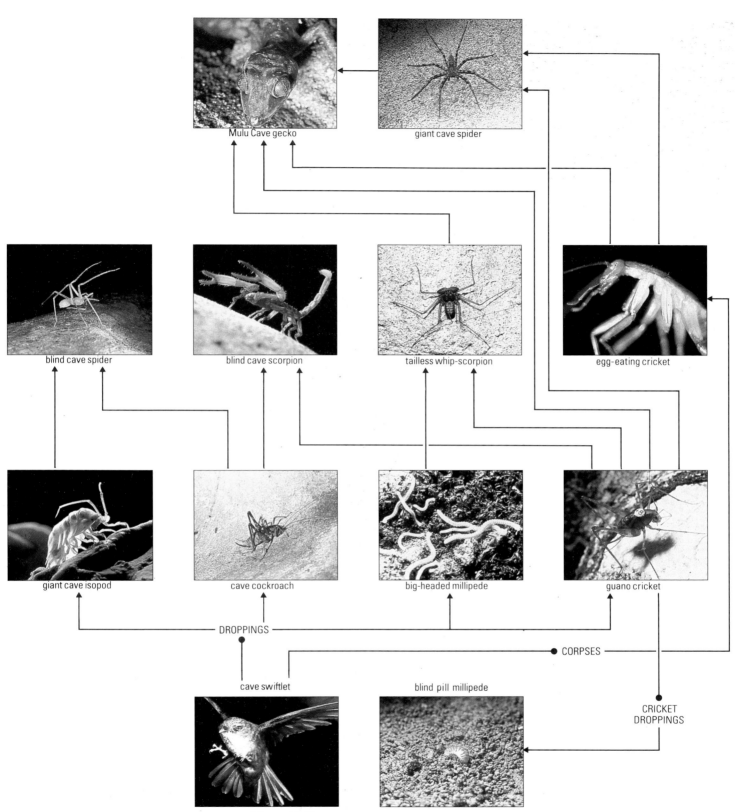

Mulu Cave gecko

giant cave spider

blind cave spider

blind cave scorpion

tailless whip-scorpion

egg-eating cricket

giant cave isopod

cave cockroach

big-headed millipede

guano cricket

DROPPINGS

CORPSES

cave swiftlet

blind pill millipede

CRICKET
DROPPINGS

Figure 15.11
All these animals depend on the swiftlets that roost in caves during daylight in the Gunung Mulu National Park, Sarawak. The cave is always dark and there is no photosynthesis taking place. Most of the organisms shown feed on the faeces dropped by the swiftlets, although some eat the dead swiftlets.

The scientists who worked out this food web had to put up with a constant "rain" from the swiftlets above for as long as they were in the cave!

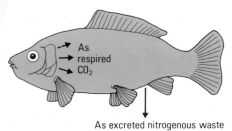

Figure 15.12
How carbon leaves a living organism.

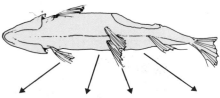

Decomposer organisms feed on dead remains. Carbon in the food becomes part of the decomposers.

Figure 15.13
How carbon leaves a dead organism.

What happens to carbon during decomposition?

All organisms contain carbon – you can discover this yourself next time you forget you are cooking something. Whatever the kind of food, once it is dry it will begin to burn, and turn black. The black, burnt food is chiefly the element carbon.

Carbon enters an organism either as carbon dioxide during photosynthesis, or in its food. There are three ways in which it can leave the body of an organism (see figures 15.12 and 15.13):

a by being released as carbon dioxide – a waste product of respiration,
b by being released as a waste product like urea which also contains nitrogen,
c by entering the decomposer which feeds on the body of the organism after it has died.

Some of the carbon that the decomposer has eaten will be used in growth or reproduction by that organism. But some of it will be given off as carbon dioxide by the decomposer as a result of respiration. In due course all the carbon that has entered organisms will be converted to carbon dioxide. This carbon dioxide will enter the atmosphere and may be taken in by plants once again during photosynthesis. Carbon is used over and over again by living organisms. This repeated uptake and release is part of the *carbon cycle* (figure 15.14). (See also Chapter **C15** in the Chemistry book.)

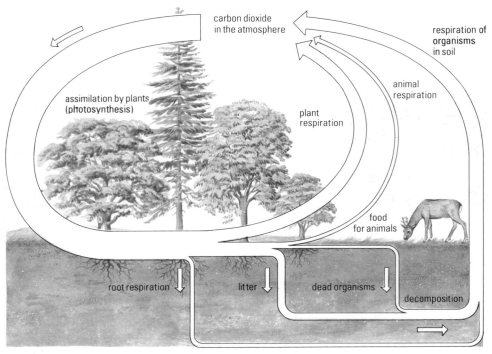

Figure 15.14
The carbon cycle.

B15.3   Water, water everywhere

A favourite topic of conversation in Britain is the weather. Sometimes it may be too hot or too cold but very often it is too wet! However, it is the amount of rain that keeps the British countryside looking so green. You can see

Figure 15.15
The drought of 1976. Here the grass is
brown but not the trees.

what happened to the colour of the countryside during the drought in 1976
(figure 15.15).

But where does the rain come from and where does it go? The answers are
provided by looking at the *water cycle*. (See also Chapter **C**10 in your
Chemistry book.)

Most living organisms contain a lot of water. Even our bodies are about
65% water. Why is water so important for life? For one thing it is a very good
solvent and many substances dissolve in it. All the chemical reactions in cells
happen between substances that are dissolved.

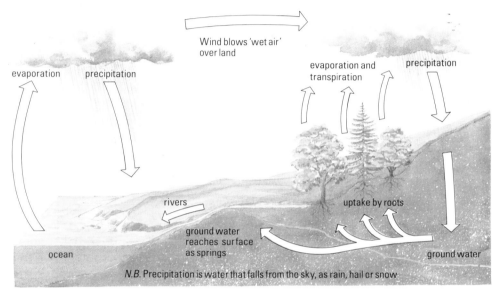

Figure 15.16
The water cycle.

10 Make a list of some of the substances you think are dissolved in our bodies. Then
do the same for a cabbage. Are there any differences in your two lists?

Another reason why water is important is that so many organisms live in it.
About 75% of the Earth's surface is covered in water, most of it ocean.

11 What other reasons are there why water is important to people?

	Volume of water in km^3
Oceans and seas	1 350 000 000
Ice	29 000 000
Ground water	8 400 000
Freshwater	200 000
Atmosphere	13 000

Figure 15.17
Volumes of water in different parts of the
water cycle.

The way that water moves through the water cycle is shown in figure 15.16.
Figure 15.17 shows you how much water there is in the different parts of the
water cycle. To get a better idea of the volumes of water involved, use a map
of where you live and see how long a kilometre is. Then think of a cube with
sides as long as that. 1 000 000 000 000 kg of water occupy 1 km^3. That's a lot
of water!

12 What difference would it make to the water cycle if there were no living organisms?

13 If the Earth were as close to the Sun as Venus or as far away from it as Mars, the water cycle would not be the same. Explain why.

B15.4   The fixing of nitrogen

Our planet is unusual in many ways. For a start, there is life here; no one has yet found evidence for life anywhere else. Another unusual feature of the Earth and very important for the existence of life, is the presence of liquid water. The Earth is neither so close to the Sun that water will always boil, nor so far away that it will always freeze. However, if an intelligent alien organism were watching the planets of our solar system from some far distant place, it might not easily detect either that there is life here or that water exists here as liquid. But if the alien had an instrument that could analyse light wavelengths it would be able to notice something else odd about the Earth compared with all the other planets circling the Sun – our atmosphere has a high percentage of nitrogen gas.

Nitrogen gas is inert, which means that it does not easily react with other chemicals. Yet life on the Earth is completely dependent upon it, for all chromosomes and proteins contain nitrogen. Chromosomes pass inherited characteristics from one generation of organisms to the next (see Chapter **B22**); this could not happen the way it does without nitrogen. All cells contain proteins and the cell activities are controlled by enzymes, which

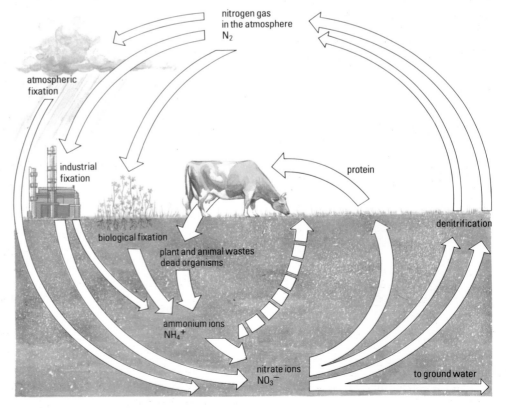

Figure 15.18
The nitrogen cycle.

Figure 15.19
Clover, *Trifolium repens*, is a legume plant and will develop root nodules.

Figure 15.20
Root nodules on clover.

Figure 15.21
Sundews (*Drosera rotundifolia*) trap insects and then digest them. They obtain some of their nutrients in this way. Here you can see some common blue butterflies (*Polymmatus icarus*) caught in sundews.

are soluble proteins. Without them metabolism would stop. This section will show you some of the ways in which nitrogen can enter living organisms. This is summarized in the *nitrogen cycle*, which is shown in figure 15.18. (See also Chapter **C**16 in the Chemistry book.)

Nitrogen is in the form of nitrate ions before it is absorbed by plants and so becomes part of other organisms via food webs. Look carefully to see where the nitrate can come from. One source is the decomposition of dead remains of organisms. In this way the nitrogen in the organisms is *recycled*.

Another very important source of nitrogen for producing nitrates is nitrogen gas from the atmosphere. It has been estimated that the total amount of nitrogen in the Earth's atmosphere is 3860 million million tonnes, so there is plenty of it! But if nitrogen is so inert, how can it find its way back into living organisms?

One way is by the action of lightning. A lightning strike might release 100 kW of power, enough for one thousand 100 W light bulbs to produce light for one hour. This provides the energy for nitrogen to react with oxygen to form nitrogen oxides. These react with rain water and oxygen and fall to the ground as nitric acid. The nitric acid then combines with minerals in the soil to form nitrates, which can be absorbed by plants.

A large amount of nitrate can be put back into the soil this way. At the Rothamsted Experimental Station the records show that 4.5 kg of nitrogen per hectare have been returned to the soil each year by this method.

Another way in which nitrogen enters the living world is by the process of *biological nitrogen fixation*, which depends on micro-organisms. These organisms (which are mostly bacteria) absorb nitrogen gas and finally produce nitrates. Some of the bacteria live in the soil – they are free-living *nitrogen-fixing bacteria*. For an account of an industrial method of nitrogen fixation, see Chapter **C**16 of your Chemistry book.

There is another group of nitrogen-fixing bacteria which are also of great importance, both in the natural world and in agriculture. These are the bacteria that colonize the roots of a family of flowering plants known as the *legumes*. It is a very large family, including common plants like pea, bean, clover, lupin and soya bean. The roots of all these plants will grow small lumps known as *root nodules* if they become colonized by nitrogen-fixing bacteria called *Rhizobium*. (See figures 15.19 and 15.20.)

This means that a legume plant can grow in soils that might lack nitrates. Legumes have their own steady supply of nitrogen from the nitrogen-fixing bacteria in their root nodules.

In Worksheet **B**15D you have an opportunity to investigate the conditions under which *Rhizobium* will colonize the roots of legumes.

You should realize the importance of nitrogen fixation. Legume crops such as peas should not need nitrate fertilizer, but of course many other crops are not legumes and they will remove nitrate ions from the soil. Most farmers in the industrialized world add nitrate fertilizer to their land to make up for this loss. Many others in poorer parts of the world cannot afford this. No fertilizers (including nitrates) are added to the land and the crop yield can become very poor because the soil is exhausted.

All plants require a source of nitrogen. If a soil has few nitrate ions, it will not support a very varied plant community. Many boggy moorland areas of Britain are lacking in nitrogen. If you visit one of these areas and look closely you are likely to find one type of plant growing very well there. These are the insectivorous plants. There are a number of kinds of such plants; the sundews (figure 15.21) are quite common ones.

Think carefully as you answer the next two questions.

14 How does the sundew plant obtain its energy?

15 The sundew does not seem to be showing the effects of a lack of nitrogen. How can you explain this?

Scientists have suggested that it might be possible in the future to have nitrogen-fixing micro-organisms growing in the roots of plants that are not legumes. This is one of the biotechnologists' dreams. Perhaps one day it will be possible to grow cereal crops without adding nitrate fertilizer to their soil.

16 What would be the advantage of this?

Figure 15.22 gives you an idea of how much nitrogen is taken out of the atmosphere each year by the different nitrogen-fixing processes.

Process	Quantity of nitrogen fixed from the atmosphere, in millions of tonnes/year
Lightning	7
Free-living nitrogen-fixing bacteria	170–270
Nitrogen-fixing bacteria in legumes	35

Figure 15.22

If a farmer adds no fertilizer to the land, the crop yield will fall within a few years and he will have a lower income. On the other hand, a natural ecosystem such as a forest has no added fertilizer, yet its production does not decline. Think of reasons why this should be so.

17 What natural environmental factors could make production fall in a natural ecosystem?

In the Middle Ages, farmers knew that if they planted peas, beans or clover one year, whatever they grew in the same field the following year would give an increased yield.

18 Explain this, using your understanding of the nitrogen cycle.

Figure 15.23
Luxuriant rain forest vegetation on the Monteverde forest, Costa Rica. This is typical of the humid tropics. It is easy to be deceived by such a scene into thinking that the soil is rich in nutrients.

Tropical rain forest soils are usually poor in mineral ions yet the forests thrive, as you can see in figure 15.23.

19 Where do the mineral ions for the plants come from?

20 Study the diagram of the nitrogen cycle in figure 15.18 and explain how nitrogen finds its way back into the atmosphere.

Fertilizer is expensive, and using it continuously as the only source of nitrogen can cause soil to deteriorate. Animal waste can be used as an alternative, and has been used for centuries in some parts of the world.

21 Make a list of as many advantages and disadvantages as you can think of, in using human waste as fertilizer.

Chapter **B16**

Staying alive

B16.1   Survival in a habitat

Most organisms seem to survive in their natural habitat very well, but the world can be a hard place and sometimes we might wonder how some organisms stay alive in certain places. Perhaps the habitat is very hot, or cold, or dry. Maybe it lacks oxygen, or is difficult to hide in, or full of predators. There are some examples in figure 16.1 and also in the coral polyps in figure 13.6b, page 160.

Figure 16.1
How do they do it? Some organisms live in what seem to us particularly dangerous or difficult habitats.
a The Morning Glory pool in the Yellowstone National Park, Wyoming, USA. The green of these hot sulphur springs comes from brilliantly coloured bacteria.
b Hydro-thermal vents in the area of the Galápagos islands. Water comes out of holes or vents in the floor of the ocean at temperatures of 7 to 17 °C, at a depth of 2500 m. Notice the rich growth of marine life, including the beard worm, *Riftia pachyptila*. None of the plant organisms can carry out photosynthesis because they live in complete darkness. Bacteria are the primary producers for the whole food web here.
c Mud at the bottom of ponds often has little or no oxygen in it. *Tubifex* worms live and feed in the mud, with one end of their bodies waving to and fro in the water above the mud. They get their supply of oxygen from this water. When the oxygen content of the water is low a greater length of the body is above the mud and its movements increase.

a

b

c

In Chapter **B**14 you can read about some of the features of parasites which enable them to survive living on our skin or in our gut. Plants, too, have features which enable them to survive in special conditions. For example, cacti (figure 16.2) live in hot, dry parts of North and South America where it is difficult to collect and keep water. Their spines are leaves that are so reduced in size and changed in structure that no water is lost from them. They also make it difficult for a thirsty or hungry herbivore to get to the juicy inside. This chapter is mainly about some of the ways organisms have of surviving in their habitats.

Figure 16.2
The Saguaro and the organ pipe cacti in the Sonora Desert, Arizona.

B16.2   Reaching a habitat

Have you ever weeded a garden? It can be a tedious job but if it is neglected, then the garden plants will not grow so well. For a gardener, weeding is a never-ending task because the weeds always seem to keep coming back.

1 Where do all the weeds come from? There are several possible answers to this question — how many can you think of?

The weeds don't appear by magic; they obviously come as seeds from a parent plant somewhere, and as soon as the conditions are suitable for their germination they start to grow.

Worksheet **B**16A gives you some details about when and where seeds germinate and suggests some ways in which you could investigate experimentally the conditions required.

The ways in which the seeds of a plant reach a new habitat are all called *dispersal*.

Dispersal of offspring

Plants have no control over where their seeds go, but there is usually some method by which these are carried away from the parent plant.

2 What are the advantages to the species if the seeds are dispersed away from the parent plants and not simply dropped from the plant onto the ground below? Chapter **B**13 might help you to answer this question.

3 What are the disadvantages in seeds being dispersed at random? Look at figures 16.3 and 16.4.

Figure 16.3
The ground is covered with common weeds. The plants have grown so close together that the soil surface is very shaded. In other words, the plants themselves have changed their own habitat.

Figure 16.4
Here you can see conditions for the seedlings that are quite different from those in figure 16.3.

There are about 575 different species of conifer plant (such as pine trees) and 285 000 different species of flowering plant (see Chapter **B**2). You might think that there would be thousands of different ways in which the seeds of plants were dispersed, but this is not so. Plants either have a structure that results in their seeds being carried away, or one that flings their seeds some distance away from them.

Dispersal of seeds by wind

There are two ways in which seeds are dispersed by the wind. Study figures 16.5, 16.6 and 16.7 to find out more about this.

Figure 16.5
Seed dispersal by wind.
a Thistle seeds are a common sight. You may have seen one drift into your classroom on a hot afternoon in the summer.
b Ground that was once cleared for industrial development or laid waste by bomb damage can become a habitat. It may be colonized by the rosebay willow herb, which you can see here in front of the gasometer, and by other plants with wind-dispersed seeds such as ragwort. In this way it loses some of its ugliness. The floating seeds are produced by all sizes of plant.

a

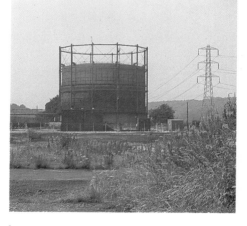

b

Figure 16.6
This boy won't learn much this way
about telling the time but he is certainly
helping in the dispersal of the dandelion.
In the dandelion the whole structure that
"floats" is a fruit because the
"parachute" is formed from the ovary
wall.

Figure 16.7
Structures with "wings" are commonly
produced by different kinds of trees. The
"wing" may be formed from a bract (a
kind of leaf). Otherwise it is formed
from the ovary wall, as in the sycamore,
Acer pseudoplatanus, seen here.

You can see from these examples that plants with wind dispersal either
have a "hairy" structure that makes a large surface area or they have some
sort of "wing".

4 How do you think such structures help to disperse seeds? Worksheet **B16B** could
help you to check if your idea is correct.

5 Why do you think the first plants to colonize waste ground like the area by the
gasometer shown in figure 16.5b almost always have seeds that are dispersed by the
wind?

Dispersal of seeds by animals

Sometimes after a walk through an area of long grass you find fruits called
burrs stuck to your clothing. They are a good example of another way by
which the seeds of plants are dispersed. See figure 16.8.

Figure 16.8
These fruits will catch on fur and
clothing.
a Cleavers, *Galium aparine*.
b Burdock, *Arctium minus*.

a   b

In all cases shown the fruit is most likely to fall to the ground some way away from the parent plant.

> **6** Explain how you think ''burrs'' disperse the seeds of plants.

There is another way in which the seeds of plants are dispersed by animals. One example is shown in figure 16.9.

> **7** Explain how you think the seeds of elderberries are dispersed. What other examples of this method of dispersal can you think of?
>
> **8** What are the special features of fruits of plants which have their seeds dispersed in this way?

Figure 16.9
Birds play an important part in the dispersal of some plants. The seeds of the elder, *Sambucus* sp., are inside the berries.

Self-dispersal

Some plants are able to fling their seeds a long way from them, when the dry fruit suddenly breaks open. This happens in all plants which have pods, and in the geraniums. There are also more spectacular examples of plants which have these "explosive" fruits, like the squirting cucumber and the balsam. (See figure 16.10.)

a   b

Figure 16.10
These seeds are flung out of the fruit by a sudden explosive action as it dries.
a Fruit of laburnum, *Laburnum anagyroides*, splitting to disperse seeds.
b Squirting cucumber, *Ecballium elaterium*. You can see where the black seeds were shot out backwards.

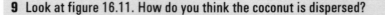

> **9** Look at figure 16.11. How do you think the coconut is dispersed?

Figure 16.11
Coconut palms grow above the high tide line along the tropical beaches. The whole coconut fruit is buoyant and waterproof.

Dispersal of animals

If plants reach suitable habitats passively (by means of water, wind or animals rather than by their own action), what about animals? Some animals

Figure 16.12
Barnacles and mussels spend nearly all their life in one spot, stuck to a rock or pier.

are dispersed in this way. Many animals which live in the sea spend most of their lives in one place, like barnacles and mussels on a rock (figure 16.12), or they don't move about very much, like cockles and lugworms. When the eggs of these animals hatch, the larvae become part of the *plankton* – the floating community in the sea. The larvae may drift for three weeks or more and travel long distances in this time. Some sea snail larvae can even cross the Atlantic from the African coast to the Caribbean (see figure 16.13). Some of these planktonic larvae may reach a suitable habitat where they can live as adults; they will be away from their parents and so will not compete with them.

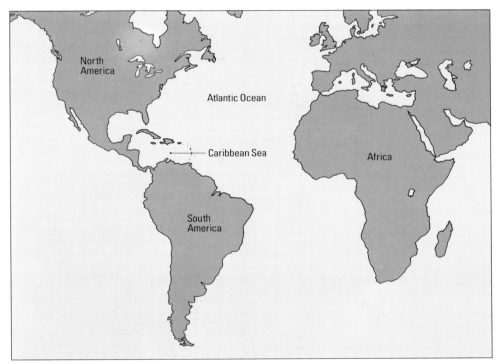

Figure 16.13
Some sea snails that live on the African coast have larvae that do not *metamorphose* (change form) into crawling snails for many months. In this time they may be taken by ocean currents across the Atlantic to the Caribbean.

Although the dispersal of the larvae of animals like barnacles (figure 16.14) is passive, they are not entirely at the mercy of the tides. When they are old enough they drop to the sea floor or onto the shore. At this stage they have some limited powers of movement; and they can distinguish between suitable and unsuitable places to settle although they don't make conscious decisions about it!

INTERPRET

10 What might be the features of a "suitable" place for a barnacle to settle?

How do animals find a suitable habitat?

This is often a surprisingly difficult question to answer. We have to assume that each species has a particular behaviour that means it ends up in a suitable habitat. It is easier to work out what is happening if we study an animal with a fairly simple behaviour. When the barnacle larvae settle, they very often do

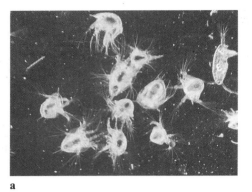

a   b

Figure 16.14
Barnacle larvae. The older larvae, on the right, are the ones which settle on rocks where the adult will live.

so on a rock where there are barnacles already, or where there were barnacles which had died and fallen off the rock. It is thought that chemicals are released from living barnacles or from the shells of dead ones which barnacle larvae can somehow detect.

11 Design an experiment to investigate if this is so. Assume that the larvae use a sense of "taste" (chemosense) to detect extremely low concentrations of chemicals in the water around them. Assume also that you have a supply of adult barnacles and their larvae.

Sometimes it is the adults which select the habitat that will be suitable for the larvae. In the examples which follow, it is the adults, rather than the larvae, that are very mobile and can travel long distances.

12 In the examples shown in figures 16.15 and 16.16, what part do the adults have in selecting the habitat of the larvae?

Figure 16.15
Blowflies, *Calliphora* sp., lay their eggs on an animal's corpse. The larvae or maggots will eat the decaying flesh.

Figure 16.16
The caterpillars of the small tortoiseshell butterfly, *Aglais urticae*, eat stinging nettles.

Worksheet **B**16C gives you a chance to investigate for yourself how animals find suitable habitats.

More about dispersal

Woodworm is a common pest of timber and furniture in houses. It is a small beetle, *Anobium punctatum*, whose larva spends up to 3 years eating and tunnelling through the wood before it finally emerges as a beetle. (See figure 15.7(**ii**) and (**a**), pages 182–3.)

---

13 How do you think the beetles find the underfloor timbers of a new house?

Look up where New Zealand is in an atlas. When the Maoris arrived in New Zealand about six hundred years ago they found an earlier race of settlers whom they displaced. They also found some bats. There were no other mammals.

---

14 What does this tell you about the powers of dispersal of bats, and of other mammals? What does it tell you about the dispersal powers of human beings?

15 Wind-blown fruits of plants like dandelions could probably reach just about all habitats in Britain. But you do not find dandelions everywhere. Suggest reasons why not.

Figure 16.17 is a photograph of sea plantain growing on the central reservation of a busy dual carriageway in north-east London. This plant is normally restricted to the sea coast, since it needs higher concentrations of salts than many other plants.

---

16 How do you think it could have reached this habitat in London, and how do you think it can survive away from the coast?

B16.3 Organisms in patches

Next time you walk across the grass in a lawn or in the park, look closely at the plants growing there. You will see grass of course, although there are probably several different species of it. But you will also find other kinds of plants. The different plants will be more obvious if they are flowering, but looking at the leaves is enough for you to see that not all lawn plants are grass. If you study the area more carefully still, you will find that the different plants are not spread evenly across the lawn. They grow in patches, and the patches themselves may all come in one part of the lawn. To find out more exactly where the plants are growing you have to carry out a *survey* of the area, counting the plants and mapping where they are very carefully.

What you will have discovered, and perhaps measured, is the *distribution* of the different plant species in the area. Look at figure 16.18b, a map showing the distribution of the common garden snail in Europe.

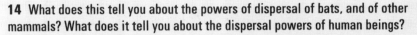

Figure 16.17
Sea plantain, *Plantago maritima*, growing by a busy road in north-east London. The verges and the central reservation here are covered by this plant.

17 Compare the European distribution map with figure 16.18c which shows the distribution of the same snail in Britain.

a   b   c

Figure 16.18
a The common garden snail, *Helix aspersa*. **b** A map showing the distribution of the garden snail in Europe. **c** A map showing the distribution of the garden snail in Britain.

Although it seems to be found throughout the southern half of Britain, you can see that there are areas where the snail is missing. In some other places, shown in mauve, it is scarce. So the distribution of the snail is patchy, just like the distribution of the plants in a lawn. This is true of the distribution of almost every animal or plant that is growing in a natural community.

18 Look at a map of Britain in an atlas. By looking at the towns, cities and villages, what would you say about the distribution of people?

19 In the community where you live, are people distributed evenly or in patches? Try to give an explanation for their distribution.

What causes this patchy distribution of organisms? To put the question a different way – if an organism lives in a particular habitat, why is it not found all over the habitat, all the time?

This is a hard question to answer. We will start with a simpler model. Consider your school at this moment. Assume that it is a habitat. There are many people who spend every working day in the school. Where are all these people now?

20 Make a list of the different sorts of people there are in the school: teachers, cleaners, pupils and so on.

21 Now write down, alongside each sort of person on your list, the places where you might find them at the moment.

22 Try to write down a general rule that seems to determine where people in the school are.

You may have decided that the distribution of the people in the school is somehow related to the jobs that they do.

Is it possible to find out similar things about an organism like a plant?

Figure 16.19
You do not see ferns growing in towns unless you look in a damp place.

---

23 Whereabouts in a woodland ecosystem would you expect to find the ferns that live there?

It is sometimes easier to see the patchy distribution of plants than animals. This is because plants do not move from where they are growing. For instance, in a city possibly the only place you would find a fern growing wild would be a drain. (See figure 16.19.)

---

24 What explanation would you suggest for the fern's distribution?

Figure 16.20
It is not surprising that sheep gather round food supplied for them during harsh winter weather.

Figure 16.21
Sand dune snails, *Theba pisana*, clustered on vegetation above the soil surface.

---

25 You can see what has caused the patchy distribution of the sheep in figure 16.20, but it is not easy to work out why the snails are clustered as in figure 16.21. Have you any ideas?

26 Figures 16.22 to 16.25 illustrate some more examples of patchy distribution. In each case, try to suggest a reason for it. (There is a clue in each photograph or caption and in figure 16.26.)

Figure 16.22
You can see rush, *Juncus* sp., growing here and there in this field. Conditions for a particular organism may only be suitable in one part of a habitat. This may be a good tip if you ever go camping!

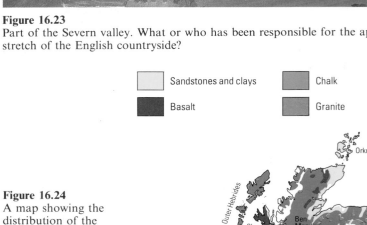

Figure 16.23
Part of the Severn valley. What or who has been responsible for the appearance of this stretch of the English countryside?

Sandstones and clays	Chalk	Metamorphic
Basalt	Granite	Limestone

Figure 16.24
A map showing the distribution of the large Roman snail in Britain.

Figure 16.25
Animals require water. Wildebeeste, warthogs and zebra drinking at a waterhole in the Mzuki Game Reserve, Natal.

Figure 16.26
A map of the different rock types in Britain.

27 Finally, write down as many reasons as you can for the patchy distribution of people. You will be able to think of some of these yourself. Use an atlas to try and work out why there are centres of population in different parts of Britain and why there are some areas where no one lives at all.

It is not too hard to make studies of the distribution of organisms yourself. Worksheet **B**16D suggests some of the ways in which you could carry out your investigations.

When a particular organism colonizes a habitat its numbers will usually increase. This is a result of reproduction (see Chapter **B**19). When there are a number of organisms of one species in a habitat we refer to them as a *population*. The remainder of this chapter will look at some of the factors that are involved in controlling the growth of populations.

Figure 16.27
Two females and four males of the guppy, *Lebistes* sp., a popular aquarium fish.

B16.4   Populations

A very popular fish to keep in a tropical aquarium is the guppy (figure 16.27). It is a great favourite with fishkeepers because it is very easy to look after and breeds easily in the aquarium.

Guppies are often chosen for population studies as they can be used to show how populations increase and decrease according to the conditions of life.

In one investigation a single pair of guppies was introduced into an aquarium; at the same time 25 pairs of the fish were introduced into a second, identical aquarium. Every environmental factor in the two aquaria was controlled so that the only difference between them was the number of fish in them to start with.

28 Suggest two environmental factors that would have to be controlled in this investigation, and explain why this must be.

After a year both aquaria were found to contain almost the same number of fish (see figure 16.28).

Figure 16.28
Population changes in guppies kept in aquaria
a starting with one pair
b starting with twenty-five pairs.

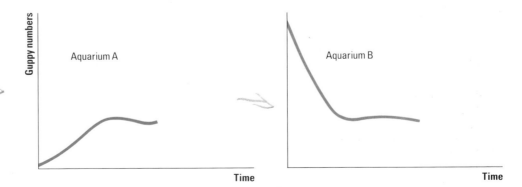

29 Explain what you think has happened in each aquarium to produce this result.

In general terms we can say that the guppies have carried out some kind of population control. Many animals and plants do this and it helps to explain fluctuations in their numbers that we can't otherwise explain very easily.

There are several answers. If the population size is small and the habitat has enough space, food and other requirements for the organisms, then the population will increase. More females will reproduce, and each one may produce more eggs and young.

Figure 16.29
A snowy owl.

30 As the numbers increase what happens to the amount of food and other requirements available for each organism?

31 What effect does this have on reproduction?

Every so often, more snowy owls than usual are seen in Scotland. (See figure 16.29.) These are predatory birds of the Arctic that feed on lemmings (see chapter **B**13).

32 How do you think the number of lemmings will relate to the numbers of the snowy owl seen?

Some populations of organisms stay at a fairly constant level – the *birth rate* equals the *death rate*. This seems to happen in human populations in places where there are no medical facilities. The underlying control mechanism is not fully understood. The size of the populations of some organisms is often anything but constant. If your cat has ever brought fleas into your house you will know just how the population seems to change from no fleas to hundreds for a week or two and then back to no fleas again.

Predators can be useful, or sometimes essential, in controlling population size. There were about 4000 deer (figure 16.31) on the Kaibab Plateau in Arizona, USA, at the beginning of this century. Large numbers of the deer's main predators were removed by hunters between 1907 and 1939 (figure 16.30). The effect on the deer population is shown in figure 16.32.

1907–1917	600 mountain lions removed
1918–1923	74 mountain lions removed
1924–1939	142 mountain lions removed
1907–1923	3000 coyotes removed
1923–1939	4388 coyotes removed
1907–1923	11 wolves removed
by 1939	Wolf extinct in the area

Figure 16.30

a

b

c

d

Figure 16.31
a Deer, *Odocoileus* sp. **b** Puma, *Felis concolor*. **c** Coyote, *Canis latrans*.
d Wolf, *Canis lupus*.

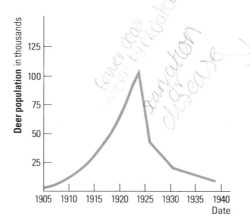

Figure 16.32
A graph showing the effect, on numbers
of deer, of the removal of their predators
on the Kaibab Plateau, Arizona. The
predators were removed between 1907
and 1939.

33 What was the result of the large increase in deer numbers when the predators were removed?

34 Why did the deer then begin to die?

Sometimes the numbers of a predator and its prey show cycles that seem to
be related. Records from the Hudson Bay Company in Canada collected over
about 90 years showed several cycles in the numbers of the snowshoe hare
and its predator the lynx (figure 16.33).

a   b

Figure 16.33
a Snowshoe hare, *Lepus americanus*. **b** Lynx, *Lynx* sp.

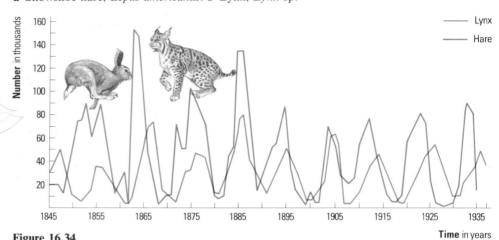

Figure 16.34
The changing numbers of snowshoe hare and lynx in Canada over about 90 years.

If you look carefully at figure 16.34 you can see that the numbers of snowshoe hare went up when the numbers of lynx had gone down. When there were large numbers of hare, the numbers of lynx increased and this was usually followed by a decrease in the number of hares.

35 Explain why the numbers of lynx increased when there were large numbers of hares.

36 When the hare population fell, the size of the lynx population also fell. Explain this observation.

37 House spiders are often found in undisturbed corners of our houses. What do they eat?

38 Why is it not a good idea to kill these spiders or remove them?

Chapter B17

Farms, factories and the environment

B17.1 Necessary damage?

Think about how you live. You may live in a house or flat; you probably travel along roads or railways, visit shops and spend a lot of time in school. What about someone your age living in your area 5000 years ago? Or 2000 years ago? The modern shops and houses, schools and roads have replaced the natural habitats that earlier people knew. Building on land will always destroy whatever habitat was there before. As soon as people began to live in large groups and stay in one place most of the time, they began to change their local environment rapidly and dramatically.

The removal of a whole forest to make paper and the massive oil pollution from a shipwrecked tanker are obvious examples of damage that people have caused to habitats. It is not always easy to see where to draw the line between **effect** on a habitat and **damage**.

We will now look at some of the ways in which necessary activities of humans have had an effect on the environment.

B17.2 Monoculture

If you think of a field of wheat, you probably imagine something like the photograph in figure 17.1.

The farmer planted only one kind of seed – wheat – in this field and so there is only one kind of crop there. This is called *monoculture*, and most crops are grown like this.

---

1 Suggest two reasons why a farmer would prefer to grow single crops in every field rather than mixed crops.

Compare the vast field in figure 17.1 with the many small ones in figure 16.23 (page 202).

---

2 What is missing from the huge fields that would encourage the survival of wildlife?

Figure 17.1
A field of ripe wheat. Farmers may prefer monocultures, but such farming methods do not encourage the survival of many forms of wildlife.

3 Give two reasons why farmers seem to prefer a few big fields to many small ones.

Figure 17.2
Caterpillars of white butterflies (*Pieris brassicae*) are a common pest of cabbage and similar crops in Britain.

B17.3   Problems with pests

In spite of the advantage of monocultures for farmers, they have some drawbacks. For example a single kind of crop grown on a large scale will attract *pests*. These feed on the crop or damage it in some way and quickly destroy it. Attacks by pests are less severe if the crops are grown in small fields, with different crops in neighbouring fields. The effects of a pest are also slower to appear if the individual plants in the crop are spaced out, although spacing plants is more suitable for some crops like cabbage, than for others such as wheat. (See figures 17.1 and 17.2.)

4 Explain why growing crops in small fields and spacing out the plants will reduce the effects of pests.

Figure 17.3
These slugs (*Agrolimax reticulatus*) will quickly ruin the cabbage as an edible plant.

The hedgerows surrounding small fields support a community of organisms; some of them, like predatory insects, may be beneficial to the farmer. If an insect pest starts to increase on a crop, then the insect predators and birds may move from the hedges into the field and eat the pest. This can quickly reduce its numbers.

5 Many farmers now leave a corner of a field uncultivated. What do they hope to gain by doing this?

Pesticides

A pest damages something that we want for ourselves. We may sow lettuce seeds in the garden. If slugs start to attack the seedlings we will want to find a way to remove the slugs. (See figure 17.3.) One way is to destroy them with a poison. A poison that kills a pest is called a *pesticide*.

Ever since farming began, farmers have had to watch their crops being eaten or damaged by pests. Usually the loss is bearable, but once in a while a pest outbreak is so serious that an entire crop may be lost.

Locusts (figure 17.4) are a well known example of insects which are pests, but there are plenty of other kinds of pests that can cause disastrous losses to farm produce.

Weeds are plants which are pests – they *compete* with crops and cause lower yields at harvest time. You can see an example in figure 23.14, page 305.

Figure 17.4
Locusts will strip a field bare before they leave.

6 Explain why weeds reduce the yield of a crop.

Figure 17.5
These Ethiopians are among the many
people who still suffer from famine.

Now, with the world human population approaching 4 000 000 000, food production is on a massive scale. But still it is not able to keep up with what is needed. Each year, pests destroy an enormous amount of food intended for people, and there is no doubt that this loss must be reduced as much as possible.

7 Pests are not the only things that prevent us from providing enough food for people to eat. Give two other reasons why some people (see figure 17.5) are still short of food the whole time.

Modern pesticides are very efficient at killing pests. However they have caused such serious ecological problems in the past, that a few farmers try to manage without using them at all.

We will now consider some of the problems.

Friend or foe, you'll have to go

Pesticides, especially the first ones to be made in the 1940s and 1950s, killed a large number of *different* animals or plants. For example, the famous insecticide, DDT, did not just kill field crop pests; it killed *all* insects. This seemed like good news for the farmers because suddenly their harvests and their profits went up.

8 Why do the farmers' harvests increase when the pests are killed?

There are at least three good reasons why killing other organisms besides the pests is harmful:

A Living organisms should not be killed without good reason. Many people have great pleasure from observing wildlife – if a pesticide spray to kill greenfly also kills all the butterflies, the environment is poorer because of this loss.

B A large number of different insects are important pollinators. Honeybees are one well known example. Many insecticides have instructions warning the farmer not to spray the crops when bees are flying (figure 17.6).

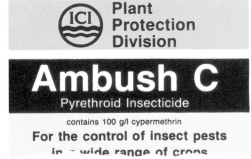

Figure 17.6
Many pesticide manufacturers warn farmers and gardeners not to spray their crops while insect pollinators are flying.

Figure 17.7
Hover fly larvae eat aphids which suck
the sap out of plants.

Figure 17.8
Each time a minnow ate a plankton
organism it took a tiny dose of DDT.
The dose stayed in the minnow's body
and built up as the minnow ate more.
A pickerel fish received however much
DDT had built up in a minnow's body,
each time it ate a minnow.
Herons ate minnows and small pickerel,
as well as other fish. Once again DDT
built up in their bodies as they received a
dose from each fish eaten. This dose was
even larger for the osprey and
cormorant, because they eat still
bigger fish.
The level of DDT in the cormorant was
500 000 times higher than the level of
DDT in the sea water.
(The numbers give the percentage
concentration of DDT.)

9 What will be the effect
   a on wild flower populations and
   b on the yield of some crop plants
if pollinating insects are accidentally killed by insecticides?

C Many insects are predators of certain insect pests (figure 17.7). If the
farmer's insecticide kills them as well as the pests, then later on, if the pests
return, there may be too few of their predators left to control their numbers.

Nowadays manufacturers can make pesticides that only harm one
particular pest – they are called *specific pesticides*.

A persistent nuisance

Another serious problem with pesticides concerns **how long** they last once
they are sprayed on to a crop. Some decompose quickly into harmless
chemicals once they reach the soil, or are absorbed by a plant. Once this has
happened they no longer kill organisms. But many of the first effective
pesticides that were made (such as DDT, aldrin and dieldrin) last for a very
long time in the environment. They retain their poisonous properties and we
call them *persistent pesticides*. When they were used they entered food webs
and became so concentrated in the tissues of the top consumers that these
animals were poisoned; their behaviour changed, their ability to reproduce
was lessened, and many of them died. Figure 17.8 shows how this happened.

Many persistent pesticides accumulate in stored fat in the body of animals.
Scientists have analysed the body fat of seals and penguins in Antarctica and
have found pesticides in the tissue. The nearest agricultural land to Antarctica
is around 1000 km away. There are no traces of pesticides in the fat of seal
carcasses that have remained frozen since they were killed during the Scott
expeditions to the Antarctic early this century.

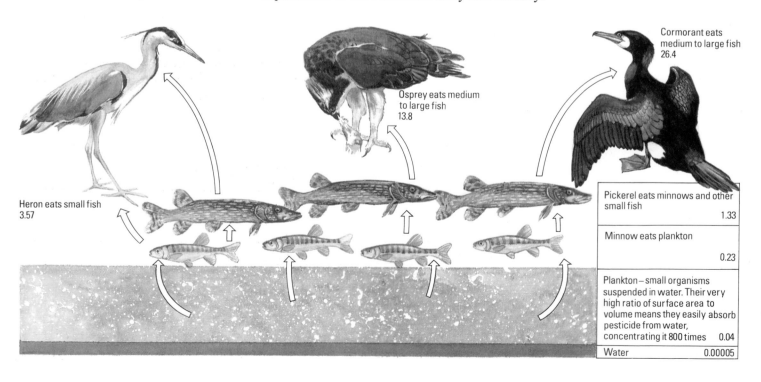

Cormorant eats
medium to large fish
26.4

Osprey eats medium
to large fish
13.8

Heron eats small fish
3.57

Pickerel eats minnows and other
small fish
1.33

Minnow eats plankton
0.23

Plankton – small organisms
suspended in water. Their very
high ratio of surface area to
volume means they easily absorb
pesticide from water,
concentrating it 800 times   0.04

Water   0.00005

10 Explain how the pesticides have now reached the seals and penguins.

Heads I win, tails you lose

Many pests, especially insects, have become *resistant* to pesticides (see Chapter **B**23). When a crop is sprayed with a pesticide most of the pests die. Often, though, just a few will survive. This is because they have a *natural resistance* to the poison. These survivors reproduce and gradually the size of the pest population increases once again. This time, however, all of the members of the population are resistant to the pesticide.

11 Explain why **all** of the pests are now resistant.

The farmer can then either increase the amount of pesticide used, or switch to another one. After a time the same thing happens with the new pesticide. Some insect pests are now resistant to many different pesticides and there is obviously a limit to how many new ones can be found. Figure 17.9 shows how many species of insects had become resistant to DDT and two other sorts of insecticides by 1967. The list is now much longer.

The insects listed in figure 17.9 include those that damage crops and those that spread diseases in humans, mostly by sucking blood.

	DDT	Dieldrin	Organo-phosphorus poison
Flies	44	68	14
Butterflies and moths	14	14	6
Bugs	10	15	14
Beetles	5	19	1

Figure 17.9

The damage that persistent pesticides can do to the environment caused many of them to be banned from use in the EEC, USA and other parts of the world. In some tropical countries where crop losses due to pests can be very serious, there are no such bans.

12 What properties do you think an ideal pesticide should have?

B17.4   Biological control

One alternative to using chemicals, which has been very successful in certain cases, is to use a *predator* or *parasite* to control the pest. This method is called *biological control*. One famous example was the control of the prickly pear cactus in Australia. This cactus was introduced from Argentina into a garden in Australia in 1840. Within a few decades it had spread so rapidly that the cactus covered millions of hectares, making the land useless for farming. The answer to this problem was a moth! In Argentina, the caterpillars (larvae) of the moth eat the prickly pear – so it is called the cactus moth. This moth was brought to Australia and was released in the areas affected by the prickly pear. Figures 17.10 and 17.11 show how successful this was.

Figure 17.10
Prickly pear, *Opuntia*, made this area in Australia useless for farming.

Figure 17.11
The same area of Australia, three years after an Argentinian moth, *Cactoblastis*, was introduced. Its caterpillar had done wonders in reducing the cactus.

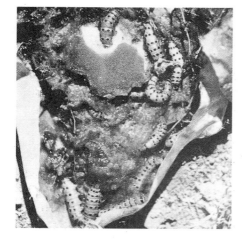

Figure 17.12
Caterpillars of the Argentinian moth, *Cactoblastis*, that finally controlled the prickly pear cactus in Australia.

13 What do you think will happen to the size of the moth population
a as it starts to eat the huge cactus population and
b as the numbers of prickly pear decrease?

A word of warning

Biological control has been very successful in some cases; at other times it has gone badly wrong. When you introduce the control organism, you are bringing an organism that was not already present into the food web of the environment where the crop is growing. In some cases you are introducing an organism from another country. It is hard to know what all its effects may be.

Here is an example that was little short of disaster. There were 41 species of tree snail in the islands of Hawaii in the Pacific Ocean (figure 17.13). They were found nowhere else in the world, and some were rare. Another kind of snail somehow became established in Hawaii. It was the African land snail, which is an agricultural pest, as well as being the giant of the snail world (figure 17.14). It began to cause havoc to the crops in Hawaii. There is another species of snail, found in Florida (figure 17.15), which is a predator rather than a herbivore, and it eats other snails. It was decided to try to use this snail to control the numbers of the African snail pest. This turned out to be a dreadful and irreversible mistake. The Florida snail attacked the Hawaiian tree snails too, and it helped to exterminate 22 of the species. Since these species were found nowhere else in the world, they are now extinct. Meanwhile, the Florida snail is an extra threat to the tree snails that are left.

Figure 17.13
Achatinella fulgens, one of the 21 remaining species of Hawaiian tree snail, *Achatinella*.

Figure 17.14
The giant African land snail, *Achatina*, an agricultural pest that has managed to spread to many parts of the tropics.

Figure 17.15
The predatory snail from Florida, *Euglandina rosea*, helped to wipe out half of the Hawaiian species of tree snail, instead of controlling the African land snail.

APPLY   PLAN

14 Imagine you are the biologist responsible for giving permission for the introduction of a predator to your country to control a pest. What questions about the predator would you want satisfactory answers to before you gave the go-ahead?

B17.5   Fertilizers

You saw in Chapter **B**15 that plants require mineral ions as raw materials, and that because crops are removed each year from farmland, these minerals have to be put back into the soil as fertilizer. This is essential if the land is to produce as much food as possible. However, adding fertilizers to farmland can cause problems. Not all the fertilizer meant for the crops stays in the soil. When it rains, some may be washed down slopes (in run-off water), and more may sink through the soil and drain away. All this water containing dissolved fertilizer eventually reaches streams or rivers. In many places streams and rivers flow into lakes. Any dissolved mineral salts in the water will collect in the lake. The nitrate in run-off water is a particular problem because there is so much of it and its effects are so rapid. See also Chapter **C**16 in the Chemistry book.

Fertilizers do not only increase the growth of crop plants. If run-off water that contains a lot of nitrates accumulates in a lake or pond (figure 17.16) the water may become very cloudy and green (see figure 17.17). We call lakes and ponds like this *eutrophic*.

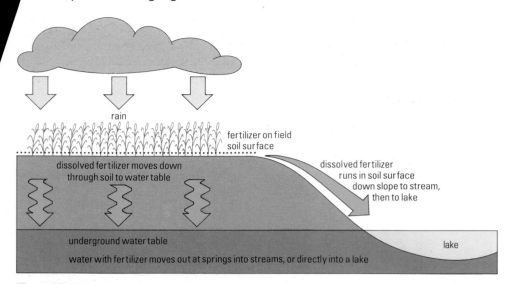

Figure 17.16
How nitrate fertilizer (as well as other fertilizers) finds its way from fields to rivers and lakes.

Figure 17.17
Single-celled algae (protists) reproduce rapidly in a lake into which agricultural fertilizers drain, and cause the water to look like a green pea soup.

15 **Explain why this change in the appearance of the water happens.**

Other water plants may also grow so much that streams become blocked. When the population of plants has increased in this way, there is an additional problem. If there are more living plants, there will soon be more dead material in the rivers as the old ones die. Dead plants are decomposed by bacteria which use up oxygen. If more plants grow, more plants die; if more plants die, more oxygen is used up by bacteria. Under these conditions there is often a shortage of oxygen for the large fish in the water. These fish, and other animals, may then either die or migrate. (See figure 17.18.) Waters that once held trout (figure 17.19) may now only have enough oxygen for less demanding fish such as roach or carp. If the oxygen levels fall too low even these fish may disappear.

Figure 17.18
These insects are the young, called nymphs, of mayflies, *Ecodyonurus torrentis*. They need more oxygen in the water than other insects, and die if the oxygen level drops.

Figure 17.19
The brown trout, *Salmo trutta salmo*, is a fish of fast-running rivers, and lakes which are low in mineral salts, normally found in hilly or mountainous districts. This fish dies if the oxygen level falls.

Eutrophication is a natural process that all lakes go through, but it usually takes thousands of years. When fertilizers find their way into a lake and cause artificial eutrophication, the process may only take a few years.

A
APPLY

16 Could any effects of eutrophication be put to good use?

Clearing for agriculture

Tropical forests are being cleared to provide land for farming (figure 17.20).
An area the size of Britain is cleared each year, or 21.6 hectares every minute;
it has been estimated that the tropical rain forests can only last for another 20
to 50 years at this rate of destruction. (See figures 17.22 and 17.21.)

Figure 17.20
A burned tropical hillside in Guyana, South America.

Figure 17.21
The soils under tropical rain forests are often shallow and
unsuitable for agriculture.

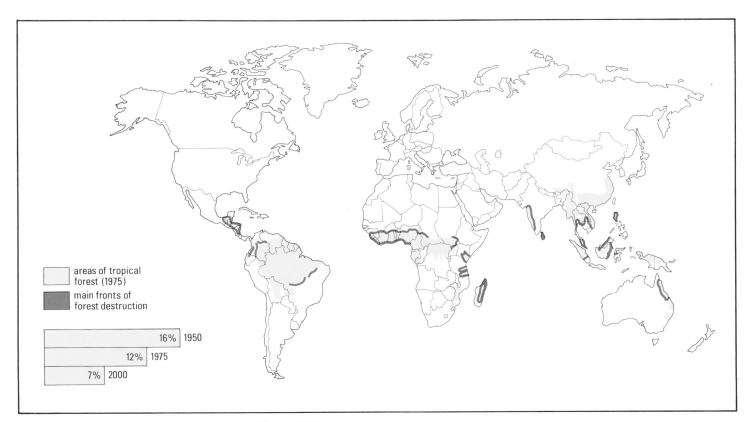

areas of tropical
forest (1975)

main fronts of
forest destruction

16% 1950
12% 1975
7% 2000

Figure 17.22
This map shows the tropical rain forests of the world and where most of the destruction
is happening.

You should not forget that humans interact with their environment in many ways, not just as farmers. In countries where there is little technology and the people are very poor, they are forced to interact very closely with it. The environment can make their survival very difficult. They may find it hard to grow enough food and very hard to keep warm and healthy. They cannot clear the forests without machinery; they cannot bring water up from deep under the ground without pumps. In some developing countries even something basic like firewood is hard to find; yet it is needed for heating at night. People also need to burn about 9 kg of wood in order to cook 1 kg of food.

If wood is not available there are other materials that can be used, and many tribes that keep cattle dry the dung and then burn it on their fires. It is possible to use dung in another way apart from drying and burning it. It can be allowed to decompose anaerobically.

---

17 What does ''anaerobically'' mean?

With a little simple technology, gas generators can be built that will allow the faeces to decompose and will collect the methane gas that is produced. Faeces of any animals, including humans, can be used.

Worksheet **B**17A gives you the opportunity to design such a piece of apparatus yourself.

B17.6   Industry and estuaries

An estuary is a place where a river meets the sea. Estuaries have two special habitats, *mud flats* at lower tide levels and *saltmarshes* further up the shore (figure 17.23). In each habitat are organisms that are adapted to estuarine conditions such as changing salinity (salt content of the water) and the presence of mud. In tropical parts of the world the mud flats are usually covered by mangrove forests (figure 17.24).

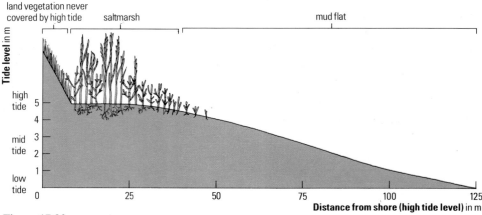

Figure 17.23
A cross-section through a saltmarsh and a mud flat showing the tidal heights.

Figure 17.24
Mud flats in the tropics are usually covered with dense mangrove forest. This one is in Grand Anse in the Seychelles.

Figure 17.25
The mud snail *Hydrobia* lives on tidal mud flats in enormous populations.

Figure 17.26
Knot, *Calidris canutus*, seen here, will eat *Hydrobia* during low tide. So will dunlin and shelduck.

Small invertebrate animals like bristle worms (which are segmented like earthworms) and the snail *Hydrobia* exist on the mud flats in huge numbers. (See figure 17.25.) Perhaps there are as many as 50 000 of these animals in every square metre, while the mud flats may cover several square kilometres. During high tide when the mud flats are covered by water, fish such as the goby and young flounder move up and feed on *Hydrobia*.

When the tide ebbs, birds come and eat *Hydrobia*. Estuaries are very important places for fish and birds because of the huge supplies of food they provide. (See figure 17.26.)

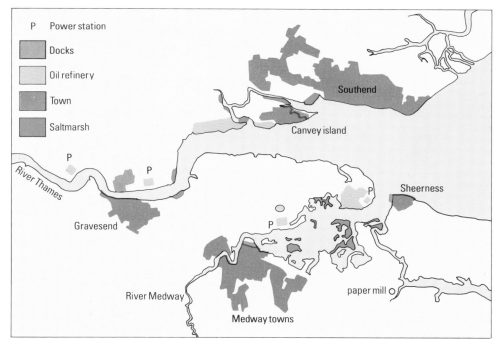

Figure 17.28
A map of the Thames and Medway estuaries showing the remains of the saltmarshes. Much of the land in this area was saltmarsh originally but was made into farm land after the building of sea defences. Later industries found this land very suitable.

Figure 17.27
Oil refineries are often built on estuaries.

In Europe, most large estuaries have been industrialized, especially if there is a port in the estuary.

18 Industries that rely on raw materials being delivered in large quantities, such as oil refineries, are often found on the shores of estuaries. (See figures 17.27 and 17.28.) Why is this?

19 Large power stations (figure 17.29) are also often sited in estuaries. Why do you think this is?

Figure 17.29
Tilbury power station on the Thames estuary.

Whenever an industrial plant has been built on an estuary, part of the habitat has been destroyed. Yet we all depend on industry in many ways. Clearly a compromise solution has to be found between the needs of industry and the requirements of wildlife.

20 Find a map showing an estuary which has industrial development along its shore. Southampton Water, which has an oil refinery on its west bank, is an example. Look at the features of the local environment that are shown on the map and draw up two lists. One should give the reasons why the industry has to be developed on the estuary rather than anywhere else; the other should list the features of the environment which you think are destroyed or damaged by the industry.

See also Chapter **C**13 in your Chemistry book.

B17.7   Acid rain

All rain is "acid rain" because carbon dioxide in the atmosphere dissolves in the rain. (See also Chapter **C**10 in the Chemistry book.) However, as rain falls through an atmosphere that is polluted with certain gases it becomes much more acidic. Pure rain water has a pH of around 5.6. *Acid rain* has a pH lower than this, perhaps even as low as 2.0. The two gases which are the usual culprits are:

sulphur dioxide (SO_2) which comes from the burning of coal and oil in power stations and smelters;

nitrogen oxides which come from the exhaust of internal combustion engines such as cars and lorries.

When they dissolve in rain these two gases produce sulphuric acid and nitric acid. Nitric acid is also made during thunderstorms. (See Chapter **B**15.)

21 Explain how nitric acid is made during thunderstorms.

The ratio of the two acids in rain water varies but in Britain it is commonly

nitric acid : sulphuric acid
    30   :   70

Some habitats onto which the acid rain falls are more sensitive than others. On chalky and limestone soils the rain will be neutralized. A lake that is on granite or basalt rock cannot neutralize the acids and the pH of the water in the lake might drop as low as 4.6.

22 How do lakes on limestone neutralize the acid rain?

The effects of acid rain

As the acid rain drains through the soil it can cause minerals such as compounds of calcium and iron to drain away with it. Also certain other minerals such as compounds of aluminium, zinc and manganese are put into solution. (See also the Chemistry Worksheet **C**15D.) Normally there are very small amounts of these metals in the soil water. After acid rain there is a marked increase. Aluminium damages the gills of fish, often fatally, and the high concentrations of the other ions damage the roots of plants.

The leaves of trees are also damaged by acid rain. Although sulphur dioxide on its own has only a small effect on the leaves, a **mixture** of sulphur dioxide and nitrogen dioxide is highly toxic. This may cause the leaves of the trees to die, which will lead to the death of the whole tree. However, scientists are still investigating the ways in which acid rain may cause the death of trees.

23 Use an atlas to try to pinpoint where in Great Britain you think the gases which cause the acid rain might come from.

24 How could acid rain from other parts of Europe be the cause of environmental damage in Scandinavia?

Worksheet **B**17B has a number of investigations into the effects of acid rain.

Chapter B18   To destroy or to conserve?

B18.1   Destruction or conservation?

It is an unfortunate fact that some animal and plant species have completely disappeared, or become *extinct*, because of humans. In Britain this happened long ago to the bear and the wolf. They were dangerous and sometimes ate farm animals. Also people enjoyed hunting them. They were driven from their habitats and killed on sight. So, gradually, their numbers dwindled. They can still be found, however, in other parts of Europe. But whereas they used to be distributed over large areas, they are now only found in very few places, chiefly in the northern forests. (See figures 18.1, 18.2 and 18.3.)

Figure 18.1
The European brown bear, *Ursus arctos*.

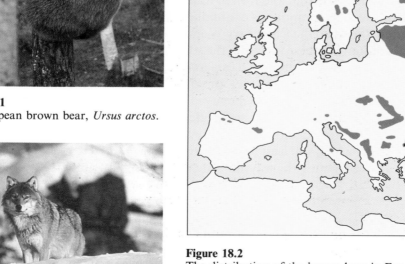

Figure 18.2
The distribution of the brown bear in Europe in the late twentieth century.

Figure 18.3
The wolf, *Canis lupus*. This animal used to be found from the Mediterranean coast in the south to the northern tundra regions.

Although there are many other similar examples of animals and plants disappearing because they were hunted or collected, by far the greatest threat to organisms now is the destruction of habitats. After all, if wolves are hunted to extinction in a forest, the other organisms still remain.

There are many reasons for the destruction of habitats, and a large number of examples. In Britain, nearly all the original oak forest that covered the land has gone and has been replaced by farmland (see figure 18.4) or moorland or it has been built on. This change was gradual, however, and farming methods often allowed some of the wildlife to remain. This is still true of farming in other parts of the world, especially where primitive farming methods have been successfully used for a very long time.

Figure 18.4
Woodland in Britain. There is plenty of evidence to show that most, if not all, of Britain was covered by forest. This map shows the proportion of land covered by forest in the whole of Britain excluding Northern Ireland, when the woodland census was carried out between 1979 and 1982.

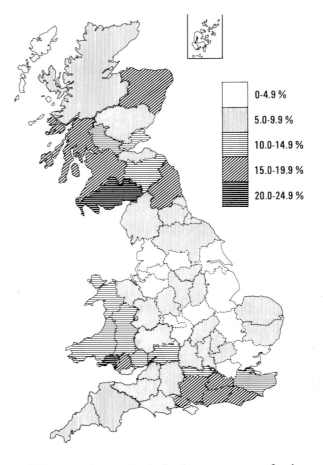

0-4.9 %

5.0-9.9 %

10.0-14.9 %

15.0-19.9 %

20.0-24.9 %

The most important single reason now for large-scale destruction of habitats is the clearing of land for agriculture. Modern machines are very efficient and they make it easy to clear the densest of forests and replace them with crops.

The following examples show some of the other ways in which habitats are lost or damaged.

Figure 18.5
Lazy, thoughtless people who will not take their rubbish to a disposal centre often throw their waste into a pond, even though the journey to the pond may be further than to the disposal centre.

Ponds

2 What could be the results of dumping rubbish in a pond? (Figure 18.5.)

Road construction

In Britain, new roads are mostly built on farmland which is bought through compulsory purchases by the government. Sometimes the road may be planned to pass through a National Park such as Dartmoor, and objections may be raised. A public enquiry may result, after which a decision will be taken whether to go ahead with the building of the road.

Figures 18.6 and 18.7 give you some information about the Trans-Amazonian Highway.

Figure 18.6
The photograph shows the construction of one of the new roads through the Amazon rain forest of Brazil. Once the road is built the forest becomes accessible to people, creating other problems (see later).

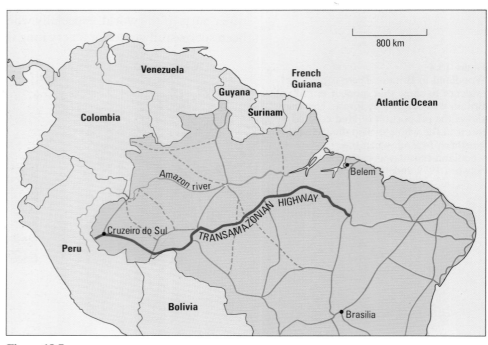

Figure 18.7
A map showing the new highway system through the Amazon region.

Burning of heathland

During the drought in the summer of 1976, fires were a serious problem on the heathlands of southern Britain. Surrey lost 29 per cent of its remaining heaths, one of which was almost completely destroyed. Figures 18.8 and 18.9 give you some idea of this problem.

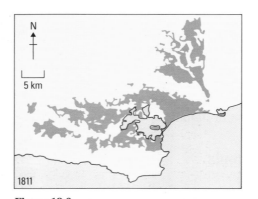 

Figure 18.8
A mature heathland takes at least 20 years to develop in Britain. If a fire starts, almost all the animals and plants may be killed, and some of the organisms will not be able to return there until the heath has had several years to regenerate. In previous centuries a local fire was not so disastrous because the heath might have covered many more square kilometres. As the burned area recovered animals and plants could recolonize it from surrounding unburned heath.

Figure 18.9
These maps show the loss of heathland in Dorset and West Hampshire between 1811 and 1960.

Tourism and leisure

Many people enjoy spending time on holiday away from home. They have earned their relaxation, and often they choose to spend their holiday by the sea or in the mountains. This is not new; the Victorians, for example, enjoyed holidays by the sea. (See figures 18.10 and 18.11.)

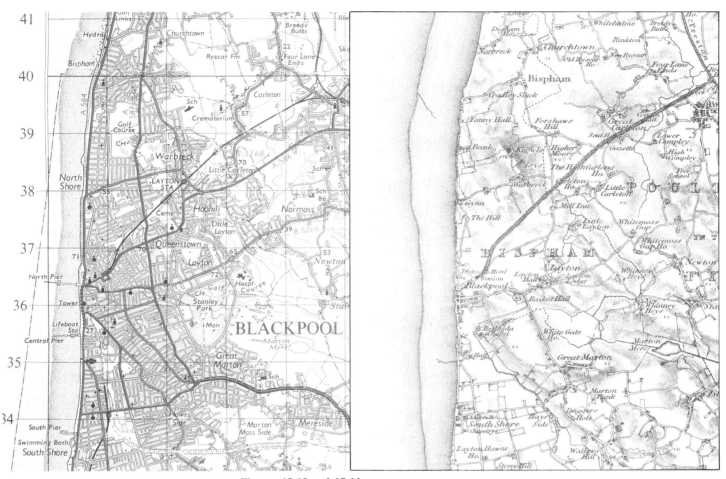

Figures 18.10 and 18.11
Some well-known seaside resorts such as Bournemouth and Blackpool were really villages or small towns until the demand for accommodation by holiday makers resulted in rapid expansion as houses and hotels were built.

Figure 18.12
In present day Benidorm, the olive groves around the village have been built on. Visiting SCUBA divers (often holiday makers from other countries) have collected vividly coloured edible marine organisms and have caused serious declines in the numbers of starfish, sea urchins, lobsters and crabs. Pollution from the summer tourist population has caused problems throughout the Mediterranean.

Figure 18.13
When this photograph of Benidorm in Spain was taken, the only demand on the sea was for fish for the people of the village and for sale in the local markets.

Figure 18.14
This is the female of the sand lizard, *Lacerta agilis*. This animal is rare because it needs a specialized habitat. It used to be found all along the coasts of Lancashire and Cheshire, on sand dunes. Now, less than 200 may survive in the wild.

Now with easy and quick travel, more leisure time and a more affluent society, far more people travel, and they often travel much longer distances. The Spanish coast is a popular destination for British holiday makers – compare the photographs of the Benidorm waterfront now, and in the 1950s (figures 18.12 and 18.13).

You do not need to destroy a habitat deliberately in order to do it considerable damage. Figure 18.14 shows an animal whose habitat has been unintentionally changed.

I INTERPRET   **A** APPLY

3 In what ways might visits from large numbers of apparently harmless people damage a habitat?

4 Can you suggest any solutions to the problems which arise from large numbers of people visiting a particular area? (Figure 18.15 might help.)

Figure 18.15
A typical scene in a popular beach in Devon on a sunny summer day.

B18.2   **Conservation**

Before human activities changed the face of the countryside, most of England was covered in dense forests of deciduous trees; most of Scotland was coniferous woodland. Wooden ships were needed for wars; people needed wood for making fires and building houses. As the human population increased the forests disappeared.

The need for more farmland caused more and more of the land to be cultivated. In spite of this, small areas of woodland remained in many farming areas and a great variety of habitats was found on farms. These habitats supported a large and varied range of wildlife. During the twentieth century there has been pressure on farmers to become more efficient. The result has been that farms have lost habitats and fewer natural habitats survive outside farmland.

5 What is meant by farming becoming "more efficient"?

If we want to preserve wildlife, then the remaining habitats become more important, and *conservation* – which means keeping habitats as they are – becomes essential.

You might think that the best way to conserve a habitat is simply to leave it alone. Sometimes this is true – the life of a rocky shore and that of a climax woodland are examples. In many cases, though, habitats are not at the climax stage, but are at an earlier stage of succession (see Chapter **B**13). They may have been kept at that stage for a long time by a particular sort of farming or use of land. One example of this is Epping Forest on the north-eastern edge of London (figure 18.16).

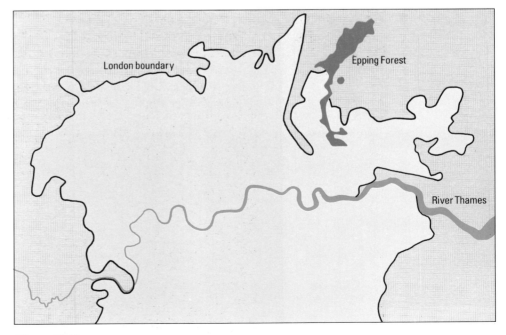

Figure 18.16
Epping Forest is an area of mature oak and beech woodland on the north-eastern edge of London.

Figure 18.17
This area was pollarded six years before the photograph was taken. You can see a dense growth of plants on the ground, now that plenty of light can reach there.

This woodland was used to provide wood for poles, and to harvest it a system called *pollarding* was used. (See figure 18.17.) Trees were cut about 1.8 metres off the ground. Fifteen years later, the re-growth of the tree had produced several branches which made stout poles when cut. After another fifteen years the cycle was repeated. This meant that the forest consisted of a patchwork of areas where pollarding had been done at different times, with each patch or area having a slightly different community. In a patch that had just been pollarded there were no leaves to shade the ground, so many wild flowers and ground plants were able to grow. As the trees grew again, the kinds of ground plants changed, since year by year the shade from the trees increased.

Different animals also occupied the different areas. Places where the trees had recently been pollarded, for example, were colonized by reptiles. Reptiles lie in the sun to warm up, and in these areas the sunlight penetrates to the forest floor.

There was also a herd of fallow deer roaming the forest. There were many rabbits, and commoners (people who had grazing rights to the forest) let their cattle wander freely to forage for themselves. These three grazing animals all helped to keep some areas within the forest free of trees, in some cases for centuries. (See figures 18.18 and 18.19.)

a   b   c

Figure 18.18
These three animals all helped to keep some areas of Epping Forest open and free of trees.
a Fallow deer, *Dama dama*. **b** Rabbits, *Oryctolagus* sp. **c** Cattle.

Any young trees that began to grow were eaten, and open areas with grasses and heather were a feature of the forest. One animal found here was the adder. (Figure 18.20.)

Figure 18.19
Sunshine Plain, an area in Epping Forest kept free of trees by grazing.

Figure 18.20
Heather and the adder are both organisms that must have unshaded habitats.

Pollarding and grazing preserved habitats and wildlife that were not present in the climax woodland. This increased the variety of organisms that lived in Epping Forest. Then, two things began to change the forest. In the first place, in 1878, pollarding stopped. It is obvious that many of the trees you can see today were once pollarded (figure 18.21). But in 100 years of growth they have shaded the forest floor so much that the plants and animals that used to live there have disappeared (figure 18.22).

Figure 18.21
This tree was once pollarded, so the main trunk now divides into several massive branches about 2 m above the ground.

Figure 18.22
This area has not been pollarded since 1878. So much shade is cast by the tree leaves that only a few ground plants will grow.

Secondly, less and less use was made of the forest for grazing. There was more than one reason for this. Myxomatosis infected the rabbit population, causing the numbers to fall sharply. The deer were put into paddocks because they were being disturbed by the increasing number of people using the woods. And fewer commoners turned their cattle out into the woods each year. So in the areas that were once open heath, bushes and then trees grew because there was not enough grazing to keep them clear. In other words, left to itself, all of Epping Forest was turning into woodland and losing its variety.

Figure 18.23
This area was kept open with few trees by grazing animals. It did not take long for these young trees in the middle foreground and centre right of the photograph to grow once the grazing stopped.

Figure 18.24
These young people are conservation volunteers, clearing young trees to restore open spaces.

The message of Epping Forest is relevant to many habitats. If the habitat is to stay as it is it must be *managed*. Conservation management in Epping Forest involves many different activities. Open areas are restored by removing young trees and bushes. Ponds that have filled with branches and leaves (and rubbish) are dredged. (Figures 18.23 and 18.24.) These jobs are often done by

a

b

c

Figure 18.25
Habitats in Britain that need conservation management.
a Water meadow. **b** Sand dunes. **c** Chalk down.

conservation volunteers. Epping Forest is unique because it has a special Act of Parliament to protect it, and a group of people employed as the "Conservators of Epping Forest". Among other activities the Conservators have restarted some experimental pollarding to try to recreate the forest patchwork which used to be there.

The main idea to understand is that conservation is usually an active process. It is necessary to watch the habitat carefully. If succession is taking place then some management is needed. The National Nature Reserves, set up by the government to preserve examples of the different habitats in Britain, all have management plans. Each plan is a book which gives details of what needs to be done, when and how, to keep the habitat as it is.

Figure 18.25 shows some examples of British habitats that need conservation management if they are to stay as they are. The pond in figure 13.5c (page 159) is another and there is a reminder, in figure 18.8, of the need to take care of heathland.

Look at each of the photographs in figures 18.25 and 13.5c and imagine that no conservation management is going to be carried out on any of the habitats for 100 years.

6 What will each habitat be like then?

7 What conservation management would you do to keep each of these habitats as it is?

8 Why is conservation management necessary for many habitats that have survived without it until now?

9 Can you think of anything that *you* do that might harm or damage a habitat? You may be able to think of ways of reducing the damage.

10 Are there any threats to a habitat near your school or home?

11 Find out about the activities of your local conservation group. Part of their work is probably to help to put right some damage to habitats.

Worksheet **B**18A gives you a chance to think about some of the ideas in this chapter so far and to make your own conservation plan for parts of your school grounds.

B18.3   Rare species

If you watch a lot of television, or if you are interested in conservation, you have probably seen programmes about **rare** species of animal or plant, with details about why they are rare and what is being done to save them. There are many examples – one is the "Save the Whale" campaign – and conservation is now a popular subject. Hardly a week goes by without there being at least one programme on this topic.

Figure 18.26
The coelacanth fish, *Latimeria chalumnae*, lives off the east coast of Africa. It has only been seen a few times and is probably rather rare. The species has survived for millions of years because its habitat is so remote and has not been influenced in any way by humans.

Figure 18.27
The rare ghost orchid, *Epipogium aphyllum*, flowering in a Chiltern beechwood in August.

Figure 18.28
Once, young orang utan, *Pongo pygmaeus*, were thought to be appealing pets. They were often collected by killing the mother. However, they were and are quite unsuitable as pets because they grow into large apes. The best place for orang utan is in their rain forest homes in Borneo.

12 Whereabouts in the sea do you think the coelacanth lives? (Figure 18.26.)

Figure 18.27 shows you an example of a rare plant.

Almost all rare species (sometimes also known as *threatened* or *endangered* species) are rare because their habitats have been destroyed by humans. That is why the conservation of habitats is so important. If the habitat is free from disturbance by people it is likely that the organisms that live there will be undisturbed as well. There will be nothing to interfere with their survival. If an animal or plant species needs special help, even if its habitat is safe, then something else may be wrong and causing a decline in numbers. Here are some examples.

A The animal or plant provides something that people want, like shells, eggs, skin (see the crocodile in figure 2.16, page 25) or pets, like the orang utan (figure 18.28). Or perhaps it may provide decoration. The Victorians collected ferns for display in large fern cases. This is one of the reasons why the polypody fern became extinct in Epping Forest.

B People may like to hunt the animal for sport. The bison (figure 18.29) is an example.

C The animal wanders from its habitat into farm land, destroying crops. Angry farmers may then destroy the animal, since to them it seems to be a pest. One such animal is the African elephant (figure 10.9, page 115).

D The animal may migrate from one habitat to another. Both of the habitats may be safe but the journey between is more dangerous. The buzzard (figure 18.30) provides an example.

Figure 18.29
The American bison was hunted until it nearly became extinct.

Figure 18.30
When the buzzard migrates some of the birds may cross the Mediterranean Sea. They use the shortest sea crossings but are forced to land wherever they can if they become exhausted.
Sometimes the landing sites are islands which give little chance of finding food or a safe place to roost. Migrating birds are often shot by hunters.

Figure 18.31
A goat on a tree top in Morocco. Medieval sailors sometimes released goats onto islands, so there would be fresh meat if ever they came that way again. The goats reproduced, causing the extinction of many island plants, and others are now very rare.

Figure 18.32
The numbers of peregrine falcons, *Falco peregrinus*, declined in the 1940s and 1950s in Britain as they became poisoned by pesticides. One effect of the chemicals was that the shells of their eggs became much thinner. When parents sat on them to incubate them the eggs were crushed.

E Some animals have very restricted or specialized habitats. If there are fires or prolonged droughts the habitat may disappear altogether. The sand lizard (figure 18.14) is at risk in this way.

F An introduced animal like the goat (figure 18.31) or a plant may destroy a rare species or its habitat.

G Top carnivores may decline because of the build-up of persistent pesticides in their tissues (see Chapter **B**17 and the photograph of the peregrine falcon in figure 18.32).

H The organism has very special ecological requirements. If its habitat is changed even only slightly, its conditions of life are altered and it begins to decline. Figure 18.27 shows one such rare plant.

Quite often, a species has become rare because of a combination of several of the given reasons. We need to study and understand the reasons before we can carry out any sort of conservation work to protect a rare species. For some species the loss of habitat is so serious that very few individuals exist in the wild. Scientists may find it possible to encourage these few remaining organisms to build up their numbers slowly.

13 You are the president of a poor tropical country of which 80 percent is covered in rain forest, with many unique plants and animals and with tribes of primitive people. There are strong economic reasons for opening the forest to prospectors who have found metal ores and oil beneath it, while cattle ranching has also been found to be successful in some parts after forest has been removed.

Develop a plan for what you intend to do with this potential wealth for your country, and be ready to defend it against your opponents.

14 Suggest measures that would encourage an animal to increase its numbers in the wild.

An alternative is to capture some of the organisms from the wild and try to breed them in captivity. It may then be possible to re-introduce them to their natural habitats.

15 What are the drawbacks of this technique?

Figure 18.33
The tuatara is a lizard-like reptile found on a few small islands around New Zealand. It breeds slowly, and needs complete protection. The New Zealand government has very strict laws for protecting the tuatara.

The numbers of the Californian condor, a huge, vulture-like bird, are so low that it is possible that by the year 2000 the bird will no longer exist in the wild.

Conservation of rare species can be expensive. It is not just money that is needed but also land. If local farmers need more space to grow more food they are unlikely to be willing to leave areas on their farms uncultivated. Without such areas rare species are unlikely to survive. It may be that some species will only get a chance of survival if humans think they can benefit from them. It is almost certainly true that many zoos were started, not to protect animals from extinction, but to provide a spectacle for which visitors were ready to pay. If a rare organism is the source of meat or wood that is in demand this may stimulate people to conserve the species. They will preserve the natural habitat of the organism and try to ensure that its numbers remain high. For some rare species though, complete protection is the only way to save them from becoming extinct. (See figure 18.33.)

16 Species have always become rare and then extinct. None of those alive during the age of the dinosaurs are alive now. What difference is there between all other times and now?

The Countryside and Wildlife Act (1981) listed some plants and animals that have complete protection in Britain since they are now so rare. They cannot even be touched, let alone dug up, collected or harmed. Figure 18.34 on the next page lists some of these.

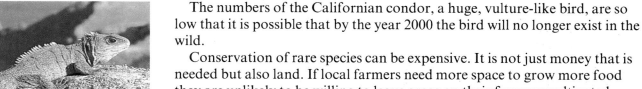

17 See whether any of these species are found near where you live.

18 Some people have suggested re-introducing the brown bear and the wolf into Britain. As you saw, both these animals used to live here but all were exterminated. What do you think of this idea?

19 You are a successful furniture manufacturer, specializing in high quality furniture made from tropical hardwoods. What is your attitude as people become more and more concerned about the destruction of the tropical forests?

20 How can you justify halting the damage or destruction of natural habitats by farming, to a peasant farmer desperate for the survival of his family?

SPECIALLY PROTECTED SPECIES

Specially protected wild plants

Adder's-tongue spearwort
Alpine catchfly
Alpine gentian
Alpine sow-thistle
Alpine Woodsia
Bedstraw broomrape
Blue heath
Brown galingale
Cheddar pink
Childling pink
Diapensia
Dickie's bladder-fern
Downy woundwort
Drooping saxifrage
Early spider-orchid
Fen orchid
Fen violet
Field cow-wheat
Field eryngo
Field wormwood
Ghost orchid
Greater yellow-rattle
Jersey cudweed
Killarney fern
Lady's-slipper
Late spider-orchid
Least lettuce
Limestone woundwort
Lizard orchid
Military orchid
Monkey orchid
Norwegian sandwort
Oblong Woodsia
Oxtongue broomrape
Perennial knawel
Plymouth pear
Purple spurge
Red helleborine
Ribbon-leaved water-
   plantain
Rock cinquefoil
Rock sea-lavender
   (two rare species)
Rough marsh-mallow
Round-headed leek
Sea knotgrass
Sickle-leaved hare's-ear
Small Alison
Small hare's-ear
Snowdon lily
Spiked speedwell
Spring gentian
Starfruit
Starved wood-sedge
Teesdale sandwort
Thistle broomrape

Triangular club-rush
Tufted saxifrage
Water germander
Whorled Solomon's-seal
Wild cotoneaster
Wild gladiolus
Wood calamint

Wild birds specially protected at all times

Avocet
Barn owl
Bearded tit
Bee-eater
Bewick's swan
Bittern
Black-necked grebe
Black redstart
Black-tailed godwit
Black tern
Black-winged stilt
Bluethroat
Brambling
Cetti's warbler
Chough
Cirl bunting
Common quail
Common scoter
Corncrake
Crested tit
Crossbills (all species)
Dartford warbler
Divers (all species)
Dotterel
Fieldfare
Firecrest
Garganey
Golden eagle
Golden oriole
Goshawk
Green sandpiper
Greenshank
Gyr falcon
Harriers (all species)
Hobby
Honey buzzard
Hoopoe
Kentish plover
Kingfisher
Lapland bunting
Leach's petrel
Little bittern
Little gull
Little ringed plover
Little tern
Long-tailed duck

Marsh warbler
Mediterranean gull
Merlin
Osprey
Peregrine
Purple heron
Purple sandpiper
Red-backed shrike
Red kite
Red-necked
   phalarope
Redwing
Roseate tern
Ruff
Savi's warbler
Scarlet rosefinch
Scaup
Serin
Shorelark
Short-toed
   treecreeper
Slavonian grebe
Snow bunting
Snowy owl
Spoonbill
Spotted crake
Stone curlew
Temminck's stint
Velvet scoter
Whimbrel
White-tailed eagle
Whooper swan
Woodlark
Wood sandpiper
Wryneck

Wild birds specially protected during the close season

Goldeneye
Greylag goose
   (in Outer Hebrides,
   Caithness,
   Sutherland and
   Wester Ross only)
Pintail

Specially protected wild animals

Mammals
Bats (all 15 species)
Bottle-nosed dolphin
Common dolphin

Common otter
Harbour (or common)
   porpoise
Red squirrel

Reptiles
Sand lizard
Smooth snake

Amphibians
Great crested (or warty)
   newt
Natterjack toad

Fish
Burbot

Butterflies
Chequered skipper
Heath fritillary
Large blue
Swallowtail

Moths
Barberry carpet
Black-veined
Essex emerald
New Forest burnet
Reddish buff

Other insects
Field cricket
Mole cricket
Norfolk aeshna dragonfly
Rainbow leaf beetle
Wart-biter grasshopper

Spiders
Fen raft spider
Ladybird spider

Snails
Carthusian snail
Glutinous snail
Sandbowl snail

Figure 18.34
The protected species list issued by the Nature Conservancy Council.

21 Does it matter if natural habitats are damaged or destroyed?

Topic B4　The continuity of life

Swans (a cob and pen) with young cygnets.

Chapter B19 — Living things multiply

a

b

Figure 19.1
Two bacterial cultures.
a 4 hours after inoculation.
b After 18 hours' incubation.
What has happened?

B19.1 Reproduction is a necessity of life

Reproduction is a feature of all living organisms. It may occur once, many times or more or less continually in an organism's lifetime. All living organisms exist only because previous generations have reproduced, and the new individuals have survived and reproduced too.

Figures 19.1, 19.2 and 17.4, page 208, illustrate the reproduction of living organisms although they tell us very little about how it is done.

Figure 19.2
Wild daffodils growing beside the river Dove at Farndale in the North Yorkshire moors in April.

B19.2 Different ways of reproducing

There is a lot of variation in the way living organisms reproduce but this is not surprising when you consider how different animals are from plants, for example. Figures 19.3, 19.4 and the photograph opposite page 234 show some of the variations.

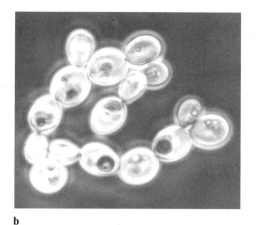

b

c

d(i)

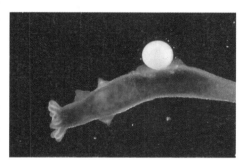

d(ii)

a

Figure 19.3
Some of the variations in the way organisms reproduce.
a An old pollard sycamore (see section **B**18.2) with a seedling growing beneath it.
b Yeast, *Saccharomyces cerevisiae*, undergoing budding. (× 100)
c Plantlets and flowers of *Saxifraga stolonifera*.
d Green *Hydra*: **i** new individuals being produced by budding and **ii** an individual releasing an egg.
Look also at the photograph of parent swans and cygnets opposite page 234.

There may be a great deal of variation in the details but there are only two basic forms of reproduction: *sexual* and *asexual*. They both result in the formation of new individuals, although by quite different methods. It is the difference between these two forms of reproduction that we will look at next.

The essential feature of sexual reproduction is that it always involves the joining together or *fusion* of two cells which are called *gametes* or sex cells.

In most organisms that reproduce sexually there are two kinds of sex cells – *female gametes* and *male gametes* – and they are sometimes, but not always, produced by different individuals, called *female* and *male*. There are some animals and many more plants in which both kinds of gamete are produced by the same individual which is called *hermaphrodite*.

In asexual reproduction there is no fusion of cells and only one individual is needed for it to take place.

Another important difference between these two types of reproduction is that the asexual method gives rise to offspring which are exact copies of their parent. Sexual reproduction results in offspring which have a mixture of characteristics from two parents. They therefore show a great deal more variation (see also Chapter **B**22).

1 For each organism shown in figure 19.3 and also in the photograph facing page 234, try to decide whether it reproduces sexually, asexually or by both methods.

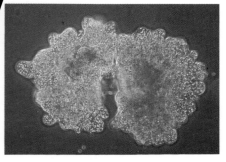

Figure 19.4
Amoeba dividing into two. (× 80)

B19.3   Reproduction without sex

The simplest kind of asexual reproduction is when one cell divides into two, as happens in bacteria and *Amoeba* (figure 19.4). In these unicellular organisms every cell is capable of reproducing.

There is another form of asexual reproduction in some multicellular organisms. The most familiar examples are to be seen among plants. There is an example in each of figures 19.2 and 19.3 and figure 19.5 shows some more.

This type of asexual reproduction, in which a part of an organism grows and gives rise to new independent ones, is called *vegetative* reproduction.

a

b

old corm

c

Figure 19.5
a Creeping buttercup (*Ranunculus repens*) with runners. **b** *Bryophyllum* with plantlets on its leaf margins. **c** New *Crocus* corms formed above old corm.

Plant growers make use of the fact that many plants reproduce vegetatively. They can grow plants asexually, not only by the natural methods already mentioned, but also by means of *cuttings* taken from stems, leaves and roots (figure 19.6) and by *grafting*, *budding* and *layering* (figure 19.7).

2 Roses, apples and various house plants are propagated vegetatively. Find out which of the four artificial methods are used for roses and apples and give some examples that you know of houseplants that can be propagated in these ways.

Few animals reproduce asexually and *Hydra*, shown in figure 19.3d, is probably the best known example. When there is plenty of food *buds* may grow on the side of this freshwater animal. They eventually break off from the parent and become separate individuals. As you can see in figure 19.3d(ii), *Hydra* also reproduces sexually. This is likely to happen when food is in short supply. The fertilized egg is then able to survive during bad conditions and its development will continue when the conditions become favourable again.

3 Explain the advantages of asexual and sexual methods of reproduction in the breeding of plants.

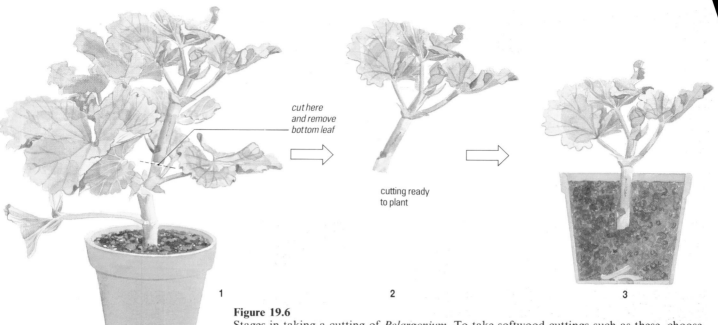

Figure 19.6
Stages in taking a cutting of *Pelargonium*. To take softwood cuttings such as these, choose a non-flowering shoot and cut it just below a node (where a leaf is attached to a stem). Remove the lower leaves before putting the cutting into compost to root.

*cut here
and remove
bottom leaf*

*cutting ready
to plant*

1

2

3

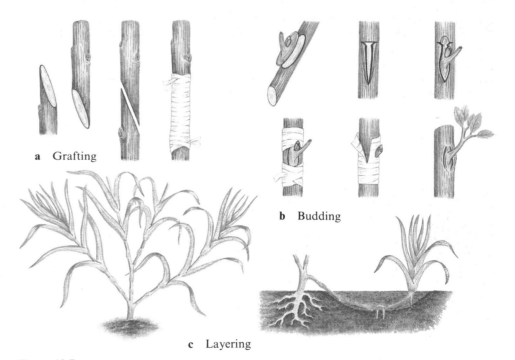

a Grafting

b Budding

c Layering

Figure 19.7
a Grafting is often used to increase fruit trees. It consists of joining a portion of the plant you wish to increase (the scion) to the chosen root system (the stock). The join is bound with some kind of tape. There are several ways of grafting but the principle is always the same.
b Budding is often used in rose breeding. Take a bud with a small piece of stem attached, from the plant you wish to increase, and put it into a T-shaped cut in the base of the stock (usually a wild rose plant). Tie the bud on and, once the buds are growing, cut off the upper part of the stock. This means that the new rose is growing on the roots of a wild species.
c Layering is a method of vegetative reproduction in which a stem or root of a plant is usually bent down into the soil and kept in position until the roots have formed. Then it can be cut from the parent plant.

B19.4 Sexual reproduction

The fusion of the two kinds of gametes, which is the essential feature of sexual reproduction, is called *fertilization*. In most organisms the male and female gametes are quite different from each other. The female gamete is the larger of the two, does not move and is called an *egg*. The smaller, male gamete moves in many organisms, but not in the flowering plants. In animals it is called a *sperm*. In the flowering plants the male gamete is in the *pollen grain*. Another difference is in the number of each type of gamete – it is typical to find that more male than female gametes are produced.

The attraction of flowers

You are probably familiar already with the structure of flowers and we are not going into any detail about it here.

Figure 19.8
Photographs of wind- and insect-pollinated plants.
a Rye grass shedding pollen. **b** Apple blossom, *Malus* sp. **c** Flowers of nettle, *Urtica* sp.
d Male and female flowers of hazel, *Corylus avellana*. The yellow catkins are the male, pollen-bearing flowers. Those with feathery red stigmas are the female flowers.
e Flowers of *Crocus* sp. **f** Catkins of silver birch, *Betula pendula*, dispersing pollen.

We are attracted by the bright colours and scent of many flowers but some flowers are much less conspicuous and we hardly notice them. Is there an explanation for these differences? To answer this question we have to find out how pollen is transferred from the anthers to the stigmas of flowers. It could simply fall from the anther onto the stigma of the same flower. When this happens it is called *self-pollination* – the garden pea is a flower which is self-pollinated. But this is not what usually happens. There are all sorts of ways by which self-pollination is prevented. One is for the pollen to ripen before the stigma is developed. It is much more usual for a flower to be *cross-pollinated*.

Two of the ways by which cross-pollination is brought about are by the **wind** and by **insects**.

4 Which of the flowers in figure 19.8 do you think are pollinated by wind and which by insects? How did you decide?

5 What does an insect collect from flowers besides pollen? What do you think may attract insects to flowers in the first place?

There is more about pollen in Worksheets **B**19A, **B**19B and **B**19C.

Very complex ways have evolved which ensure that flowers are cross-pollinated and it would take a whole book to describe them. Insects and wind are not the only means by which pollen is transferred, although they are the main ones. Birds, bats and water are also known to act as carriers of pollen.

If pollination is successful – which means that pollen has been transferred to a stigma of the same kind of flower at the right time – then the male gamete still has to reach the female gamete in order for fertilization to take place. Figure 19.9 shows what may happen next. If the pollen grains are ripe and the stigma is also at the right stage then tubes may grow from the pollen grains down the style to the ovary.

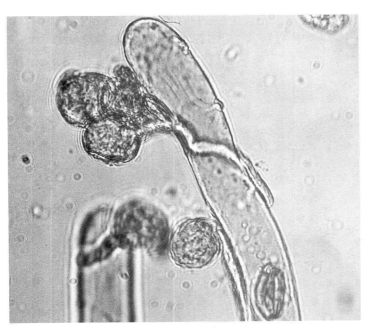 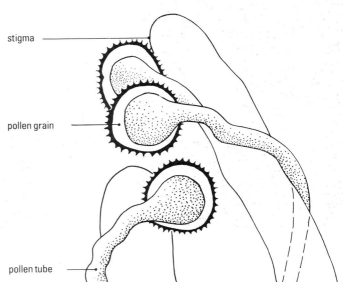

Figure 19.9
A photomicrograph and a diagram of pollen grains germinating on a stigma. The pollen tubes have started to grow between the finger-like processes of the stigma.

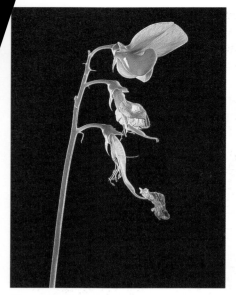

Figure 19.10
Here you can see what happens after
the fertilization of a sweet pea flower.

The *pollen tubes* carry the male gametes to the ovules. Once they reach the ovule, fertilization – or fusion of the male gamete and egg – may follow. Figure 19.10 shows what happens to a flower once this happens.

6 Describe all that you can see happening to the flower of sweet pea in figure 19.10 after it has been fertilized.

It is even more important to understand that as a result of fertilization a plant *embryo* is formed in the ovule and this is protected inside the ovary. The ovule and its contents (embryo and a food store) form the seed.

7 One could say that the function of a flower is to prepare for the future. In what way does seed production do this?

The mating of animals

One of the differences between male and female animals is in the kind of gametes they make. Sperms are made in the *testes* of the males, and eggs in the *ovaries* of the females. The sexes are usually separate but there are hermaphrodite animals, like earthworms, in which ovaries and testes are found in the same individual. Eggs are larger than sperms and rather fewer of them are produced.

In animals the eggs and sperms are brought together as a result of behaviour of the male and female, called *mating*.

A requirement for successful mating is to find a partner of the **same species** and the **opposite sex**. The senses of sound and smell as well as sight are all used in attracting a suitable partner. In many species of frogs and toads, the males croak to attract females of the same species to the breeding site. The females of some moth species produce chemicals (pheromones) which the males of that species can detect as far as 11 km away.

Female glow worms give out a light signal which attracts the males to them. Male bower birds, which live in New Guinea, make beautiful bowers. These

Figure 19.11
The male satin bower bird decorates its bower with a collection of objects as part of its courtship, in order to attract a mate.

are quite different from their nests, and they decorate them with flowers or other bright and vividly coloured objects to attract females (see figure 19.11). These are just a few of the many ways animals attract a mate.

Hermaphrodite animals also mate and sperms are exchanged between the two individuals.

Figure 19.12 shows mating in a variety of animals. See also the brown trout in figure 19.13 and the toads in figure 19.15.

a   b   c

d   e   f

Figure 19.12
All of these photographs illustrate behaviour which is connected with mating.
a Earthworms, *Lumbricus terrestris*. **b** Barnacles, *Balanus crenatus*, feeding and mating.
c A pair of domestic fowl, *Gallus gallus*, mating. **d** Lions, *Panthera leo*. **e** A pair of damsel flies, *Coenagrion* sp. **f** Giant tortoises, *Geochelone* sp., in the Alcedo crater, Galápagos islands.

Figure 19.13
Brown trout, *Salmo trutta fario*, spawning. The male, releasing sperms, is on the left. You can see the eggs released by the female, on the right.

Mating behaviour depends very much on where the egg is fertilized. If this happens outside the female's body it is called *external fertilization*. Many animals which live in water simply release large numbers of their eggs and sperms at the same time and place. Species that do this include sea urchins, sea anemones and many fish (figure 19.13). It is a feature of these species to produce very large numbers of gametes. A single female sea urchin may produce tens of millions of eggs and the male produces even more sperms.

8 Why is it important for the eggs and sperms to be released at the same time?

9 In spite of the very large numbers of eggs produced the number of sea urchins in the sea remains constant. Why is this?

Sometimes mating that results in external fertilization of the eggs is more complex and involves *courtship*. The courtship of sticklebacks is illustrated in figure 19.14.

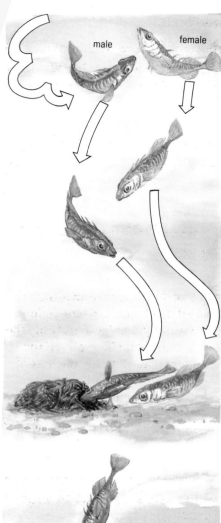

female lays eggs in nest

male fertilizes eggs

Figure 19.14
The courtship of the three-spined stickleback consists of a series of stimuli and responses between the male and the female.

A
APPLY

10 After studying the drawings of the sticklebacks' courtship write an account of it in your own words.

11 What advantages are there when external fertilization is preceded by courtship?

Figure 19.15
Toads mating. The male climbs onto the female's back and clasps her tightly with his front legs for several days. As the female lays eggs the male sheds sperms.

12 Frogs and toads show another variation of mating in which, again, the eggs are fertilized externally. What advantages does it have? (See figure 19.15.)

In many animals the eggs are fertilized inside the female's body and this is called *internal fertilization*. When fertilization is internal the male puts his sperms into the female's body – an act which is called *copulation*.

13 What are the advantages of internal fertilization of eggs?

14 In which of the animals shown in figure 19.12 does internal fertilization of the eggs take place as a result of copulation?

All reptiles, birds and mammals copulate when they mate and so do many other animals as well.

15 Why is internal fertilization essential in reptiles and birds?

Internal fertilization is also essential in mammals because the fertilized eggs develop inside a special part of the female's body called the *uterus*.

What happens when an egg is fertilized?

It is not mating but fertilization which is important in reproduction. It is therefore worth while looking at what happens in some detail. A mature sperm consists of three parts – a head, mid-piece and tail – which you can see in figure 19.16.

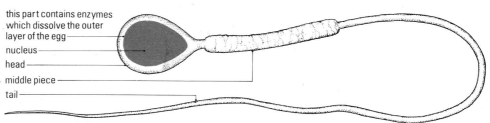

this part contains enzymes which dissolve the outer layer of the egg

nucleus

head

middle piece

tail

Figure 19.16
The structure of a human sperm. ($\times$ 4900)

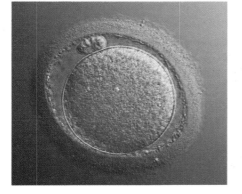

Figure 19.17
A human egg being fertilized. ($\times$ 34)

It is the head which plays the most important part in fertilization although the tail and mid-piece enable it to move. The head produces enzymes which digest the egg membrane; the tail and mid-piece usually break off and only the head containing the nucleus enters the egg. Once one sperm has entered the egg no other sperm can do so. Fertilization is completed when the nucleus of the egg fuses with the sperm nucleus.

You can see in figure 19.17 how much larger the egg is than the sperm. The egg is the largest cell found in an animal and this is because it has a store of food for the developing embryo. We call this food store *yolk*. The amount of food stored varies from species to species.

O
OBSERVE

16 Birds have the largest eggs (only the yolk is the true egg). See figure 19.18. Which bird do you think produces the largest animal cell of all?

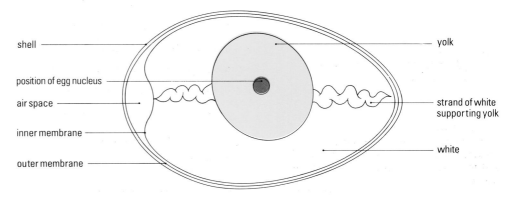

shell

position of egg nucleus

air space

inner membrane

outer membrane

yolk

strand of white supporting yolk

white

Figure 19.18
The structure of a hen's egg. The egg has been cut into two, lengthwise.

The sperm has no food store but it contributes to the new individual which develops as the result of fertilization. This is because the nuclei of the egg and the sperm contain chromosomes through which characteristics from both parents are passed on to the new individual. This important aspect of fertilization is considered in Chapter **B**22.

B19.5   Sexual cycles in mammals

We have seen that in flowering plants, ripe pollen has to be transferred to mature stigmas if fertilization is to occur. In animals male and female gametes must also be mature at the same time. Most organisms have a breeding season which results in seeds germinating, eggs hatching or young being born at a time of year when they are likely to survive.

Most wild mammals have a breeding season. The clearest sign that the breeding season is beginning is that the female shows a willingness to copulate. She is said to be "on heat" or in *oestrus* (pronounced *ee-strus*). This is when *ovulation* normally occurs and one or more eggs are released from the ovary.

17 What is the advantage of copulation only taking place when the female is in oestrus?

Deer and lions have one period of oestrus a year while mice and rats come into oestrus several times during the breeding season. If you keep a cat or a bitch you will know that they are on heat two or three times a year. Between each oestrus, other changes take place in the reproductive system, which prepares the uterus to receive an embryo. This cycle of changes is called the *oestrous cycle*.

We shall see in the next chapter that human beings are different, because they do not mate **only** when an egg is ready to be fertilized.

B19.6   What happens as a result of fertilization?

Figure 19.19
What happens after a frog's egg (*Rana temporaria temporaria*) is fertilized? Shortly after the egg nucleus has fused with a sperm nucleus, the fertilized egg undergoes a series of rapid divisions called *cleavages*. Photographs **a**, **b** and **c** show the first, second and third cleavages.

From what has been said so far it should be clear that both plants and animals develop from a single cell – the fertilized egg. This begins to divide very soon after fertilization. As soon as the fertilized egg starts to divide it becomes an *embryo*. You can see in figure 19.19 that as the cells divide they become smaller and no growth takes place.

a

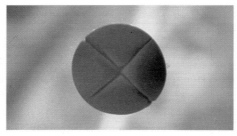

b

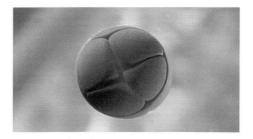

c

Eventually the embryo begins to grow and recognizable structures can be seen (figures 19.20 and 19.21).

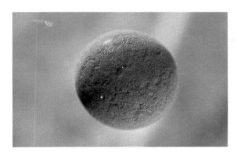

a

b

c

Figure 19.20
The embryo of a frog develops into a tadpole.

a

b

c

d

Figure 19.21
Four stages in the development of a chick embryo.

Figure 19.22
Eastern hognose snakes, *Heterodon platyrhinos*, hatching from their eggs.

The development of the frog embryo is completed rapidly. It does not develop into an adult frog, however, but into a tadpole, which is called a *larva*, and this continues to develop while feeding itself. The larva does not look much like the adult but it eventually undergoes a dramatic change called *metamorphosis*, to become an adult.

18 What other animals have eggs which hatch into larvae and undergo metamorphosis to become adults?

Eggs with large yolk supplies, which develop externally, hatch into small versions of the adult (figure 19.22).

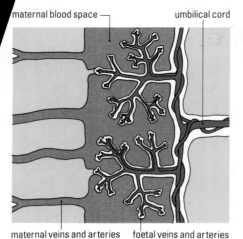

maternal blood space — umbilical cord

maternal veins and arteries　foetal veins and arteries

Figure 19.23
The placenta of a mammal is formed.

Mammals have very little yolk in their eggs and development of the embryo takes place within the uterus. Soon after fertilization a close connection develops between the embryo and the wall of the uterus and a structure called the *placenta* is formed (figure 19.23). The embryo obtains its supply of food and oxygen from the mother's blood, and gets rid of waste products into the mother's blood, through the placenta. But although the blood of the embryo and mother come very close they never normally mix. The embryo also produces a bag-like structure, which is filled with a fluid, and this gives it some protection from being damaged if it is knocked.

The length of time the embryo develops in the uterus before it is born is called the *gestation period*. Worksheet **B**19D gives you some more information about the length of the gestation period.

a

b

Figure 19.24
a The newly born young of the rabbit, *Oryctolagus cuniculus*. They are born bald and blind, underground.
b 3-day-old leverets of the brown hare, *Lepus capensis*. They are born above ground. They have fur and they open their eyes immediately.

Review

In this chapter we have looked at what reproduction involves and we have seen that there are only two basic methods – sexual and asexual. At the same time we have seen that there is a great deal of variation in the details, among both animals and plants. In the next chapter we look at human reproduction in detail. This is of particular interest and importance to us as human beings and it often raises questions which need to be discussed. We hope you will be able to consider them with the help of your teacher as you study the next chapter.

Chapter **B20**

People are different

B20.1   What is it that makes sex different for us?

Why do you think it is that human beings are so interested in sex? We read books, watch films, tell jokes and ask questions about it. We make rules about it, and we even have laws about it.

You have seen that in all other mammals sexual activity is linked to the oestrous cycle. The female only mates at times when there is a good chance that she will become pregnant. In fact, sexual activity in other animals is concerned entirely with reproduction.

In humans, sex is different because it need not be linked with reproduction. Men and women can enjoy sexual intercourse, not just on the few days the woman is likely to be fertile, but at any time. The fact that humans enjoy sexual intercourse for its own sake, and use it as a way of expressing loving feelings, makes it very important to them. But it can also make it more complicated. In the rest of this chapter we shall start by looking at human reproduction, and then go on to look at some of the problems that arise because there are these two sides to sex.

B20.2   Sexual development

Almost everyone has some worries at some time about his or her sexual development. You may worry that you are not "normal" if you start to develop later than your friends, or feel conspicuous and uncomfortable if you are way ahead of them.

1 Describe an average boy or girl of your own age.

2 How nearly do you think you correspond to this?

(See Worksheet **B20A**.)

3 If you have completed Worksheet B20A for the whole class, what do you notice about the results?

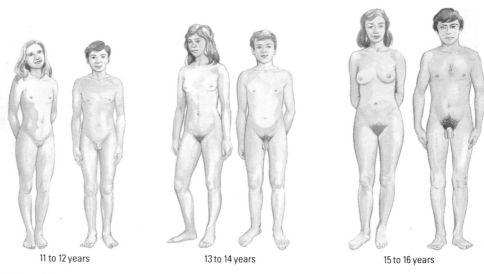

11 to 12 years   13 to 14 years   15 to 16 years

Figure 20.1
Girls generally notice that their bodies are beginning to show signs of sexual development two years before boys notice any changes. However, there is a great deal of variation in the age at which these changes begin in both sexes.

One of the things that should strike you is that there is really no "normal" size. There is almost certainly a huge variation in size and shape amongst your friends. Also look at the photograph opposite page 6.

The *growth spurt*, when girls and boys suddenly start to "shoot up", outgrowing all their clothes from one term to the next, does not happen at the same age for everyone. Girls usually start their growth spurt at about 10 or 11 and boys about two years later; this period of rapid growth continues for about five years.

This growth spurt is the first visible sign of *puberty* – the time when the secondary sexual characteristics (for example, breasts in girls, the deepening of the voice in boys) begin to appear and a child starts to become an adult. And, just as with the growth spurt, there is no normal age for any of these signs of sexual development to appear – the range of ages at which these things happen is enormous.

4 If you are in a mixed class, do the boys in the class tend to be taller than the girls, or the other way round? If your class is not mixed, think of the girls or boys you know of your own age and try to decide which group is taller.

Let's take a more detailed look at the physical changes of puberty, always remembering that the ages given are the *average* ages at which they occur, not the *normal* ages. (Are you clear about the difference?)

5 By studying the graphs in figures 20.2 and 20.3, can you explain why it is that although girls tend to be taller than boys during adolescence, boys are usually taller as adults?

6 The graphs show the main physical signs of growing up. Have you noticed any other changes in yourself?

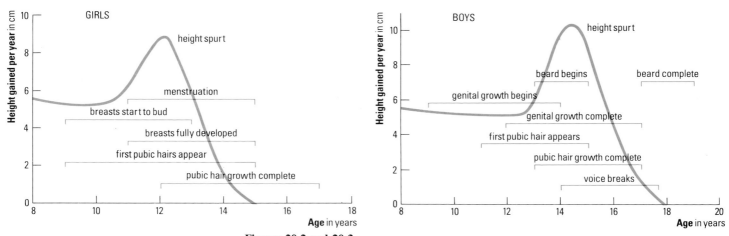

Figures 20.2 and 20.3
The normal range of physical development in boys and girls.

It's quite possible that your parents find it hard to get you out of bed in the mornings! They may even complain that you are moody, or lazy, or difficult. You may feel "different" even if you don't believe you are difficult! And you will almost certainly have to suffer a few spots (acne), even if you've never had them before.

All the changes at this stage, which is called adolescence, are controlled by various *sex hormones*: these are produced by the *adrenal glands*, and the *testes* or the *ovaries*. This sudden increase in the amount of hormones circulating in the body can have all kinds of side-effects. Acne is one of these, and the "up and down" feelings you may have are all due to the hormones too.

The starting signal

The signal for puberty to start comes from a part of the brain called the *hypothalamus* (see section **B**12.2). This directs the nearby *pituitary gland* to increase the production of certain hormones which control other glands. In boys these hormones make the testes start to produce sperms. They also act on the *adrenal cortex* and testes to produce male sex hormones. It is these hormones which are responsible for all the signs of sexual development in boys which are shown in the graph in figure 20.3.

In girls the pituitary hormones stimulate the adrenal cortex and ovaries to produce female sex hormones. These are responsible for the characteristic female shape. The ovaries also start to produce *oestrogen* and *progesterone* – the hormones which start and control the *menstrual cycle*. (See figure 20.4.)

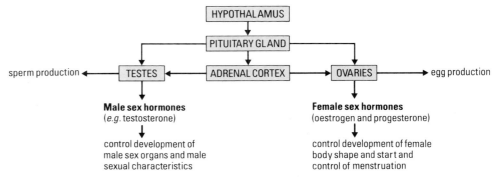

Figure 20.4
Sexual development is controlled by hormones in males and females.

The menstrual cycle

Each month from puberty, when a girl has her first period, until the *menopause*, when periods stop (usually between the ages of 45 and 55), one egg is produced by an ovary, and the woman's body prepares for a possible pregnancy. (See figure 20.5.) This series of events takes about 28 days in most women, and is called the *menstrual cycle*. And as you have already read, it is controlled by oestrogen and progesterone, the hormones produced by the ovaries in a regular, monthly cycle. The cycle begins on the first day of the woman's period.

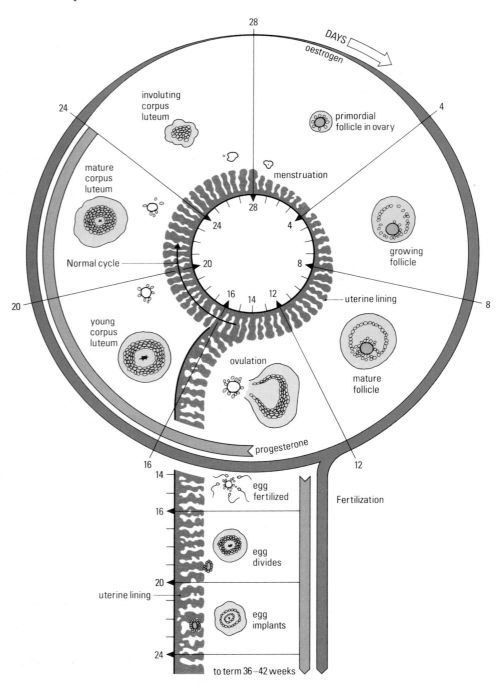

Figure 20.5
A summary of the events which happen during the menstrual cycle and what happens if the egg is fertilized.

For the first half of the month, oestrogen is produced. During this time, an egg appears in a small swelling (called a *follicle*) on the surface of the ovary, and starts to grow. About half way through the month, the mature egg bursts from its follicle (this is called *ovulation*) and enters the funnel-shaped opening of the *Fallopian tube* (the egg tube; see figure 20.6).

After ovulation, the ovary starts to produce progesterone as well. The two hormones together make the lining of the uterus thicker and more richly supplied with blood vessels.

7 **Why do you think this is necessary?**

Figure 20.6
The release of the egg from the ovary at ovulation.

However, if the egg is not fertilized, there is no need for this thickened lining. Less and less oestrogen and progesterone are produced towards the end of the cycle; without them the uterus lining breaks down and is shed, with some blood, through the vagina. This is the woman's *period* of *menstruation* and it usually lasts about 5 days.

The hormones that control the menstrual cycle can affect different people in different ways. Some girls feel no change during a period. Others may notice that they have more spots than usual, or that they feel very "bloated", or tearful and irritable, when a period is about to start. In fact, nearly all women show a gain in body mass just before a period and this is because more water than usual is retained in the body. Girls quite often have mild "period pains" on the first day or two of a period – if these are very bad a doctor will usually prescribe medicine which will help to relieve them. But even though periods can be a nuisance, girls usually find that they do not interfere very much with their normal activities. Most girls now wear tampons (cottonwool cylinders which plug the vagina), which means that even activities such as swimming are no problem during a period.

The first sign of pregnancy a woman notices is usually a missed menstrual period.

8 **What would happen if she continued to menstruate after she became pregnant?**

Once the fertilized egg becomes embedded in the wall of the uterus, another hormone is produced which ensures that the ovaries continue to produce oestrogen and progesterone.

Occasionally **TWO** eggs ripen and are released at ovulation. If both these eggs are fertilized they will develop into twins. Sometimes **ONE** fertilized egg will divide to form twins.

9 **What will be the difference between these two kinds of twins? (See page 283.)**

A look at the reproductive systems

You probably know the "geography" of these systems perfectly well. If you don't, study the diagrams in figures 20.7 and 20.8 before going on to answer the questions.

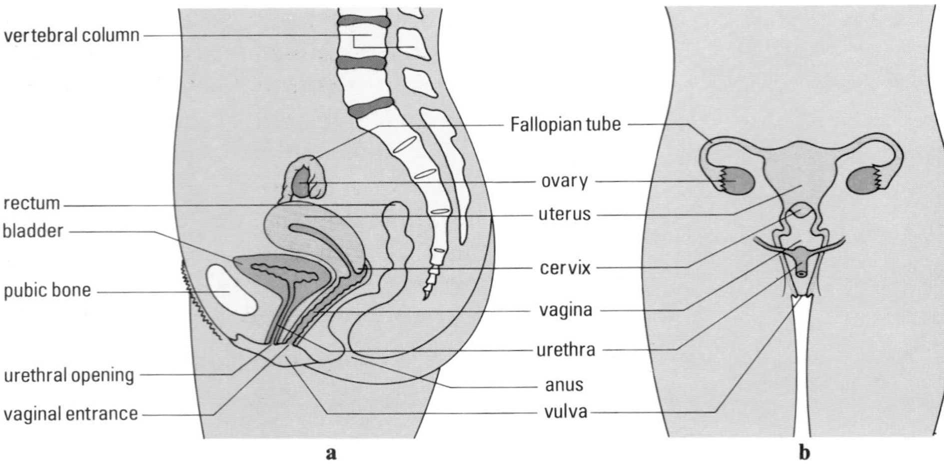

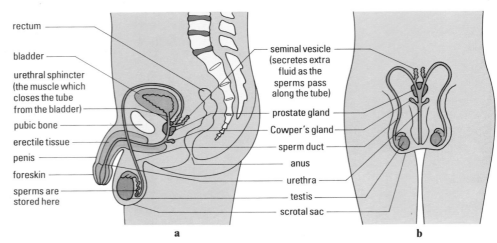

Figure 20.7
The female reproductive organs **a** from the side. **b** from the front.

Figure 20.8
The male reproductive organs **a** from the side **b** from the front.

---

10 What are the functions of the different parts of the male system?

11 What are the functions of the different parts of the female system?

12 Extra organs are needed for the extra functions the woman's reproductive system has to perform. What are they?

The special "birth passage" – called the *vagina* – leads from the uterus and opens between the two fleshy "lips" which form the woman's external genital organs or *vulva*. The vagina has very elastic, folded walls – no matter how large the baby, the vagina can easily stretch and allow it to pass through.

You can see from figures 20.7 and 20.8 that, while the ovaries (which produce the eggs) are inside the woman's body, the testes (where the sperms are made) hang outside the man's body.

INTERPRET

13 Can you suggest a reason for this?

As the sperms travel from the testes to the urethra, fluids secreted by glands near the beginning of the urethra (see figure 20.8) are added to them. These secretions make up the bulk of the fluid containing the sperms which is called *semen.*

14 Look at the *bladder* and *urethra* – the tube down which urine passes – in both the male and female. What differences do you notice?

15 What does this tell you about the function of the urethra in the male?

16 The female reproductive system has developed quite separately from the urinary system. What is the advantage of this?

There is no male organ that corresponds to either vagina or uterus. There is, however, a tiny, female equivalent of the penis – the *clitoris*, which develops from the same tissues as the penis. The clitoris plays no essential part in reproduction. But it is very sensitive to touch and so provides much of the woman's pleasure during sexual intercourse.

Growing up early

People are becoming physically mature now much earlier than in the past. In the eighteenth century it was quite usual for menstruation to begin at about 18. As you know most girls nowadays start to menstruate between the ages of 11 and 14.

17 Why do you think that girls now begin to menstruate earlier than they used to?

Think about the problems that this earlier maturity can cause. Part of the growing up process is to have strong sexual feelings, and a good deal of curiosity about sex.

Dealing with sexual feelings

Why do you think that young teenagers so often have crushes on pop stars, whom they are unlikely ever to meet?

This kind of crush provides a good way of dealing with all the romantic and sexual feelings which everyone has. The usual teenage sex life is a mixture of "petting", fantasizing and masturbation. And these are all normal ways of coping with the surge of sexual feelings which almost everyone has. You may have heard that masturbation (achieving an orgasm – see page 257 – by stimulating the penis or the clitoris by rubbing with the hand, for example) is harmful, or something to be ashamed of. It isn't – in fact it is the way most people learn about their own bodies and sexual feelings. It is also the usual way that boys ejaculate their semen. Semen is also ejaculated sometimes when a boy is asleep, and this is called a "wet dream".

Homosexuality

It is usual to feel attracted to people of the opposite sex. But during their teenage years people quite often have romantic feelings about someone of their own sex or feel attracted to the same sex. This is especially likely if you don't have much opportunity to meet people of the opposite sex, or feel very ill at ease with them. It is a stage that will usually pass as you do begin to meet people of the opposite sex and grow more confident with them. It does **not** mean that you are bound to have homosexual feelings when you grow up. No one knows why some adults are homosexual (attracted to people of the same sex) rather than heterosexual (attracted to people of the opposite sex). But we do know that people can't choose whether they will be hetero- or homosexual. It is somehow built into their own personal make-up. Some people are attracted both to their own and the opposite sex; they are called bisexuals.

Starting too soon

In Britain it is illegal to have sexual intercourse with anyone under the age of 16 – this is called the "age of consent".

18 Have you ever thought about the main reasons behind this law?

There are health risks involved for girls who have sexual intercourse before their bodies have developed to full physical maturity which is probably not before they are 16 or 17. Pregnancy in young girls is more dangerous for both the baby and the mother. And women who start to be sexually active at a very young age are more likely to develop cancer of the cervix.

Sexual intercourse

Figure 20.9 shows you how the penis fits into the vagina when a man and woman have sexual intercourse.

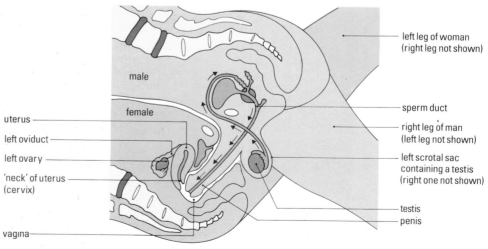

Figure 20.9
A drawing showing the position of the male and female organs during sexual intercourse.

Normally the penis is quite small and limp. It is made up of spongy tissue. When the man becomes sexually excited a reflex action makes this tissue fill with blood and the penis becomes enlarged and stiffened ready for intercourse. (This is called an *erection*.) As the woman becomes sexually excited, her vagina becomes moist and slippery, so that the stiffened penis can slip in easily.

As the man moves his penis inside the woman, they both feel the sensations of pleasure and sexual excitement increasing. Once excitement reaches a certain level, the body's reflexes take over to produce a series of involuntary contractions in the penis and vagina – the *orgasm* (or climax).

As the man reaches orgasm these contractions force the semen through the urethra and into the vagina. About a teaspoonful of semen containing millions of sperms is *ejaculated* at orgasm. But only a hundred or so will survive the journey through the uterus and Fallopian tubes to meet the egg, and only one will finally penetrate the outer membrane of the egg and *fertilize* it.

B20.3   Fertilization and development

The egg has a relatively short life – not much more than 12 to 24 hours. But sperms can survive inside the woman's body for about five days, or even longer.

19 If a woman ovulates on day 14 of her menstrual cycle, on which days will she be fertile (that is, on which days may she become pregnant if she has intercourse)?

Compared with the egg, which is just large enough to be seen with the naked eye, each sperm is minute – about $\frac{1}{200}$ cm long. It is tadpole-like, with a head, which contains the nucleus, and a tail (see figure 19.16, page 245). At fertilization the tail is shed and the nucleus – which contains the chromosome – fuses with the nucleus of the egg (see figure 19.17). At this moment, too, the sex of the baby will be determined, depending on whether the "successful" sperm was X-bearing or Y-bearing. (See Chapter **B22**.)

The questions you might now ask are:

Once the egg has been fertilized, is pregnancy inevitable?
What else might happen to it?

Fertilization is only the beginning of the story. The egg starts to divide and develop immediately it has been fertilized. But it may take up to a week for it to complete the journey down the Fallopian tube to the uterus and bury itself in the lining – this is called *implantation*. Unless the fertilized egg does become implanted, it will not survive and develop further. Once implantation has occurred, the fertilized egg is called an *embryo*. (Figure 20.10.)

Even after implantation, the very young embryo may be dislodged so that the pregnancy ends naturally – this is called *abortion*. This nearly always happens fairly early, usually before the woman even realizes she is pregnant. Once the embryo is firmly established and developing normally, these spontaneous abortions (or miscarriages) seldom happen.

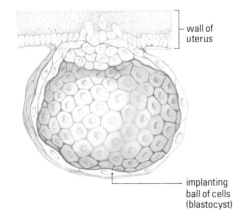

wall of uterus

implanting ball of cells (blastocyst)

Figure 20.10
The fertilized egg is implanted in the lining of the uterus.

Pregnancy

Most babies develop normally and are born healthy. Throughout the nine months of development in the uterus they have their own safe environment, almost always unaffected by anything that happens to the mother. (See figure 20.11.)

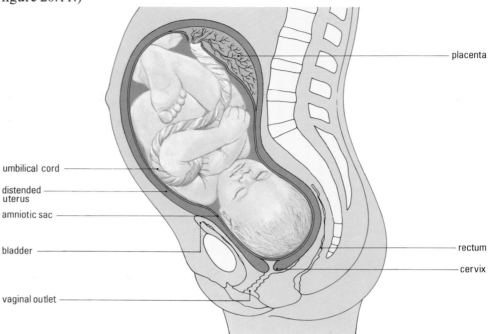

placenta

umbilical cord

distended uterus

amniotic sac

bladder

rectum

cervix

vaginal outlet

Figure 20.11
The foetus lies within a fluid-filled sac, the amniotic sac. It is attached, by the umbilical cord, to the placenta. Within this plate-shaped organ, blood vessels from the foetus absorb nourishment from the mother's blood. Waste products from the foetus are excreted into the mother's blood.

The *placenta* acts as:

a means of obtaining food
an organ for gas exchange
an excretory organ

In order to make this possible, the blood vessels of the mother and those of the embryo must come very close to one another in the placenta although the blood of the two never mixes. See figure 19.23, page 248.

The placenta also acts as a barrier, allowing some substances to pass through to the embryo, but not others.

Why is it important to have such a barrier?

The placenta is the baby's main "defence mechanism" and acts as a barrier to most harmful substances and infections. But it is not a perfect barrier. Some drugs and viruses and other harmful substances may pass through, as we shall see later.

OBSERVE

20 In what other way is the embryo protected?

The embryo develops very rapidly indeed. Most systems of the body develop during the first twelve weeks and by the end of the third month, it looks recognizably human and is called a *foetus* (pronounced *f-ee-tus* and some times spelt *fetus*). For the rest of the pregnancy the organs already formed become more elaborate, but the main change is a steady increase in the size and mass of the foetus.

You probably know that pregnant women are always advised not to drink alcohol and should not take drugs or any medicine, unless it is absolutely essential, in case they damage the baby.

A

APPLY

21 Why is this risk especially high in the first few weeks of the pregnancy?

22 Why is it risky for a woman to smoke **at any time** during her pregnancy?

23 Why is it important for girls to be vaccinated against rubella (German measles)?

Worksheet **B20B** gives you an opportunity to find out more about the growth of the human embryo and foetus.

Birth

No one knows exactly what triggers off the process of birth, which begins with remarkable accuracy, after the baby has completed 266 days of development in the uterus.

Until the baby's birth, the passage from the uterus to the outside world is completely closed. This protects the baby and prevents infections from reaching it. During the first (and longest) stage of *labour* (the process of birth) contractions of the uterine muscles cause the tightly closed "neck" (or cervix) of the uterus to widen and stretch so that uterus and vagina form one continuous passage. Once this passage is open, the contractions of the uterus start to push the baby out through the cervix into the vagina, and finally out of the mother's body. During the final stage of labour, some minutes after the baby is born, the placenta becomes loose and it too is expelled through the woman's vagina. (See figures 20.13 and 20.14.)

Figure 20.12
Madonna and child, by Dieric Bouts (1415–1475).

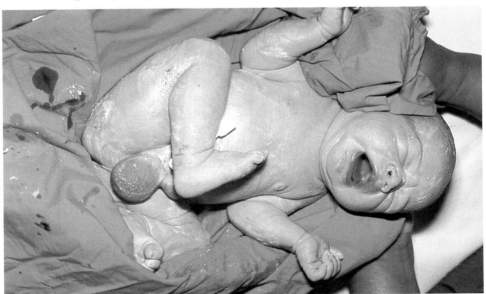

Figure 20.13
This baby has just been born.

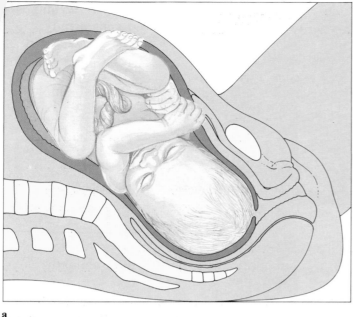

a

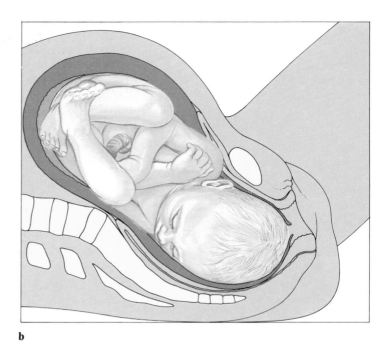

b

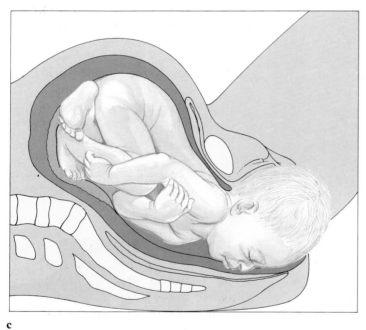

c

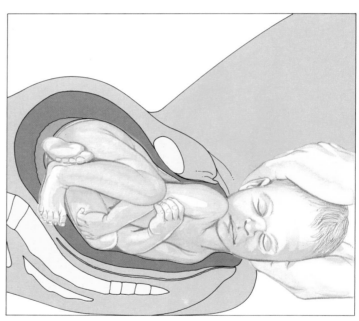

d

Figure 20.14
The stages of birth.
a The first stage of labour begins with the dilatation of the cervix. This is the longest stage.
b During the second stage of labour the baby's head passes through the birth canal (vagina). This is usually the shortest stage.
c The third stage is when the head has cleared the birth canal and the body rotates to allow the shoulders, arms, body and legs to pass easily through the birth canal. This stage is usually over quite quickly.
d The baby is born.

It has been suggested that babies may be soothed by rhythmic sounds because they have become used to the rhythmic beat of their mother's heart while in the uterus. It is said that mothers instinctively hold their babies on the left side of their bodies, near to the heart, so that they can hear the soothing rhythm.

24 How would you check whether there is any truth in this suggestion? You should think of ways of checking that babies really are soothed by rhythmic sounds and you could collect evidence by observing mothers and their babies and by looking at paintings as well.

B20.4   The human population

Boys or girls?

Perhaps you come from an all-girl or all-boy family. It may even be that your whole street seems to have far more than its fair share of boys or of girls. But in the population as a whole the sexes balance each other remarkably well.

> **25** Count the numbers of males and females in your family. Now add together the totals for everyone in the class. (The larger your sample the more likely you are to get a result which is similar to that of the country as a whole.)
>
> **26** How well do the numbers balance each other?

More male babies than female babies are born each year – about 106 boys for every 100 girls. But females – at all ages – survive rather better than males. So by the age of about 50, the number of women begins to exceed the number of men. In Britain, at the time of publication, the population consists of

Males: 27 064 000
Females: 28 701 000

Worksheet **B20C** looks at the human population in more detail.

B20.5   Contraception

Conception is easy *

Although a few couples do not conceive as quickly or have as many babies as they would like, for most couples, conception is easy. Their problem is to avoid unwanted pregnancies, so that they have only the number of children they want, spaced at the intervals they think will suit them best. Without some way of preventing conception and pregnancy – *contraception* or *birth control* or *family planning* – this would be impossible.

Each year, out of every 100 young couples using no contraception at all, 90 are likely to become pregnant. Each year there are about 200 000 unplanned pregnancies in Britain.

How contraception works

Contraception can work at a number of different "sites" in the body.

The next question is one for you to discuss with the help of your teacher.

> **27** Can you suggest some of these "sites"? (Look at figures 20.7 and 20.8 to help you.)

28 What do you think is the most essential characteristic of any method of birth control?

For most couples – certainly all those who have not yet either started or completed their family – the most important thing about any method of birth control is that it should be **reversible**. The couple must be able to stop using the method and start a family when it suits them.

29 What else do you think is important for any method of contraception?

Besides being reversible, most people want their contraceptive method to be **reliable** (it must work) and everyone wants it to be **safe** (not to damage their health). It should be **convenient** too – if it is not, the couple may be tempted not to use it, or find they can't be bothered to use it properly. If this happens it probably won't work properly either. The different methods of contraception fall into four groups.

1   The barrier methods

The simplest methods of birth control are the barrier methods. They work because either the man or the woman wears a special device to prevent the egg and sperms ever coming into contact. They are **reliable** and **very safe**. They may be **less convenient** than some other methods because they have to be used every time the couple have intercourse.

a   The condom or sheath

Condoms are made of thin rubber, and must be rolled onto the man's erect penis before sexual intercourse begins. When the man ejaculates, the condom prevents the sperms from entering the vagina. The condom is very reliable if used with a *spermicide* (see later). Condoms are easy to buy and easy to use which makes them **very convenient**. And in addition, a condom can stop sexually transmitted disease organisms passing from one partner to the other (see later).

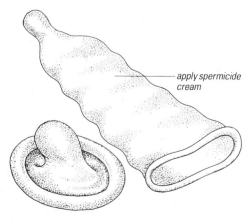

apply spermicide cream

Figure 20.15
Condoms (sheaths).

b The cap or diaphragm

The cap is a rubber dome with a flexible metal rim. The woman puts this into her vagina before intercourse so that it covers the cervix and stops sperms from entering the uterus. The cap is just as reliable as a condom if it is used carefully, with a spermicide (see below). A cap must be fitted by a trained doctor or nurse, to make sure it is the right size for the individual woman.

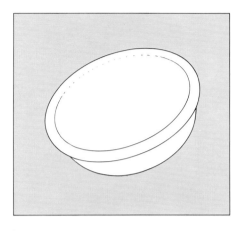 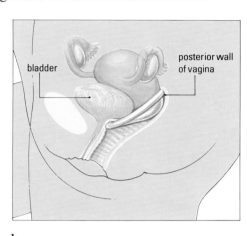

posterior wall
of vagina

bladder

a   b

Figure 20.16
a A contraceptive cap. **b** The cap in position.

Spermicides

Spermicides are sperm-destroying chemicals which should be used with a condom or cap. They come in the form of a tablet (pessary), cream, jelly or aerosol foam. The spermicide is spread over the woman's cap before insertion. Alternatively (if the man uses a condom), the spermicide is put into her vagina. Spermicides on their own **are not a reliable method of contraception**.

2   The medical methods

Medical methods work by altering the natural reproductive functions of the woman's body so that pregnancy does not occur. These methods are **reliable**. They are **reversible** and **very convenient** because the couple don't have to worry about taking precautions every time they have intercourse.

a The coil or intra-uterine device (IUD)

A coil, or IUD, is a small plastic or copper device which has to be inserted into the uterus by a doctor. It prevents a fertilized egg from implanting in the uterus. The device stays there until the woman wants to have a baby. Then the doctor will remove it. An IUD does sometimes cause side effects and infections. Because there is a small chance that infections can cause infertility, it is not a good method for young girls or women who have had no children.

b The pill (oral contraceptive)

Birth control pills work by altering the balance of hormones that control the menstrual cycle so that ovulation does not happen. If it is taken every single day as prescribed, without fail, the pill is the most reliable method of contraception. Provided it is taken under a doctor's guidance, it is also very safe.

3   Natural or rhythm methods

In natural methods, no artificial or medical means are used to prevent conception. Instead, the couple try to avoid intercourse when the woman is most likely to conceive. Natural methods have no health risk but most people find them very **unreliable** and **inconvenient**.

The aim of a natural method is to predict when ovulation will occur, so that intercourse can be avoided at that time. This is called using the "safe period". Ovulation may not occur at exactly the same time every month. And it can be difficult to predict it accurately. The most reliable way of doing this is for the woman, first thing each morning, to record her body temperature, which rises slightly just before an egg is released. She also has to learn to recognize various bodily changes which occur at ovulation. But stress, excitement or illness can all throw the woman's cycle – and her calculations – out. Natural methods are difficult to use reliably.

4   The permanent methods

There are two permanent methods of birth control – male and female sterilization. These both involve a small operation to cut or block the tubes through which the sperms or egg travel on the way from the testes or ovary. Couples who have completed their family and are quite sure they want no more children may choose this method of birth control. But this means that they can **never** have any more children – so it is something they have to think about very carefully.

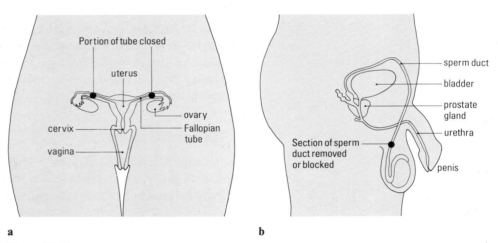

a   b

Figure 20.17
Sterilization in **a** a woman, and **b** a man.

Unreliable methods
There are a few methods you may have heard of, but they are so unreliable that you should not really think of them as methods of birth control at all. One is the withdrawal method in which the man tries (but does not always succeed) to withdraw his penis from the woman's vagina before he ejaculates.

Spermicides, used on their own, are not effective. Neither is doucheing (trying to wash the sperm out of the vagina after intercourse). Don't believe any old wives' tales you hear about birth control either – for example that a woman can't conceive if she is breast feeding, or if she has sexual intercourse standing up, or during her period. She can. Plenty of women have done so.

Morning-after birth control

If a couple do have "unplanned" sexual intercourse, using no contraceptive, they may be able to prevent an "unplanned" pregnancy if the girl visits her doctor or a family planning clinic within 72 hours (3 days). The girl will be given two special doses of a pill which will alter her hormonal balance and prevent pregnancy.

It is important to know about this method, but it's just as important to understand that it should **ONLY** be used in an emergency. Anyone who needs it more than once needs a proper, regular method of contraception.

Success and failure

A lot of contraceptive failures are really "user failures". The method is often blamed ("the sheath must have had a hole in it") when the user is really at fault ("I'd run out of spermicide jelly"). Even the pill can't work if you go away for the weekend and forget to take it.

B20.6   Sexually transmitted diseases

People sometimes worry needlessly that they may catch a sexually transmitted disease.

"It's no use standing on the seat,
The little germs can jump ten feet."

This piece of graffiti quite often decorates the walls of public lavatories. But the truth is that most of the organisms that cause sexually transmitted diseases cannot survive outside the body for more than a few minutes, and thrive only in moist, warm conditions. It is almost impossible to become infected through contact with a lavatory seat, or by drinking out of the same cup as someone who is infected.

It is quite normal for the reproductive system, like many other parts of the body, to contain micro-organisms. Some of them can cause uncomfortable or unpleasant symptoms, if they are able to multiply. For example, the fungus that causes thrush (a common infection in women), is very often present in the vagina. But its growth is usually inhibited by the small amounts of acid produced by the numerous harmless bacteria which are also present.

Figure 20.18
Is it fact or fiction that you can't catch sexually transmitted diseases in any of these ways?

a

b

c

Sometimes a course of antibiotics taken for an infection elsewhere in the body may destroy many of these bacteria, making it possible for the fungus to grow and thrive.

It is possible that harmful micro-organisms may be transferred from person to person during sexual intercourse. So the diseases they cause are called *sexually transmitted diseases*. You can't catch a sexually transmitted disease merely by holding hands or even kissing someone who is infected. There must be direct contact with the infected part, and because this is almost always the penis or vagina, this usually means sexual intercourse. Because these infections can only be passed between sexual partners they have always seemed frightening and shameful.

People who are promiscuous are much more likely to acquire sexually transmitted diseases than those who are not. This is not surprising since promiscuous people have many casual sexual encounters.

Signs and symptoms

How does someone know that he or she has caught a sexually transmitted disease?

Genital herpes produces painful blisters and *syphilis* produces painless sores, on the penis or vulva. But the only symptoms of most of the other diseases are a discharge from the penis or vagina, or discomfort in passing urine (as in *non-specific urethritis*). Sometimes there are no symptoms at all (*gonorrhoea* is often symptomless in women), and this, of course, means that the infected person can pass on the infection without realizing it. So both members of a couple are always treated, even though only one may have symptoms. Even if you have symptoms you may not be suffering from a sexually transmitted disease. Other diseases can cause similar symptoms and only a doctor can make the diagnosis.

It is impossible to acquire immunity to sexually transmitted diseases. Having the disease once does not mean that you cannot have it again. In some cases it actually makes it more likely. After one attack of genital herpes, for example, other attacks often follow, though they may not be so severe. But the real problem of sexually transmitted diseases is that they can lead to other much more serious conditions. Some can cause infertility. Non-specific urethritis and gonorrhoea, for example, can infect and sometimes block a woman's Fallopian tubes and make it less easy or even impossible for her to become pregnant. Others may lead to cancer. Genital warts and genital herpes increase the risk of a woman developing cancer of the cervix.

With the exception of AIDS (acquired immune deficiency syndrome – see below) and untreated syphilis (which is rare nowadays), people do not die from sexually transmitted diseases. But they are unpleasant and uncomfortable for the person concerned, and spread easily from one person to another. That is why it is important for anyone who thinks they or their partner may have been infected to go straight away to their doctor, or to one of the clinics which specialize in treating sexually transmitted diseases.

30 What advice do YOU think should be given to young people about sexually transmitted diseases?

AIDS – Acquired Immune Deficiency Syndrome

Many people are frightened about AIDS, because it is incurable at the present time and is very often a fatal disease. But many people worry unnecessarily. People who have the disease almost always belong to one of the following groups: men and women who have many sexual partners (these, of course, may have other sexually transmitted diseases); drug users who share hypodermic needles to inject themselves; haemophiliacs who have accidentally been given blood infected with the AIDS virus; babies born to mothers who have the disease. Men and women in any of these groups can pass the infection on to a partner during sexual intercourse. There is virtually no chance of becoming infected through ordinary everyday contact with someone who has the disease. Even those people who are exposed to the virus do not always develop the disease and some develop it only in a mild form.

The symptoms of AIDS are quite different from those of other sexually transmitted diseases. AIDS can affect any system of the body and symptoms do not appear for months, even years, after the initial infection.

An AIDS infection can only be acquired if the virus responsible enters the bloodstream. This can be through a very small cut or abrasion indeed. The disease suppresses the body's defence system so that it can no longer fight infections. The sufferer is likely to develop various infections and some forms of cancer.

It would be a good idea to keep yourself up to date with the latest information about AIDS available through your local Health Authority.

Review

In this chapter we have concentrated on the biological aspects of human reproduction. We have seen that sexual intercourse in humans is not just about reproduction. This is why people are different from other animals. Humans are perhaps unique in that they may have sexual intercourse simply because it is pleasurable and rewarding for both partners. Because of this, long term and loving relationships may be established between two people. Contraception is very often important in the context of such a relationship. The availability of contraceptive methods means that a couple can regulate the size of their family without having to restrict their physical enjoyment of each other. With the development of reliable and safe techniques of contraception it has become possible to avoid the physical and emotional stresses of the unplanned and unwanted pregnancies that are otherwise the likely outcome of any sexual relationship. We should not lose sight of the fact that human reproduction is the beginning of the establishment of family groups in which living together, caring for each other and sharing things are part of everyday life.

Chapter **B**21   **Growing up**

B21.1   **Growth and development**

All living organisms *develop*; the young mature and become adults. They become old (or *age*) and finally they die. In some species the differences between the young and the adult of the species are very striking; in others the young is close to a small version of the adult. The ducks in figure 21.1, the tree in figure 19.3 (page 237) and the photograph of swans opposite page 234 give you some examples.

Figure 21.1
A mallard duck and ducklings.

1 What differences can you see between the adult and the young in these examples?

Development means *all* the changes that go to produce a mature, fully developed organism. Some of these changes are difficult to measure; growth, however, is a change which can usually be measured quite easily.

2 Suggest ways in which you could measure the growth of the organisms shown in figures 21.1 and 19.3 and the photograph opposite page 234.

What is growth?

The bodies of organisms are made of cells, and the organisms grow bigger because the cells divide and make more cells and each new cell increases in size. Growth is often defined as an increase in the living material of an organism. A graph showing the increase in cell numbers as a result of cell division is drawn in figure 21.2. This is a theoretical graph but it is the shape of graph you would expect to get if you plotted a graph of the measurements of any feature of an organism which grew as a result of cell division.

Graphs showing the growth of different parts of barley seedlings are drawn in figure 21.3.

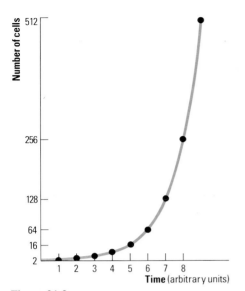

Figure 21.2
A graph showing the increase in cell numbers as a result of cell division.

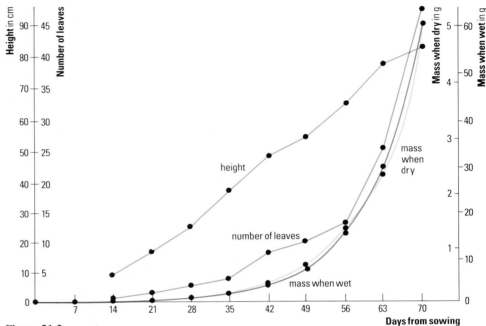

Figure 21.3
Graphs showing the development of different parts of barley seedlings.

3 Compare the graphs of barley development with the one of cell division in figure 21.2. Which graphs show a similar pattern and which ones are different?

4 What can you conclude about the pattern of development in barley seedlings? Is it just the result of cell division or is it likely that other processes affect it as well?

B21.2 Different patterns of development

We probably know most about the pattern of human development because that is most familiar to us. We know that after birth we develop as children and you can see in Chapter **B**20 how boys and girls become adolescent and sexually mature until finally they are adult. Later in this chapter we see how the adult body changes as we get older. In other words, there is a normal sequence through which our body changes during our lifetime.

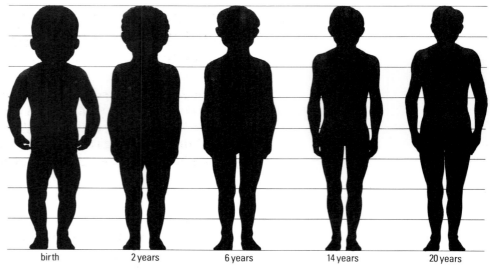

birth   2 years   6 years   14 years   20 years

Figure 21.4
Changes in the proportions of a male human being at different ages.

5 For each of the diagrams of the humans in figure 21.4 measure, in millimetres, the length of the head from the top of the head to the chin and the length of the body from the neck to the feet.

6 Devise a suitable table to record your results.

7 Plot a graph, with age on the horizontal axis and length on the vertical axis, to show the relative length of the head at different ages and the relative length of the rest of the body.

8 What happens to the relative lengths of **a** the head and **b** the body as a person becomes older?

Other patterns of development are seen in insects and amphibians, about which you probably already know something.

B21.3   Telling the age of an organism

People are often interested in how old organisms are (see Chapter **B**1) and there are various ways we can use to find out. You may know some of them.

Telling the age of a fish

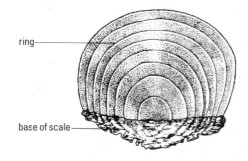

Figure 21.5
The scale of a herring, *Clupea harengus*, showing the rings.

We can tell the age of fish that have scales, like herrings. We do this by looking at the rings on one of the scales. Tiny scales appear on young fish when they are about two and a half centimetres long. The scales grow larger as the fish grows. In spring and summer when there is plenty of food the herring grows rapidly and the scales grow faster as well. In winter, when food is scarce, the scales stop growing and this shows as a ring on the scales. A ring marks the end of a year's growth, so by counting the rings on the scales we can tell the age of the herring. (See figure 21.5.)

9 How old was the herring from which the scale in figure 21.5 was taken?

The life span of animals and plants varies tremendously and you can find out about how long some animals live in Worksheet **B**1B. Some plants like groundsel live only a few weeks while trees like yews and cedars can live for over a thousand years. The longest life span of any tree is that of the giant Californian redwood which can live for over four thousand years.

B21.4   How are growth and development controlled?

Most people know that plants must have light and water in order to grow at all, and that giving them some fertilizer may produce bigger and better ones.

Light, water, and fertilizer are all obtained from the environment of the plant, but for a plant to grow and develop normally certain internally produced chemicals called *auxins* are also needed.

Auxins are only needed in very small quantities. Since the first auxin was isolated in 1934 many other chemical substances have been discovered which influence and control plant growth and development. All these chemical substances, including auxins, are known generally as *growth substances*.

You can see the effect of an auxin on the growth of shoots by putting the young shoots of a cereal like oats or wheat into different concentrations of an auxin and measuring their growth. The results can be plotted on a graph as in figure 21.7.

Auxins are also used in hormone rooting powders to promote root growth. Figures 21.8 and 21.9 show how effective they can be.

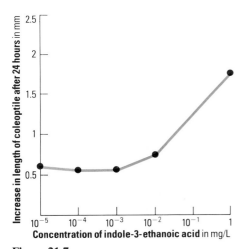

Figure 21.6
A germinating barley grain, showing the shoot.

Figure 21.7
A graph showing the effect of auxin on the growth of a shoot.

Figure 21.8
Dipping a cutting of *Clematis montana* in hormone rooting powder.

Figure 21.9
The *Clematis montana* plant on the left has been grown from a cutting with hormone rooting powder, the other plant without it.

In a typical shoot with a terminal bud, auxin is produced at the tip and passes down the stem, stopping the side buds from developing. If the terminal bud is "pinched out" the flow of auxin stops, and side shoots develop. (See figure 21.10.) Gardeners make use of this to get bushy plants rather than spindly ones.

Figure 21.10
The *Pelargonium* plant on the left has been left to grow unchecked.
The one on the right has had its terminal bud removed. Note the side shoots which are
developing and the bushy growth, compared with the other plant.

So growth substances do not always increase growth in plants – they may
stop it, especially if used at higher concentrations.

Plant growth substances have many other effects as well as increasing or
stopping growth. Some, or chemicals very like them, are now made in
factories and are used as weed killers. Others are used to stop hedges and the
grass on lawns from growing quickly. They can also be used to produce dwarf
pot plants, to keep vegetables like cabbages and lettuces fresh for longer, to
make cut flowers last longer, and to help ripen fruit. These substances are
therefore very important in horticulture as well as to gardeners.

Hormones in the growth and development of animals

You may already have learned about some of the functions of hormones in
animals in Chapters **B**12 and **B**20. They are also needed in very small
amounts for normal growth and development.

In 1785 a giant, whose name was Patrick Conner, put himself in an
exhibition in London. A hundred years after his death his skeleton was
removed from his grave and a doctor who examined it found that his leg and
hand bones were about half as long again as those of a normal man. The clue
to the cause of this could be seen in the bony cavity in the floor of the skull in
which the *pituitary gland* is housed: in Patrick Conner's skull this cavity was
much larger than normal. We now know that the pituitary gland, found on
the under side of the brain (Chapter **B**11, section **B**11.9) secretes a most
important hormone which controls growth. It is called *growth hormone*.

INTERPRET

10 Suggest the reason why Patrick Conner was a giant.

11 What do you think the result of too little growth hormone in a child would be?

Figure 21.11 shows the heights of a normal child and one who lacks enough growth hormone.

Age, in years	Height of normal boy, in cm	Height of boy with growth hormone deficiency, in cm
Birth	52.0	52.0
2.0	86.0	76.0
3.0	94.0	80.0
4.0	102.0	85.0
5.0	109.0	90.0
6.0	115.0	91.0
7.0	121.0	95.0
8.0	126.0	100.0
9.0	131.0	104.0
10.0	137.0	106.5
11.0	142.0	108.5
12.0	147.0	110.0
13.0	153.0	111.0
14.0	161.0	114.0
15.0	169.0	116.0
16.0	173.0	118.0
17.0	174.0	124.0
18.0	175.0	128.0
19.0	175.0	129.5
(19.5	175.0	130.0)
20.0	175.0	130.0

Figure 21.11

12 Plot two line graphs to compare the growth of these two children.

Fortunately, if children who lack growth hormone are given carefully controlled amounts of it at the right stage in their development they will grow to a normal height.

There is another hormone that plays an important part in the development of animals. The changes that take place when tadpoles become adult frogs and toads are dramatic. The fully aquatic tadpole suddenly changes into an adult and lives on land. In 1912 a scientist fed an extract of the *thyroid gland* to frog tadpoles and found that they became adult frogs much sooner than expected. This suggested that something in the thyroid extract might be causing the change. At the time the chemicals we now call hormones were not known. We now know that a hormone secreted by the thyroid gland is involved in the control of metamorphosis of amphibians.

Thyroid hormone plays a vital part in the development of all vertebrate animals (see Chapter **B**6). If thyroid hormone is lacking at birth the animal fails to develop normally, both mentally and physically. If the hormone is given early enough normal development is partly, if not fully, restored.

Other animals have hormones which control development: for instance, insects have a hormone called *juvenile hormone* which prevents moulting and another one which stimulates it. Timing of moulting in insects is brought about as a result of a balance between the two.

B21.5   Uncontrolled growth

At the beginning of the chapter we saw that growth may be the result of cells dividing. Usually cell division happens in a controlled way. Sometimes cell division gets out of hand and a mass of cells, called a *tumour*, forms. Tumours are of two kinds. One kind stays in one place and is called *benign*. Benign tumours cause little trouble except occasionally to press on surrounding tissues, which is why they sometimes have to be removed surgically. With the other kind, which is called *malignant*, some of the cells break off and move into the lymph or blood. This is how tumour cells spread to other parts of the body where new tumours may grow. *Cancer* (or *carcinoma*) is an example of a malignant tumour.

People often get very worried about cancer and it is a very common cause of death in this country. But nowadays there are many possible treatments for cancer. The earlier a developing cancer can be detected, the more likely it is that the treatment will be successful. Someone who notices symptoms like the following should probably seek advice:

a lump;

coughing up blood;

a cough lasting a month or more in a person who has not previously had a persistent cough;

a change in the regularity of bowel action in someone who has previously been very regular in this respect;

passing blood in the faeces or urine.

None of these symptoms necessarily means that a person has got cancer, but it is sensible to have an early check and find out whether treatment is necessary.

The treatment may mean an operation to remove the tumour. *Radiotherapy* (the use of radioactivity to kill the tumour cells or to stop them dividing) and *chemotherapy* (the use of drugs) can also be very successful in the treatment of cancer.

In women, two of the commonest types of cancer can often be detected very early on, at a stage when the results of treatment are very good. A condition that precedes *cervical cancer* (though not cancerous itself) can be detected by the cervical smear test; this is why women should be tested regularly (every three to five years). And *cancer of the breast* would be far less common if every woman was taught how to examine her breasts in order to detect the first sign of any change about which she should seek her doctor's advice.

There is no single thing anyone can do to prevent cancer because there are so many possible causes. The risks of getting certain cancers can be reduced, however, by avoiding what appear to be the causes: for example, not smoking to avoid the risk of getting lung cancer (see Chapter **B**7). More positively, eating a high fibre diet may reduce the likelihood of developing cancer of the colon.

B21.6   More about human development

About a quarter of our lives is spent in developing to reach physical and intellectual maturity. As you have seen earlier in the chapter, "development"

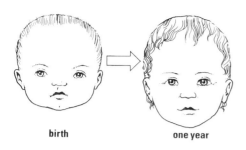

birth   one year

brain mass

Figure 21.12
The relative increase in mass of the human brain in the first year of life.

does not just mean growth. It is the process of learning new and more complex skills which make us able to deal with new and more complex situations.

By the time a baby is born, most of the bodily systems have matured so that the baby can survive outside the mother's uterus. Even so, the newborn baby is a helpless bundle of reflex action, and this is because the central nervous system is much less developed at birth than other systems are.

The pattern of development in humans

All babies develop according to the same pattern, passing the same "milestones" in much the same order. They all learn to roll before they learn to sit, and to sit before they can stand. But they all develop at different rates. Figure 21.13 shows the time span over which children normally learn each new skill.

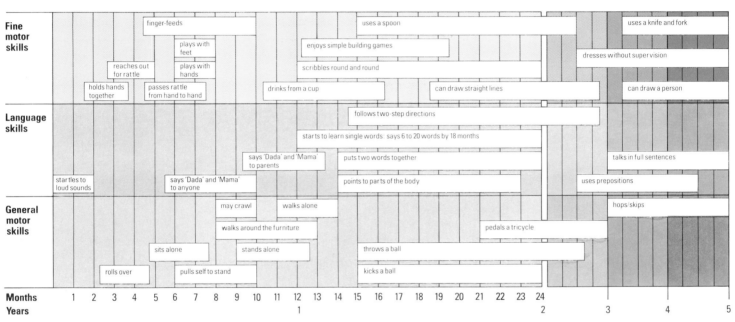

Figure 21.13
The time span over which children learn new skills.

OBSERVE   INTERPRET

13 When do children learn most of their movement (motor) skills?

14 What is the "busiest" year for learning language?

Some skills are learned most easily at a particular stage of development (there is very little use, for example, in trying to toilet train children before the age of two, when they begin to have control over their bowels and bladder). For some skills, such as language, there is a "critical" learning period – if they are not acquired at a particular stage, they cannot be learned later in life.

APPLY

15 Can you explain why children who are deaf from birth may never learn to speak properly?

Figure 21.13 shows the pattern of a child's physical and language development. But maturity implies more than this.

16 In what other ways do you think a child needs to develop to become a fully mature adult?

17 Can you suggest the age range over which these new skills are learned?

B21.7   Parental care

Here are three questions about parents and families it may be helpful to think about and discuss.

18 What is a good parent?

You will probably have your own ideas about what a good parent "ought" or "ought not" to do. They will depend partly on your experience of your own and other people's families, and partly on your own personality. When you become a parent yourself you may try to avoid the mistakes you think your parents have made. And you'll most certainly make other mistakes – every parent does. But children are amazingly adaptable and nearly always survive their parents' efforts to bring them up!

19 Could you describe a normal family?

Every home and every family is different from every other. But to nearly every child their own family is "normal" and their home is the one they feel most comfortable in. What does this suggest to you? Perhaps there is no single "right" way to bring up a family.

20 What do you think of the following definition?
"The job of a good parent is to protect the children when they are young, and to encourage them to be increasingly independent as they grow older."

This is all right as far as it goes, but it leaves out one essential feature of parental care. Children need to be **loved**. One of the reasons they need to be loved is so that they can, in their turn, learn to love. It is easier for people who have had a happy and loving childhood to pass this on to their own children.

Making attachments

Here are some more questions for you to think about and discuss.

---

21 Do you think that most parents love their children as soon as they are born, or do parents learn to love as they care for their babies?

22 If parents learn to love their children, why do we talk about the "maternal" *instinct*? Is there a "paternal" instinct too?

There seems to be no reason why a man should not have paternal instinct just as strong as a woman's maternal instinct. The problem is that he may not have as many opportunities to develop it.

---

23 Think about what happens during a baby's first few days. List the opportunities each parent has to spend time with the baby.

You will probably come to the conclusion that in most families the mother, especially if she is breast feeding, spends far more time in close contact with the baby than the father does. The mother usually has every opportunity to develop her maternal instinct and form a close bond with the child.

---

24 Do you think it is important for a man to try to develop his paternal instinct? How do you think he might do this?

There is some evidence that men who have watched their children being born tend to become more involved with them.

Parents certainly grow to love their children more through being with them and caring for them in the early days and weeks of the child's life. This attachment between parents and child, which develops through early contact with each other, is called *bonding*. Maternity hospitals now recognize the importance of contact during these early days. Even babies who are so small or premature that they have to be kept in special incubators are looked after and handled by their parents as much as possible. (Figure 21.14.)

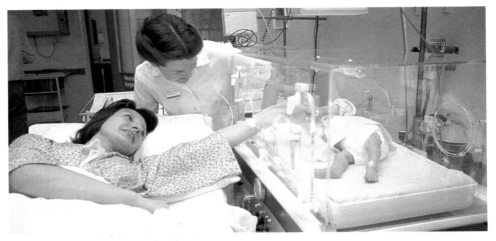

Figure 21.14
A mother touching her premature baby in an incubator.

under 6 weeks

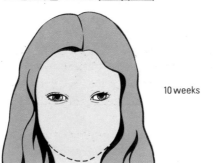

10 weeks

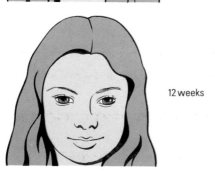

12 weeks

Figure 21.15
Faces at which children smile at different ages.

Babies are utterly helpless and dependent on their parents' care, so the attachment between parents and child is very important to the baby.

25   What can babies do to make their parents attached to them?

Babies smile at human faces very early in their lives – when they are about one month old. It seems that the baby's smile is important – it "rewards" the parents and strengthens the affectionate bond between them. Blind babies smile less and don't gaze into their mother's eyes. Their mothers often feel rejected and unhappy.

26   Do you think babies become attached to just one person?

By the age of ten months, a child has usually become attached to several people, though some will be more important than others and one person may be especially important. Usually this is the person who cares for the child most of the time. This need not be the mother. It could just as easily be the father or grandmother. And a child does not necessarily become most attached to the person who provides physical care – changing nappies or feeding. What the child responds to more than anything is the emotional warmth – the love – he or she is given.

What should parents do?

The most important thing parents can do (apart from loving their child) is to get along with each other. Most children are happier in a contented "one parent" family than they are with two parents who are constantly quarrelling. It is very good for a child to have two parents, however – and it is certainly easier for the parents if there are two of them to share parental care.

27   Do you think that when there are two parents they have different ''roles'' to play with their children?

One of the greatest advantages of having two parents is that they are **different**. They may balance each other. One may be more inclined to present challenges, encourage risk-taking, and the other to be more cautious, inclined to play safe. Children need to be played with – to be stimulated and to have their interest aroused in different things. Two parents are more likely to have the time to do all this than one alone. Having two parents helps a child to get along with and understand the opposite sex, too. And it provides a "model" of the same sex for the child to identify with.

28   How do you think parents should change as their children grow older? Or don't you think it is necessary for them to change?

Children grow up very quickly, but not all at once. One of the most difficult things parents have to do is to recognize the ways in which their son or daughter is maturing and needs more independence, and ways in which he or she is still a child needing protection. Parents have to change continually, altering their own attitudes and behaviour to keep pace with their developing children.

Patterns of family care

In *The story of the amulet*, a children's story by E. Nesbit published in 1906, the author describes her vision of London in the future: "men as well as women seemed to be in charge of the children and were playing with them."

E. Nesbit's future has arrived and it seems to be working well. More fathers now take part in caring for their children than ever before. Sometimes the parents share the care of their children because both are working. Sometimes a father has to care for his children on his own because the family has broken up through death or divorce. Men seem able to "mother" just as well as women, and children seem to fare just as well with a male care-giver as with a female one.

In fact there are all sorts of different patterns of family care. Take some of the following as a basis for class discussion.

29 What about role reversal – the woman goes out to work, the man becomes the "househusband"?

30 Or the merging of roles, where jobs and child care are shared completely, with no "his" or "her" areas?

31 Or the kibbutz system, where the children of the community are cared for in a communal nursery during the day?

32 How important do you think it is for a woman to stay at home and care for her children full time during the early years?

33 If the mother goes out to work, what sort of substitute care do you think should be arranged for the children?

Growing up and growing old

A human life is often seen as having three phases – development, followed by a period of maturity during which there is little physical or mental change, and then a period of aging or *senescence*. But in fact the aging process starts almost as soon as we reach adulthood. Even during the twenties the mass of the brain and the number of nerve cells starts to decrease and the nerves start to conduct impulses rather more slowly. From the thirties onwards there is a gradual slowing down of all the body processes. The basal metabolic rate (see Chapter **B9**, section **B9**.7) slows down, so that the body does not transfer energy as quickly and body temperature is slightly lower. The senses – smell, sight, hearing, and taste – become less acute. The skin loses its elasticity. But until late middle age these changes are so slow and gradual that they are scarcely noticeable.

Most people want to live a long time, though no one wants to be old. Any number of myths and legends tell of man's search for eternal youth. But the

Figure 21.16
"When I get older, losing my hair…"

search is always in vain – aging is inevitable. No one knows exactly what makes us age, but it is probably built into us as part of our genetic programming. A tendency to live a long time seems to run in families, which suggests that it may be genetically controlled. Part of the process of aging is that the body seems to lose some of its ability to "copy" cells efficiently, so there is a gradual running down in its capacity to renew itself. (See figure 21.17.)

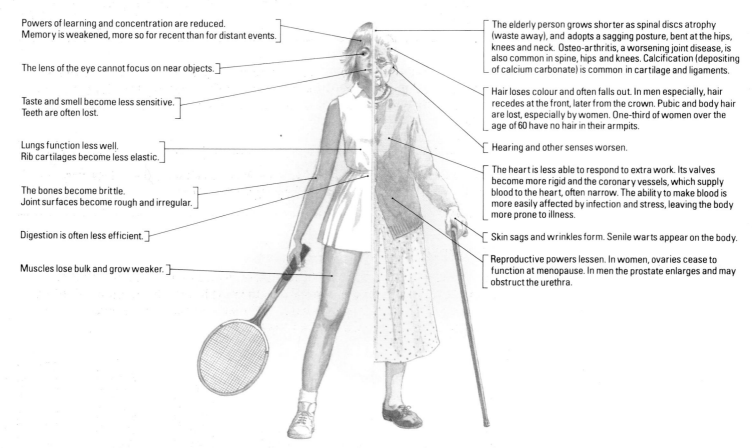

Powers of learning and concentration are reduced. Memory is weakened, more so for recent than for distant events.

The lens of the eye cannot focus on near objects.

Taste and smell become less sensitive. Teeth are often lost.

Lungs function less well. Rib cartilages become less elastic.

The bones become brittle. Joint surfaces become rough and irregular.

Digestion is often less efficient.

Muscles lose bulk and grow weaker.

The elderly person grows shorter as spinal discs atrophy (waste away), and adopts a sagging posture, bent at the hips, knees and neck. Osteo-arthritis, a worsening joint disease, is also common in spine, hips and knees. Calcification (depositing of calcium carbonate) is common in cartilage and ligaments.

Hair loses colour and often falls out. In men especially, hair recedes at the front, later from the crown. Pubic and body hair are lost, especially by women. One-third of women over the age of 60 have no hair in their armpits.

Hearing and other senses worsen.

The heart is less able to respond to extra work. Its valves become more rigid and the coronary vessels, which supply blood to the heart, often narrow. The ability to make blood is more easily affected by infection and stress, leaving the body more prone to illness.

Skin sags and wrinkles form. Senile warts appear on the body.

Reproductive powers lessen. In women, ovaries cease to function at menopause. In men the prostate enlarges and may obstruct the urethra.

Figure 21.17
The changes that take place in aging.

Reaching your peak

Humans reach their physical peak around the age of thirty – this is the age of greatest athletic achievements.

34 Try to find out the age of some Olympic athletes who have won the men's 100 m, 1500 m, and marathon races and the 50 km walk.

Intellectual and scientific ability seems to peak between the ages of thirty and thirty-five, which are often the most productive years in a person's life. One study of chemists found that it was between these ages that most made their greatest contributions to their field. After this their achievement started to decline.

35 Make a list of five leaders of British industry – the chairmen of British Coal, for example, British Steel, ICI, Shell, or any large company. Try to find out the age of these people and then work out their average age.

36 List the last five British Prime Ministers, try to find out how old they were when they came to power, and work out the average age.

37 People in positions of power are often in their late sixties. What qualities do you think they have to make up for any deterioration in their mental or physical capacity with age?

Traditionally, a society has always been ruled by its "elders". The oldest members of the tribe were respected because they had lived the longest, and they knew the most. The rest of the tribe looked to them for guidance and authority.

38 Do you think attitudes have changed towards the oldest members of our own society? If you do think so, can you suggest why they have?

Life expectancy

Humans live longer than any other mammal and longer than most other animal species. The Indian elephant is the next longest lived mammal, often surviving for sixty or seventy years, and a few tortoises are believed to have outlived humans. See Chapter **B1**, section **B1.2**.

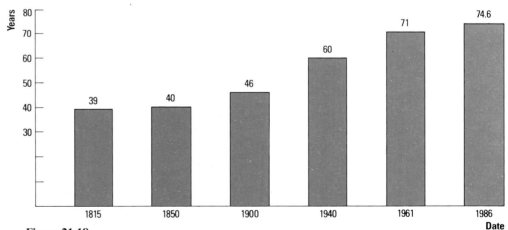

Figure 21.18
Changing life spans.

Early in this century life expectancy started to rise, and it has gone on rising gradually ever since. (See figure 21.18.) Today men can be expected to live, on average, for 71.6 years and women for 77.6.

39 What do you think has changed? What reasons can you suggest for the fact that people are surviving longer than they used to do?

We can start to see part of the reason for this by looking at the main causes of death a hundred years ago and comparing them to the foremost causes of death today.

1880s

1 Tuberculosis
2 Diarrhoea and dysentery
3 Scarlet fever

1980s

1 Heart disease
2 Cancer
3 Stroke

40 What is the most striking difference between these two lists?

A hundred years ago, few people had a chance to grow old. Most died of infectious diseases before their bodies had started to degenerate and wear out. Modern medicine with its use of antibiotics, immunizations and sterile operating conditions, together with today's much improved living conditions, mean that few people nowadays die of infections. They live long enough to develop a different set of diseases, which were not common in the last century simply because they involve a slow deterioration of the body systems over a period of time. Over half all deaths are caused by these diseases of old age – heart disease, cancer and stroke.

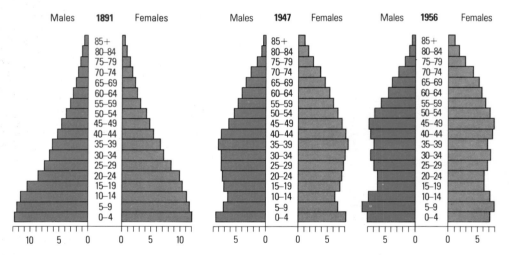

Figure 21.19
Population pyramids showing how the age distribution of the population of Great Britain has changed.

41 What else can be done to help people to live longer?

42 Would it be desirable to prolong life for much longer than its present span? What are the problems this could bring?

Chapter B22

Handing on to the next generation

B22.1 Alike or not alike?

All the cows in a herd may look very much alike to us but the farmer who owns them can tell them apart.

Figure 22.1
A herd of Jersey cows.

OBSERVE

1 What is it about particular individuals that makes you able to identify them?

2 Make a list of the features by which you can distinguish different people in the crowd shown in figure 23.8 (page 303).

3 What is it that often makes people **look** the same?

Two kinds of twins

The pairs of twins in figure 22.2a look alike. They are both of the same sex and so alike in appearance that they may confuse their friends – and certainly their teachers. But what about the others (figure 22.2b)? They are no more alike than any brothers or sisters in a family, they just happen to be the same age. The twins who look alike are called *identical*; the others are *non-identical*. What happens if identical twin babies are adopted separately and brought up in different homes? The information given in figure 22.3 should help to provide an answer.

a

b
Figure 22.2
Two pairs of twins:
a identical
b non-identical.

	Difference between identical twins		
	average height	average mass	average head length
Brought up together	17 mm	2.0 kg	2.9 mm
Brought up apart	18 mm	4.5 kg	2.2 mm

Figure 22.3
Some differences between identical twins brought up together and identical twins brought up apart.

4 Which characteristics remain almost the same, even when the children are brought up in different homes?

5 Which characteristic is changed when the twins are brought up separately? Suggest an explanation for this.

B22.2   Environment or heredity?

Figure 22.4
A crop of potatoes, some grown with fertilizer and some without.

Variations are seen in all living organisms and are brought about in two ways. Some variations are caused as a result of the surroundings (*environment*) and some are the result of what the organisms have inherited from their parents (*heredity*). All keen gardeners know the effect of fertilizer, water and pesticides (all part of the environment) on the growth of their flowers and vegetables, even when all the plants come from the same parent plant (heredity). (Figure 22.4.)

6 Which of the differences shown in figure 22.4 are caused by the effect of environment and which are inherited?

It is often difficult to be sure how much of the variation is due to heredity. Thus, when investigating what is inherited, scientists must use carefully controlled conditions, in order to reduce the effects of the environment.
Here are some ways in which humans can vary:

blood group	curliness of hair
eye colour	favourite foods
good or bad temper	hair colour
height	interest in music
mass	regional accent
shape of ear lobes	freckles
sense of humour	skill at games

7 In each case, do you think the variation is due to environment or heredity or do both have an effect? (See Worksheet **B22A**.)

Why do people look like their parents?

Every new individual begins as the result of fertilization, so the "instructions" for inherited characteristics must be in the egg and sperm. In fact, the instructions are in the nuclei of these cells. When these two nuclei fuse at fertilization they become the nucleus of the first cell of the new individual. This nucleus is exactly copied as the cell divides to form the embryo and then the foetus. In this way every cell in the body contains the same instructions. Identical twins are the result of a fertilized egg separating into two sets of cells, both of which continue to divide, so two identical embryos come from the same egg and sperm. Non-identical twins occur when two eggs are produced at the same time and each is fertilized by a different sperm. (Figure 22.6.)

Figure 22.5
Three generations – is there such a thing as family likeness?

	One baby	Ordinary twins (fraternal twins)	Identical twins
Each egg is fertilized by a sperm…	1 egg, 1 sperm	2 eggs, 2 sperms	1 egg, 1 sperm
the cell divides…			
and divides…			
again and again…			
until nine months later a baby has grown from each group of cells.		These twins may not be any more alike than ordinary brothers and sisters. This is because they come from different eggs and sperms.	These twins will look *exactly* alike. They will be the same sex because they came from the same egg and sperm.

Figure 22.6
How twins occur.

If cells are specially treated and then stained when they are dividing, it is sometimes possible to see in them, under a microscope, long threads, called *chromosomes*. The chromosomes are in the nucleus. They carry the "instructions", which are called *genes*, for all the inherited characteristics.

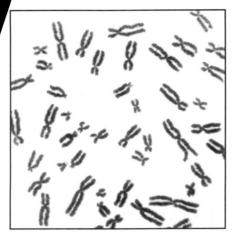

Figure 22.7
Chromosomes of a human female – you can see that they are not all alike.

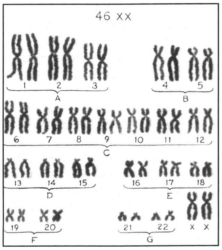

Figure 22.8
Chromosomes of a human female. The chromosomes have been arranged in pairs.

As you can see in figure 22.7, the chromosomes are not all alike. If a photograph of all the chromosomes in one nucleus is cut up, they can be sorted into pairs as shown in figure 22.8.

---

8 How many pairs of chromosomes do humans have?

The members of each pair of chromosomes are not only the same size; they also carry the same genes.

B22.3   Halving and doubling

All human cells have the same number of chromosomes, except for the gametes (eggs and sperms). They only get half shares. After all, if there were 23 pairs in both the egg and the sperm, when they joined together to make a new person there would be 46 pairs. The next lot of children would have twice as many, until finally the nucleus of each cell would be bursting at the seams with chromosomes.

So eggs and sperms are made with 23 **single** chromosomes instead of 23 **pairs**. This means that the new baby contains the same number of chromosomes in each cell as its parents' body cells did. (Figure 22.9.)

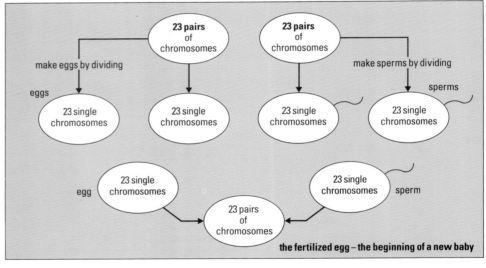

Figure 22.9
This shows how the number of chromosomes stays the same when fertilization takes place.

APPLY

B22.4   Cloning – science fiction or fact?

Human clones may belong to the world of science fiction but clones that provide food crops and forests – and plants for the amateur gardener – are part of the real world.

What is cloning?

In Chapter **B**19 you saw that many plants can reproduce from one parent only, by asexual (vegetative) methods. One advantage of vegetative reproduction is that all the offspring are identical to the parent. Sugar cane and potatoes are two important crop plants which are grown by using vegetative methods.

Cloning is not new. Indeed it is an ancient art and if you have ever taken a leaf from an African violet and kept it in water until a new plant has grown on it – you have done it!

---

9   What other examples of cloning are used in growing new plants?

A new plant produced by cloning has chromosomes identical to those of the parent plant from which it came. If its chromosomes are identical, so are its genes. A *clone* therefore comes from one parent and has **all** the genes of that parent (see page 286). This is unlike the animals which develop from an unfertilized egg, as in the case of the drones in a hive of bees. They are not a clone because they only have half the usual number of chromosomes found in bees. They only have the chromosomes found in the egg so they are not identical to the parent.

Cloning plants is quite easy. It is now done on a large scale in a laboratory by using a technique called *tissue culture*. One of the first plants to be grown by tissue culture was the carrot. The secret is to use a sterile technique in the laboratory. A sterile razor blade can be used to cut away a tiny piece of stem from a carrot seedling. This is put on to sterile nutrient agar (which contains a "cocktail" of all the things needed for the carrot to grow) in a sterile Petri dish. Clumps of cells called a *callus* grow from the cut stem pieces. The cells of a callus are all the same and each one can be grown into a whole new carrot plant. (Figure 22.10.) All of those plants would therefore be exactly alike. They would be a clone.

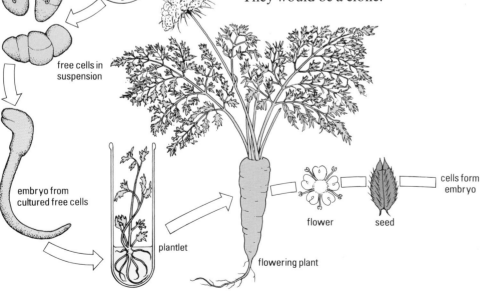

a

b

Figure 22.10
a The tissue culture of carrot. **b** Regrowing carrot from a small piece of carrot tissue.

a

b

Figure 22.11
a Stages in the tissue culture method of cloning an oil palm. **b** Young cloned palms in Unipanwe Kluang in Malaysia.

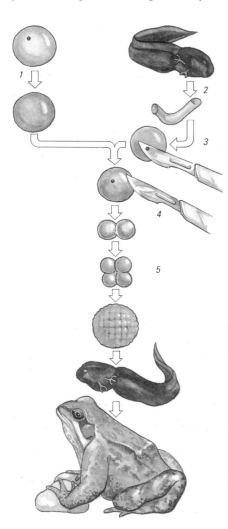

The oil palm story

Oil palm oil is used in large quantities in industry to make margarine, soaps and detergents. Under the best growing conditions some oil palms will yield 6 tonnes of oil per hectare. Others yield much less. If the plants are grown from seed there will always be variation in the yield from the crop. The obvious thing to do, to be sure of getting a high yield from all of the plants, is to clone the high-yielding oil palms.

10 Explain why this is the case.

It took English scientists at Unilever 10 years to find a way of using the tissue culture method to clone oil palms. Figure 22.11a shows stages in tissue culture.

Oil palms grown in this way are already bearing fruit in plantations in Malaysia (figure 22.11b). As well as food crops, whole forests of trees can be produced by cloning. The possibility of cloning Norway spruce trees which are resistant to acid rain is already being investigated. Other plants, including roses, orchids, bananas and pineapples, have also been cloned.

11 What other advantage is there in cloning besides getting plants which are identical and which have all the features you want?

What about animal clones?

Cloning animals is not as easy as cloning plants. The reason for this is that whereas **any** plant cell will develop into a whole new plant, animals have to grow from an egg cell. So to clone an animal cell you have to use an egg. The egg's own nucleus is first removed, and then the nucleus of the cell you want to clone is put into the egg. Figure 22.12 shows how this has been done in the frog.

Cloning mammals is more difficult still because they have to develop in a uterus.

At the present time perhaps the greatest value of cloning techniques is that they help scientists to learn more about cells. There is a great deal still to be learned about what happens to cells when they get old (aging) and when they form cancers. So that although cloning humans will remain the subject of science fiction films and novels – indeed it is illegal to try to clone humans – tissue culture is an exciting technique from which a great deal will be learned which will be of benefit to us.

Figure 22.12
Cloning a frog. **1** The nucleus is removed from a frog egg. It is now called an enucleated egg. **2** A section of intestine is taken from a tadpole. **3** A cell is taken from that intestinal tissue and its nucleus is removed. **4** The nucleus (with all its hereditary instructions) from the tadpole cell is put into the enucleated frog egg. **5** The egg, with its new nucleus, begins to divide and develop into a tadpole and then an adult frog. The frog's genes are exactly like those of the tadpole because its instructions came only from the nucleus of the tadpole. The frog is a clone.

B22.5 Boy or girl?

The two chromosomes in each pair are similar in size and shape, except for the 23rd pair, called the sex chromosomes. In the male these two are of different sizes and are given the names "X" and "Y" because of their shape. In females there are two X chromosomes.

Before you look at what is printed under figure 22.13, answer the next two questions.

12 Is figure 22.13 a photograph of the chromosomes of a man or a woman? How can you tell?

13 How can you tell the sex of the person whose chromosomes are shown in figure 22.8?

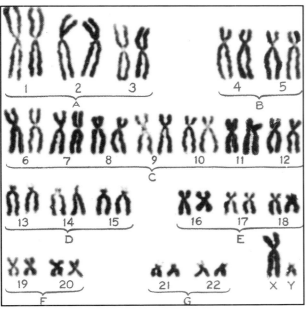

Figure 22.13
Chromosomes of a human male. These chromosomes have been arranged in pairs in the same way as those of the female in figure 22.8.

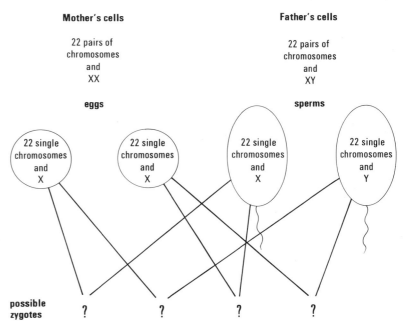

Figure 22.14
Fertilization of an egg with an X and a Y chromosome.

As you can see from the photograph in figure 22.13, the Y chromosome is much smaller than the X chromosome, so it cannot carry many genes. In fact, most of the genes on the X chromosome are not found on the Y chromosome at all.

14 How many X chromosomes are present in each egg produced by a woman?

The way in which the sex chromosomes behave when sperms are produced decides the sex of the unborn child. (See figure 22.14.) It is possible, though very difficult, to separate sperms into two different kinds.

15 What do you think the difference in their chromosomes would be?

16 Is it the egg nucleus or the sperm nucleus which determines the sex of a baby?

A girl inherits one X chromosome from each parent.

17 From which parent does a boy inherit his one X chromosome?

18 From which parent does a boy inherit the Y chromosome?

B22.6   Patterns of inheritance

Different sexes are determined by differences between whole chromosomes but most inherited variation is brought about by much smaller differences between parts of chromosomes.

A pair of large chromosomes has many genes; a pair of short chromosomes has fewer. The genes occur in a fixed sequence on each chromosome and the two members of a matched chromosome pair have exactly the same sequence of genes. The two genes at any one position on a pair of chromosomes may be exactly the same as each other, or slightly different. *These different forms of the same gene are called alleles.* The alleles provide slightly different instructions for the same character. For example, the gene for hair colour exists as several alleles, one of which provides the instruction "red hair" while another provides the instruction "brown hair". If differences in alleles of a gene produce differences which we can recognize then it is possible to study patterns of inheritance.

These patterns of inheritance are simplest to understand when the characteristic is easy to see, as in the family tree in figure 22.15, showing the inheritance of red hair. An allele whose effect can be "hidden" by the presence of another allele is called *recessive* and will only show when the other allele (the *dominant* one) is absent. In this case the recessive allele is for red hair colour and the dominant allele is for brown hair. Many inherited characteristics in all living things show this pattern of dominant and recessive alleles.

The allele for red hair may be handed on to the next generation from mother, father or both parents. The other allele is for brown hair.

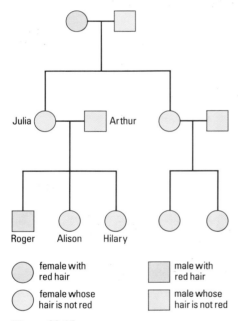

Figure 22.15
A family tree showing the inheritance of red hair.

19 How many alleles for red hair did the red-headed boy inherit? (Remember, the allele for red hair is recessive.)

20 What two alleles for hair colour might each of his sisters have inherited?

21 From which of his mother's parents was the allele for red hair inherited?

22 What do you know about the recessive allele carried by the boy's parents?

23 Would you expect the boy's father to have any red-haired relatives?

The first experiments in genetics

Gregor Mendel was a monk who later became abbot of a monastery in what is now Czechoslovakia. His photograph is shown in figure 22.16. In the 1850s he carried out some of the earliest and most important breeding experiments, using pea plants. For eight years he grew his plants in the monastery garden – tall and dwarf, red flowered and white flowered; he studied seven different characteristics in all. (See figure 22.17.)

Mendel cross-pollinated tall and dwarf plants. He showed that when the seeds produced by this cross are grown, plants of the next generation are all tall. If these tall plants are allowed to flower, self-pollinate and produce seeds, a second generation of plants can be grown. If a large number of plants are grown we find that most of them are tall but one out of every four is dwarf. (See figure 22.18.)

Is there a pattern to be seen in the inheritance of recessive alleles? All the first generation (F1) plants are tall but they must also carry a recessive allele for dwarfness which they inherited from the dwarf parent. The plants which carry two different alleles for height are called *heterozygotes*. The parent plants, each of which carry two copies of the same allele, either for tallness or dwarfness, are called *homozygotes*.

Figure 22.16
Gregor Mendel.

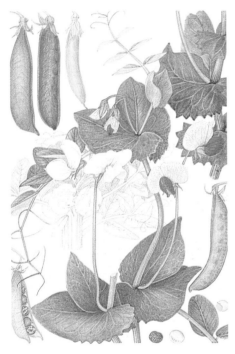

Figure 22.17
Mendel's peas.

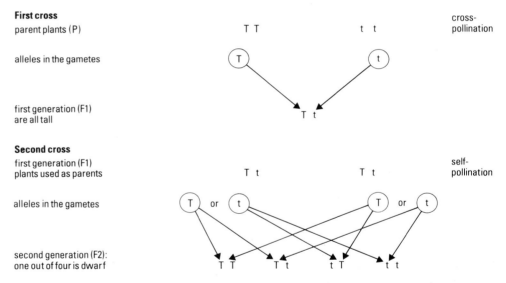

T = allele produces a tall plant   t = allele produces a dwarf plant (but only if T allele is absent)

First cross
parent plants (P) TT   tt   cross-pollination

alleles in the gametes T   t

first generation (F1) are all tall T t

Second cross
first generation (F1) plants used as parents T t   T t   self-pollination

alleles in the gametes T or t   T or t

second generation (F2): one out of four is dwarf T T   T t   t T   t t

Figure 22.18
An explanation of Mendel's experiment.

Appearance of plant	Alleles which the plant carries	Homozygote or heterozygote?
Tall (parent)	TT	homozygote
Dwarf (parent)	tt	homozygote
Tall (Fl)	Tt	heterozygote

Figure 22.19
The description of the appearance of the plant – tall or dwarf – is called its phenotype but the alleles the plant actually carries are called its genotype.

In the second generation (F2), the tall plants are of two kinds, though you can't tell them apart by just looking. Some are homozygotes, with two alleles for tallness. Some are heterozygotes, with one allele for tallness and one recessive allele for dwarfness. (See figure 22.19.) The only way to tell which is which is to carry out breeding experiments with each of them and see what kinds of plants are produced when the seeds grow into new plants.

Worksheets **B22C** and **B22D** allow you to investigate patterns of inheritance.

---

24 When a tall plant of the F2 generation is crossed with a dwarf plant, what kinds of plants will be produced if the tall plant has a recessive allele?

25 Would the result be the same if the tall plant had two alleles for tallness, and no recessive alleles?

26 A plant which shows the recessive character is always a homozygote. Explain why this is so.

27 If a large number of F2 plants is grown, what proportion of the tall ones would you expect to carry the recessive allele?

Human blood groups and inheritance

So far we have only considered the inheritance of two alleles of a gene, such as tallness and dwarfness (height) in pea plants. Genes often have more than two alleles. An important example of a gene with three alleles is the one which determines blood groups in humans. There are three alleles, "A", "B" and "O", of which each person has only two. The "O" allele is recessive to both "A" and "B". If "A" and "B" alleles are both present, both have an effect so the blood group is AB. A person of blood group A might carry the alleles "AA" or "AO", and a person with blood group B might carry the alleles "BB" or "BO".

---

28 What alleles must be carried by a person of blood group O?

Children of all four blood groups – A, B, AB and O – can occur in the same family although this is unlikely.

---

29 What blood groups must the parents have if all four blood groups could occur in their children? What alleles must the parents carry?

Sex-linked inheritance

Do you know anyone who is colour blind? (See figure 22.20.) If so, is the person male or female? Colour blindness is a common example of what we call sex-linked inheritance – about 1% of females and 5% of males are colour blind. This difference between the sexes is because the allele for this condition happens to be on the X chromosome (the Y chromosome is so small that it does not carry an allele for colour vision at all).

If a colour blind man marries a woman with two alleles for normal colour vision, none of their children will be colour blind, though they may have colour blind grandchildren. (See the family tree in figure 22.21.)

Figure 22.20
A test for colour blindness.

Figure 22.21
A family tree which shows the inheritance of colour blindness.

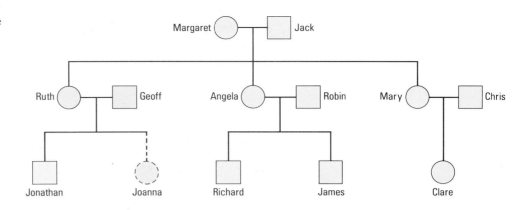

 female with
normal colour vision

 adopted daughter with
normal colour vision

colour-blind male

male with
normal colour vision

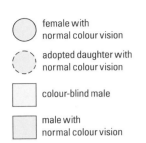

30 Is the allele for colour blindness dominant or recessive?

31 What alleles for colour vision do all of Jack's and Margaret's daughters have?

32 From which of his parents did James inherit his normal colour vision?

33 From which of their parents did Jonathan and Richard inherit their colour blindness?

34 Could Clare have an allele for colour blindness?

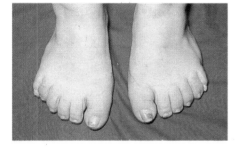

Figure 22.22
A woman with six toes on each foot.

B22.7 Five toes, or maybe six?

Most people have five fingers and toes but sometimes a baby is born with six. Figure 22.22 gives an example. This happens because the allele controlling the character "number of fingers" has changed. Such a change in an allele is called a *mutation*. Sometimes whole chromosomes mutate.

Figure 22.22 gives an example. This happens because the allele controlling the character "number of fingers" has changed. Such a change in an allele is called a *mutation*. Sometimes whole chromosomes mutate.
The chromosomes in figure 22.23 are those of a child with Down's syndrome.

Figure 22.23
a Unlike her brothers the child in the centre was born with Down's syndrome.
b The chromosomes of a female child with Down's syndrome.

a

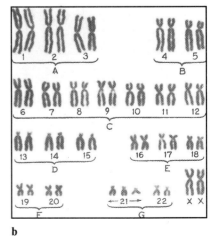

b

35 Can you see what makes this child's chromosomes different from normal ones?

Mutations are taking place all the time. We can only tell when a mutation has happened if it has an effect on the individual. Because many mutations produce recessive alleles they only show up if two mutant alleles happen to occur in the same person.

We do not always know why mutations happen but we do know that atomic radiation, X-rays, ultra-violet light and some chemicals can all cause mutations in different ways. Worksheet **B22E** allows you to investigate the effect of radiation on seeds.

Marrying in the family

The allele which produces an albino person (figure 22.24) is recessive and will only show if it is inherited from both parents.

The family tree in figure 22.25 shows albino children whose parents were first cousins. These cousins share the same grandparents on one side of the family. A mutant allele in one of these grandparents may be passed to two cousins and so two copies of the same allele may be found in the child of a first cousin marriage.

Figure 22.24
An albino negro.

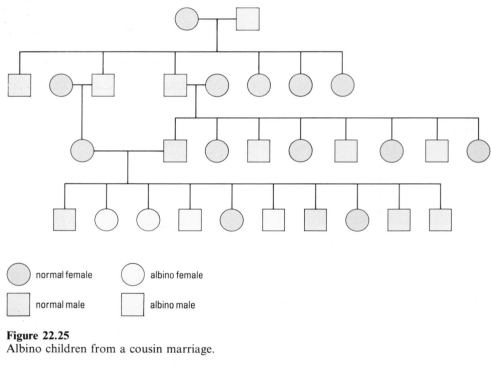

 normal female   ○ albino female

 normal male   □ albino male

Figure 22.25
Albino children from a cousin marriage.

I
INTERPRET

36 Which members of the family must have carried the recessive allele for albinism?

37 Which members of the family might pass on the allele to their children?

A
APPLY

B22.8   Genetic counselling

Most of the time it doesn't matter what alleles you hand on to your children but just sometimes it matters a great deal. This is when one or both parents pass on an allele which means that their child may have a serious mental or physical handicap. Fortunately this does not happen very often but if there is any risk then a couple can talk to a doctor who is specially trained to give information, help and advice. This is called "genetic counselling".

Who needs counselling?

If two parents already have a child with an inherited disease, or if it is present in any member of their families, then they will want to know the chance of another child being affected. There are a very few cases where the risk is high, and then the parents may need to consider whether it is right for them to have more children.

An inherited disease

Most inherited diseases are caused by recessive alleles which are mutant forms of the normal alleles found in healthy people. An important example of such a condition is cystic fibrosis. Children with this disease produce "sticky" mucus in their lungs and pancreas. This means that they have a greater risk of getting bronchitis and cannot digest their food properly.

38 Why do you think the sticky mucus causes these problems?

Another effect of the disease is that it makes the sweat much more salty than usual, though this is not usually a problem unless the person lives in a hot country.

39 Why would salty sweat be more of a problem in a hot country than in England?

Between 1 in 10 and 1 in 25 of the population of north-west Europe have the recessive allele for cystic fibrosis and are therefore "carriers" of the disease although they themselves are healthy. (Cystic fibrosis is not sex-linked.) It is only when **both** parents happen to be carriers of the recessive allele that there is a risk of an affected child being born. (See figure 22.26.)

If the mother is a carrier, any eggs she produces will either carry the dominant normal allele or the recessive mutant allele which causes the disease. The sperms produced by the carrier father will also be two kinds, normal sperms and the kind carrying the allele for the disease. If both egg and sperm happen to carry the cystic fibrosis allele then the child will have the disease.

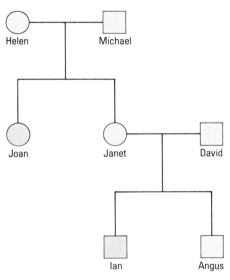

Figure 22.26
A family tree showing the inheritance of cystic fibrosis. Janet's sister Joan died of the disease when she was six years old. Ian also had cystic fibrosis but Angus was completely normal.

INTERPRET

40 What chance is there that a child with cystic fibrosis will be born to a couple who are both carriers?

41 What chance is there that they will have a normal child?

42 If their child is normal, what chance is there that it has a hidden recessive allele and is therefore a carrier?

43 What chance is there that the harmful allele will not be passed on to the child from either parent?

Since family size is usually small it is quite possible that all the children of carriers will be normal, though they could also be unlucky enough to have more than one child with the disease. It is sometimes possible (though not yet with cystic fibrosis) to tell if the foetus has inherited a particular disease. A small amount of the amniotic fluid surrounding the foetus is removed from the uterus. The fluid contains cells from the skin of the foetus, and these cells can be grown in the laboratory. By looking at the chromosomes, and from other tests on the cells, it is possible to diagnose some genetic defects. If tests show that the foetus is not normal the parents may wish to have it aborted so that a handicapped child is not born.

44 Should parents have the right to decide to terminate a pregnancy when it is known that their developing foetus has inherited a major handicap?

Dominant mutant alleles

Sometimes a dominant allele causes the abnormality. The allele which causes six fingers (see section **B22.7**) is dominant over the normal recessive allele present in five-fingered people. The six-fingered person usually carries a hidden recessive allele for the normal number of fingers.

45 If a six-fingered person has children, what chance is there that the child will also have six fingers?

46 If the child has five fingers can it pass on the allele for six fingers?

As scientists develop better techniques for finding out about chromosomes and mutant alleles, it should be possible to diagnose more problems at the foetal stage and so reduce the number of genetic defects in future generations. An even more useful test is one which will identify a recessive allele in a healthy carrier. Brothers and sisters of an affected person can then know for sure whether or not they have a recessive harmful allele which they might pass on to their own children.

B22.9   Are you just your genes?

Fifty years ago, people in the poorest families each had about one pint of milk a week. The very poorest only had half a pint, while better-off people drank about five pints each. At that time poor children were on average nearly eight centimetres shorter than children from better-off homes. The average height of people born after 1940 is nearly five centimetres taller than the average height of those born before 1930. These changes cannot possibly be due to heredity, in only one or two generations; what they do show is the enormous effect of improved nutrition, just one part of the environment. Figure 22.27 shows another part. Human genes cannot be altered deliberately, but the environment can be changed, so that all people have the best chance to make the most of their genetic inheritance.

Despite our knowledge of genetics, which can help to produce new varieties of crop plants and domestic animals by breeding experiments, it is still easier and quicker to alter the environment of an organism than to alter its genes.

a

b

Figure 22.27
In the environment, good and bad housing have an enormous effect.

You never know till you try

What's special about the things you can do? Do you enjoy sport or music? Did you become interested in something just because the opportunities happened to be there? Were you encouraged by your parents or your teachers? Are other members of your family good at the same things? With humans it is very difficult to know just how much of a person's ability is the result of inherited genes and how much is due to the opportunities which that person has, of making the most of his or her genetic potential.

So if you have the chance to try something new, go ahead and see how you get on. Not everyone has the inborn ability to be a top athlete or an expert dress designer, but you'll never know if you don't try, and everyone has to start somewhere.

Chapter B23 Changing with time

B23.1   Unanswerable questions?

The first people (that is, the first members of the genus *Homo*) who lived on the Earth were very different from the people who live on it today. (See figure 23.1). However, the place where they probably lived – the grassland plains of Africa – has changed very little. The other animals which live on the African grasslands today are also very different from those which lived there 2 million years ago.

Figure 23.1
Homo erectus – "upright Man" – lived on the plains of Africa.

Humans have probably always wanted to know the answers to questions about **how** they came to be on the Earth, **when** they first appeared, and **what** they were like.

It is only quite recently – during the last hundred years or so – that people have used scientific methods, based on observation and experiment, to try to answer these questions. Before then all cultures had their own beliefs and myths about how life began on the Earth.

We can never know exactly what happened in the past but the more evidence we can collect that is based on observation and experiment, the more accurate our understanding is likely to be. This scientific approach has led to

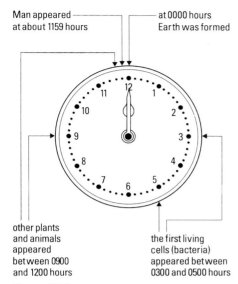

Man appeared at about 1159 hours

at 0000 hours Earth was formed

other plants and animals appeared between 0900 and 1200 hours

the first living cells (bacteria) appeared between 0300 and 0500 hours

Figure 23.2
On this clock face 12 hours = the age of the Earth, which is 4600 million years.

new theories both about the history of the solar system and about the beginning of life on our planet.

Among the things we need to know are how long ago the Earth was formed and how long living things have been on it.

B23.2 How old is the Earth?

The oldest rocks in the world were formed over 4000 million years ago. The first living organisms are thought to have appeared about 3000 million years ago. Set against this time scale, our own history of about 2 million years from caveman to spaceman is very short indeed.

The time scale of Earth history is hard to grasp and the model in figure 23.2, using a clock, may help.

> 1 For what part of its history has there been life of any kind on the Earth? (One hour on the clock is about 380 million years.)
>
> 2 What kinds of organisms have been on the Earth for the greatest part of this time?
>
> 3 For what part of the Earth's history have most plants and animals been on it?

A walk back in time

Another way to try to understand the enormous lengths of time we are dealing with is to take an imaginary walk back into the past, using the scale of 1 mm for each year we travel. On this scale your own life is about 1.5 cm; you would pass William the Conqueror before you had gone 2 metres, and the ancient Egyptians probably before you got to the door of the laboratory. It is difficult to realize that on this scale you would have to travel a journey as long as from London to the Midlands in order to meet a dinosaur.

million years

4000 — the oldest rock in the world
the oldest unaltered sedimentary rock
the oldest fossils
3000 — the oldest rock in Britain

the oldest algal reefs

2000 —

the first green algae
the first soft-bodied animals
the first shell-fish
1000 — the first vertebrates
Precambrian — the first land plants and animals
Cambrian — the age of reptiles
the age of mammals
Carboniferous — the age of Man

Cretaceous —
Tertiary —
Quaternary —
the build-up of oxygen in the atmosphere
mountain-building activity
the build-up of life

Figure 23.3
A table of geological time.

4 How far would you have to walk to get back to the time when the white cliffs of Dover were made?

5 How long a journey would it be to the oldest rocks in England?

B23.3   What evidence is there of change?

To take the grasslands of Africa shown in figure 4.1 (page 42) as an example, the plants and animals found there today are thought to be descendants of the earlier forms which lived there 2 million years ago (figure 23.1).

6 How many differences can you think of between the organisms which live there today and those which lived there about 2 million years ago?

B23.4   What's Darwin got to do with it?

Nearly everyone has heard of Charles Darwin but without Alfred Wallace he might not have published the famous book which changed the way people thought about natural history.

    In the history of science there are many examples of two people, who do not know of each other's work, hitting upon the same idea at the same time. This is what happened with Wallace and Darwin.

    Charles Darwin (figure 23.4) was born in 1809. His father was a doctor and he wanted his son to follow in his footsteps. Like so many sons, Charles thought differently. Charles's father was wealthy and sent him to medical school in Edinburgh where he stuck it for two years. Then his father relented and Charles was allowed to go to Cambridge to take a degree, with the idea that he might become a clergyman. The young man himself, however, was more interested in natural history and an outdoor life. After leaving Cambridge Charles was chosen to go as naturalist on a voyage to South America on HMS *Beagle*. The main purpose of the voyage was to survey and chart the coasts of South America for the Admiralty. The post was unpaid and his father did not want him to go. Charles was 22 years old when he left England, just after Christmas 1831, and he did not return home for five years. He was a bad sailor and went ashore whenever he could; half of the five years away was spent in overland expeditions, long journeys on horseback, rough camps and dangerous mountain climbing.

    Alfred Russel Wallace (figure 23.5) was born in 1823. His parents were poor and he left school when he was fourteen, the year after Charles Darwin returned to England. He went on courses at Working Men's Institutes and with his brother's help trained as a land surveyor, which was a good job in the 1840s when many new railway lines were being planned. Working out of doors in the countryside, Alfred, like Charles, became interested in natural

Figure 23.4
Charles Darwin as a young man, painted by George Richmond, 1840.

history. A friend introduced him to the study of beetles; he was surprised to find that there were hundreds of different kinds, and more still to be discovered. When he was twenty-five, Alfred Wallace and his friend Henry Bates decided to leave England and try to make a living collecting specimens to sell to museums at home.

With £100 between them they set off for South America. They travelled together for a thousand miles up the Amazon before going their separate ways. In the end Alfred spent four years in the Amazon basin and later travelled and collected in the islands of the East Indies.

It was the immense variety of animals and plants and the differences between them that led both Darwin and Wallace to think about how these differences could have come about. Darwin developed his theory two years after his return to England but he did not write a proper account for another six years. He then put the paper away with the instructions that it was only to be published after he died. Perhaps he realized how deeply shocked his wife would be to know that his theory cast doubt on the account of Creation set out in the book of Genesis.

In 1858, fourteen years after Charles Darwin had written – but not published – the first account of his theory of the origin of species, he received a paper from Alfred Wallace who was at that time working in the East Indies. This paper was an account of Wallace's own theory, and it was just the same as Darwin's, though he knew nothing of Darwin's work.

What was Darwin to do? For twenty years he had collected information in support of his theory and now the first paper on the subject had been written by someone else! In the end it was arranged that two papers, the one by Wallace and the other by Darwin, should be presented at the same scientific meeting in London. No one showed much interest at the time but at last Darwin had been forced into action and a year later his famous book *On the Origin of Species by Means of Natural Selection* was published. It was a best-seller and it provoked religious and scientific discussion throughout the rest of the nineteenth century.

This is how Wallace first wrote about his idea:

"It occurred to me to ask the question, why do some die and some live? And the answer was clearly that on the whole the best fitted lived. From the effects of disease the most healthy escaped; from enemies, the strongest, the swiftest or the most cunning; from famine, the best hunters or those with the best digestion; and so on. Then I at once saw, that the ever present variability of all living things would furnish the material from which, by the mere weeding out of those less adapted to the actual conditions, the fittest alone would continue the race. There suddenly flashed upon me the *idea* of the survival of the fittest."

This sums up what we now call the *theory of evolution by natural selection.*

Figure 23.5
Alfred Russel Wallace.

B23.5   The Darwin–Wallace theory of evolution

Over millions of years, selection leads to changes in species; in other words, *evolution* takes place. We cannot cram the work of twenty years into a few days but we can look at some of the evidence for ourselves.

What are the facts on which Darwin and Wallace based their theory of evolution? They may be summarized as follows:

1 organisms are able to produce vast numbers of offspring;
2 variations exist among organisms of the same type;
3 some of the variations are inherited;
4 the environment affects the survival of organisms.

(See figure 23.6.)

a

b

c

d

Figure 23.6
a More than enough offspring. **b** Not all the same. **c** A question of inheritance.
d The effect of the environment.

From these facts it follows that:

offspring which are best adapted to their environment tend to be the ones that survive and reproduce;
those which are most successful are likely to leave the most descendants.

Therefore there is *selection* of organisms which are most fitted for a particular kind of environment.

How many offspring can an organism produce?

The rate of growth in the human population can be seen in the graph in Worksheet **B20C**.

One of the slowest-breeding animals is the elephant. Charles Darwin worked out that if you started with only one pair of elephants their offspring **could** number 19 million after 700 years – if they all survived. You may be able to find out for yourselves the number of eggs produced by a fish, or seeds

	Number of eggs
Cod	3 000 000 to 4 000 000
Frog	1000 to 2000
Adder	10 to 14
Crocodile	50 to 80
Pheasant	14
Thrush	4 to 5
Rabbit	8
Human	1

Figure 23.7

Figure 23.8
The crowd at an Inauguration Day parade in Washington D.C. Every one of the 4000 million people in the world has millions of harmless bacteria both inside and outside his or her body. People and bacteria are just two of the enormous number of living things.

produced by a plant. (See Worksheet **B23A**.) Figure 23.7 shows the number of eggs produced at any one time by some other animals. (This number may be produced several times during the animals' lifetime.)

---

7 Women produce one egg each month for about forty years. How many eggs in a lifetime is this? Compare this with the number of children in most families.

Figure 23.9
A wild type fruit fly which has a grey body and red eyes.

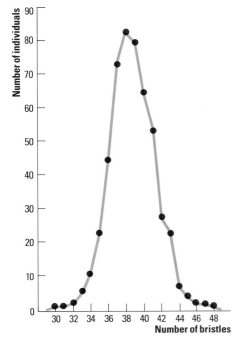

Figure 23.10
The number of bristles on the bodies of fruit flies.

B23.6   Are all offspring the same?

A quick look at brothers and sisters, aunts and uncles, makes it easy to answer "no" to this question. But what about simpler organisms? The fruit fly shown in figure 23.9 is only 3 mm long. This little fly is used in many genetics experiments because it has only 4 pairs of chromosomes. Scientists love it. More is known about its appearance and its chromosomes than is known about any other kind of fly in the world. Someone once counted the number of bristles on the bodies of 511 fruit flies and plotted the results on a graph.

Use the graph in figure 23.10 to answer the following questions.

---

8 What is the most common number of bristles?

9 How many fruit flies have this number of bristles?

10 What are the lowest and the highest numbers of bristles? (This is called the *range*.)

We can see from these results that fruit flies show *variation* in the number of bristles on their bodies.

a   b   c

Figure 23.11
Mutant forms of fruit flies. **a** White eye. **b** Ebony body. **c** Vestigial wings.

The photographs in figure 23.11 show some other variations which are found in fruit flies.

11 Which of these variations might make it harder for the fly to survive in the wild? Explain your answer.

Another example of variation is seen in human blood groups; each person belongs to one of the four main blood groups, A, B, AB and O.

Although there are only four main blood groups, the number of people within each blood group varies in nations in different parts of the world. This information is often useful when studying the migrations and history of groups of people.

	Blood group (% of population)			
	O	A	B	AB
English	47	42	8	3
Welsh	49	38	10	3
Scots	52	34	11	3
Irish	54	32	11	3
Gypsies in Europe	31	27	35	7
Indians	33	24	34	9

Figure 23.12

The table in figure 23.12 shows the percentage of people with each blood group in a number of different populations.

12 Where do you think the gypsies in Europe came from originally?

13 Which blood group do you think was most common in the early inhabitants of the British Isles?

Figure 23.13
A Burmese woman weaving.

Are variations inherited?

14 Burmese babies are never born with long necks. How do their mothers (figure 23.13) get their long necks?

15 From your work on variation and inheritance, can you explain why a variation caused by the environment is not passed on? Can you think of any examples?

B23.7   How do new variations happen?

When Darwin and Wallace did their work, scientists knew very little about the inside of the nucleus of the cell and the word "chromosome" had not even been invented. They knew that variations existed and that new variations could suddenly appear, but that was all. We know now that new variations come about because of mutations (see section **B**22.7). Mutations happen at random and not very often. Although they are often harmful, some may have good effects and these are the ones which are likely to be handed on to the next generation. Any mutation which makes an organism unable to grow or reproduce is not going to be present in the next generation.

Many varieties of pot plants and garden plants are grown just because of their variegated foliage.

16 Suggest why variegated plants are not often found growing wild.

How many survive?

We have seen that plants and animals produce enormous numbers of seeds or eggs, but very few of them survive the hazards of growing to maturity.

Poppies

Figures 23.14
Poppies growing among wheat.

The common field poppy (figure 23.14) produces around 17 000 seeds on each plant. Each one is very small and easily blown by the wind, and of course many of them never land in places where they can germinate. However, about 3000 of the 17 000 produced by each plant are different from the rest and will not germinate at all, whatever the conditions, until several months or even years after they have been produced. No seeds will germinate if they are washed too deep into the ground by the rain. Germination will only happen when the seeds are brought up to the surface again perhaps by ploughing, or when a new road is built.

17 What advantage is it to the plants if their seeds do not all germinate at the same time?

There may be as many as 100 million poppy seeds lying dormant in each hectare of soil where poppies have flowered in the past. "Poppy Day" on 11th November (when we remember those who have died in two World Wars) originated because of the many poppy flowers which grew from previously buried seeds when trenches were dug in the cornfields of northern France during the 1914–1918 war.

Frogs

In the spring, frogs lay vast numbers of eggs, which we call frog spawn. In late summer, there often seem to be hundreds of little frogs jumping about in long grass close to ponds. Most of these young animals will die during their first winter. The ones which survive represent only a fraction of the huge number of eggs laid as frog spawn in the previous spring.

18 Why doesn't all the frog spawn develop?

19 Make a list of reasons why some offspring survive and others don't.

These observations about poppies and frogs suggest that it is quite difficult for organisms to survive. This is true for all organisms.

How does the environment affect organisms?

When the environment changes, features which have been useful may no longer be so and organisms with these features will tend to disappear from the population. Different variations may be an advantage in the new environment so these are selected. Then the organisms which possess them become more common in the population than they were before. Darwin called this process *natural selection*.

Figure 23.15
Different forms of the white-lipped snail, *Cepaea hortensis*.

B23.8   Natural selection in action

Changes in our own environment are happening all the time and we can try to find out if they are having any effect on plants and animals. Here are some examples of selection in action.

Snails and thrushes

Snails of the species *Cepaea* are found in different colours – brown, pink and yellow. The differently coloured snails may be found with or without dark bands on their shells. The four most common types are shown in figure 23.15.

Thrushes search for these snails, take them away to a special stone or "anvil", bang away at the shell until it is broken and then eat the soft body of the snail, leaving the broken bits of shell behind. (See figure 23.16.) If you collect shells from a thrush's anvil you can find out what proportion of the differently coloured snails the thrush has found and eaten at different times of the year.

Figure 23.16
A thrush's anvil with broken shells of three species of snails: garden, *Helix aspersa*; brown-lipped, *Cepaea nemoralis*; and (mostly) Kentish, *Monacha cantiana*.

Month	Collected shells that were yellow (%)
April	42
June	22

Figure 23.17

Shells were collected from a thrush's anvil in a wood near Oxford and were sorted according to their colour. Figure 23.17 shows the results.

At both of these times of year the proportion of yellow snails living in the wood was the same, so the difference was not because there were fewer yellow snails in the wood in June.

20 Why do you think the thrushes caught fewer yellow snails in June than in April?

21 What changes would have taken place in the wood during the spring?

These snails are also found in grassland and hedgerows as well as woods.

22 Where would you expect to find more yellow snails, in woods or grassland?

Look at figure 23.18.

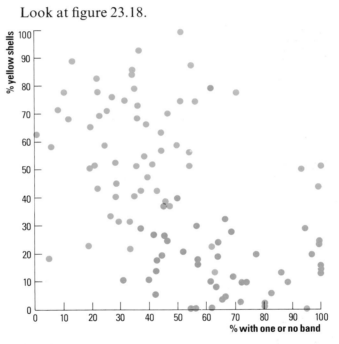

Figure 23.18
A graph showing different kinds of snails from two habitats.

23 In woodland, are you likely to find more banded or unbanded snails?

24 Which snail is least common at any of the sites? Why do you think this is so?

25 At nearly all the sites all four kinds of snail are found. Why is it an advantage to have a population with more than one kind of shell?

26 What might happen to the numbers of yellow snails if the amount of woodland in England became very much less?

In Worksheet **B23B** you can investigate camouflage for yourselves.

Malarial resistance

Humans have played a major part in changing the environment of very many species by using pesticides and medicines to protect themselves. For example in areas where malaria is common, insecticides were used to kill the mosquitoes which spread the disease. Eventually, however, mosquitoes which were no longer killed by the insecticide appeared in the population. In other words they had become *resistant* to it. These resistant forms came about because of mutations in the mosquito population. The mutant mosquitoes were the ones which survived to reproduce, so eventually most of the population was made up of mosquitoes that were resistant to the insecticide. A different insecticide could be used to kill them, but forms resistant to the new insecticide would soon appear. Eventually you would be left with a situation such as that found in Denmark where the house fly is resistant to all but one of the insecticides which can be safely used.

Antibiotics

The first antibiotic – penicillin – was discovered in 1928, but it was not until the 1940s that it was used to treat patients suffering from bacterial infections. Now there are many different kinds of antibiotics. Some of them no longer kill bacteria, or only do so if given in very large doses.

27 Explain how antibiotic resistance has arisen in bacteria.

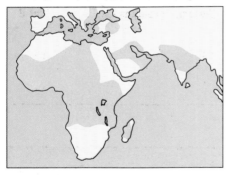

Figure 23.19
A map showing the distribution of sickle cell anaemia.

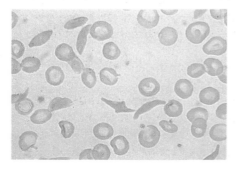

Figure 23.20
A photograph showing both normal red blood cells and sickle cells.

Sickle cell disease

There are several kinds of sickle cell disease and the one we are going to look at is sickle cell anaemia. Sickle cell anaemia is most common in people who live in, or who come from, parts of Africa. It also occurs in people living in, or who come from, India, Pakistan, the Middle East and the Eastern Mediterranean (see figure 23.19). It is not a disease you catch like measles; it is inherited.

First of all you need to know some facts about the disease. You already know from Chapter **B**8 that your blood contains millions of red blood cells. Normally they are round in shape. In sickle cell disease they look quite different. They are shaped like a sickle – which is, of course, how the disease got its name. (Figure 23.20.)

What makes the cells this shape? The answer lies in the structure of the haemoglobin, the red pigment in the red blood cells which carries oxygen around the body (see Chapter **B**8). The normal form of haemoglobin is called HbA. A slightly altered form, which has arisen as the result of a mutation, is called HbS. People who inherit an A allele from both parents will be AA and their haemoglobin will be normal. People who inherit an S allele from both parents will be SS and all their haemoglobin will be abnormal. When the cells containing this abnormal haemoglobin give up their oxygen they collapse and become sickle-shaped. The collapsed cells stick together in long chains which may block small blood vessels – a serious effect of the disease. Eventually the sickle cells may lose their haemoglobin and this is what causes the anaemia.

A person who has sickle cell anaemia rarely survives to have children.

28 Therefore, what would you expect to happen to the number of S alleles in the populations where sickle cell anaemia occurs?

29 Give possible genotypes (figure 22.19) for the two types of haemoglobin.

In people who are AS, some of the red blood cells may become sickle-shaped when the oxygen concentration in their blood is low but these people are not anaemic and they lead normal lives.

30 Suggest how a person can inherit one allele of each type from his or her parents.

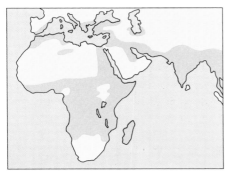

Figure 23.21
A map showing the distribution of malaria.

Sickle cell anaemia presents us with something of a puzzle, because you might expect the sickle cell S allele to disappear from the population as a result of natural selection. But this is not what happens. The key to this puzzle was found in 1954 when A. C. Allison, who was interested in this disease, pointed out that the distribution of sickle cell anaemia was almost the same as that of malaria. Compare figure 23.21 with figure 23.19.

Allison carried out what may be considered a risky experiment on two groups of brave volunteers. One group had normal red blood cells (AA) and the other had some sickle cells (AS). Both groups were artificially infected with malarial parasites and observed for forty days. There were 15 people in each group. The results are shown in figure 23.22.

	Developed malaria	Did not develop malaria	Total
People with sickle cell (AS)	2	13	15
People with no sickle cells (AA)	14	1	15

Figure 23.22

31 What do these results suggest?

Malaria is caused by a parasite which spends part of its life history inside the red blood cells. If the cells are sickle-shaped it seems that the parasite is not usually able to complete its development and therefore the person does not develop malaria.

We are now in a position to see how natural selection acts in a balancing way in the case of sickle cell anaemia and malaria.

Consider the following statements and then answer the questions.
a People who are AA have normal red blood cells. They can get malaria and may die from it.
b People who are AS are not so likely to get malaria; nor will they develop sickle cell anaemia.
c People who are SS will have sickle cell anaemia and are likely to die from this condition before they reach the age of 25.

> **32** Explain how natural selection removes
> **a** the A allele
> **b** the S allele from a population
>
> **33** Natural selection also keeps the A and S alleles in a population. Explain how this is so.

There is therefore a balance between these two effects of natural selection on the A and S alleles in the population.

> **34** What does this balance depend upon?

The disease is no longer unknown in Great Britain because many people have come to live there from areas where sickle cell anaemia occurs. Children who have it need help and support from their parents, doctors and other health workers and friends. There is also a Sickle Cell Society from which further information may be obtained.

a

B23.9   The fossil record

Fossils are the remains of organisms preserved in the rocks of the Earth's crust. Usually it is the hard parts of the organisms which are preserved but sometimes the fossil can be a cast of the soft parts. Charles Darwin found many fossils in South America. Here is an extract from his diary:

> "23 September, 1832. A large party was sent to fish in a creek…. I walked on to look for fossils; and to my great joy, I found the head of some large animal, imbedded in a soft rock. It took me nearly three hours to get it out. As far as I am able to judge, it is allied to the rhinoceros. I did not get it on board until some hours after it was dark."

This is what the *Beagle*'s captain wrote in his "Narrative" about Darwin and his fossils:

> "Notwithstanding our smiles at the cargoes of apparent rubbish which he frequently brought on board, he and his servant used their pick-axes in earnest, and brought away what have since proved to be most interesting and valuable remains of extinct animals."

b

Figure 23.23
a A fossil ammonite, *Hildoceras sublevisonii*, preserved in calcite. It was found near Yeovil in Somerset.
b The fossilized footprint of an iguanodon.

What can we learn from fossils?

We know from fossil remains that many kinds of plants and animals which once lived on the Earth are no longer alive today (among them the ammonite and the iguanodon in figure 23.23). We know something of what these animals and plants were like and as we know the age of the rocks in which the fossils are found we can also tell the age of the fossils. Models of the animals can be made and artists have drawn pictures of what they think the landscape was like when the animals were alive. (Figure 23.24).

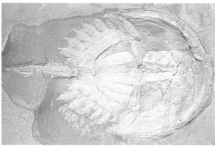

a

b

Figure 23.25
a A fossil horseshoe crab, *Mesolimulus walchii*.
b A present day horseshoe crab, *Limulus polyphemus*.

Figure 23.24
An artist's impression of tree ferns in a Carboniferous forest.

35 Do you think that artists' drawings based on fossil evidence can give us a true picture of what life was like in the past?

36 Can you think of any ways in which these models or drawings might be wrong?

Something else we can learn from fossils is how much (or how little) different organisms have changed. The fossil of the horseshoe crab, which lived 350 million years ago, is not much different from the horseshoe crab of today, which is found living in shallow water along sandy and muddy shores along the east coast of North America. See figure 23.25.

37 Why do you think the horseshoe crab has changed so little in 350 million years?

About 160 million years separate the fossil leaf of the ginkgo tree from the one living today. (Figure 23.26.)

38 Trace the outlines of the fossil and present day ginkgo leaves. What differences are there?

Is Man just another animal?

The pictures in figure 23.27 show two examples of human abilities.

39 Make a list of the things humans do which other animals do not.

a

b

Figure 23.26
a The fossil leaf of a ginkgo tree.
b A leaf from a present day ginkgo tree.

40 What answers would you give to the questions ''Have humans changed?'' and ''Are humans like other animals?''

There are many people who would accept the observations on which Darwin and Wallace based their theory of evolution by natural selection, but they would not agree that they add up to a theory of evolution. We should remember that however much factual evidence there may be there are also large gaps in our knowledge and there are some theories which we can never test.

Perhaps the most important thing about the evidence for the Darwin–Wallace theory of evolution is that it may help us to have a better understanding of the consequences of altering our environment. In this way we could perhaps prevent ecological disasters and use the knowledge to our advantage – for example, by increasing our food production.

a

b

Figure 23.27
Human achievements.
a A space shuttle: Orbiter Atlantis in the 51-J mission.
b A painting: Claude Monet in his floating studio, 1874, by Edouard Manet.

Index

Index